WHOSE GLOBAL VILLAGE?

Whose Global Village?

Rethinking How Technology Shapes Our World

Ramesh Srinivasan

NEW YORK UNIVERSITY PRESS

New York

NEW YORK UNIVERSITY PRESS
New York
www.nyupress.org

References to Internet websites (URLs) were accurate at the time of writing. Neither the author nor New York University Press is responsible for URLs that may have expired or changed since the manuscript was prepared.

ISBN: 978-1-4798-6296-2

For Library of Congress Cataloging-in-Publication data, please contact the Library of Congress.

New York University Press books are printed on acid-free paper, and their binding materials are chosen for strength and durability. We strive to use environmentally responsible suppliers and materials to the greatest extent possible in publishing our books.

Manufactured in the United States of America

10 9 8 7 6 5 4 3 2 1

Also available as an ebook

CONTENTS

ACKNOWLEDGMENTS

It was nearly five years ago when I had a vision of sharing the incredible stories, experiences, and lessons I have learned from working with diverse communities and cultures across the world. I imagined that as a first time author the book could best be written in isolation in the redwood forests of Northern California. I was wrong. The book came to write itself while I was active in the world rather than removed from it. It has been written across many countries, and it is through my experiences of fieldwork that it blossomed.

I am truly grateful for those who have hung through it all with me. This book has witnessed my engagement and marriage to the inspiring, beautiful, and powerful Syama Meagher. I thank her for being there for me every day since we met on an amazing Brooklyn night in June 2012.

My parents, Seenu and Sita, and brother, Mahesh, have been there for me since I was so young, along with my grandparents and family in South India. Their compassion and support of my process as I shifted from a young engineer to now humanist, scholar, and activist has been a foundation that has allowed this book to blossom. My father and brother's academic careers complement my own, making for wonderful and hilarious dinner table conversation!

Thank you to NYU Press, and in particular Alicia Nadkarni, who has been a fantastic editor with whom I have greatly enjoyed collaborating. The mentorship of media scholar Henry Jenkins, my professor from many years back, brought NYU Press into my life and early on helped cement the intellectual foundations of this book. Henry has gone above and beyond the responsibility of any mentor to support me, particularly for a student from the past!

I am truly grateful for the support of my colleagues. There are so many of you whom I admire for the brave positions you take, for the intellectual transformations you facilitate, and the presence you have had as true interlocutors. Thanks to my dear friend and colleague Robin

Boast, and Adam Fish with whom I will soon be releasing a book titled *After the Internet*. Thank you also to the many coauthors with whom I have developed fantastic collaborations over the years. UCLA, and the Department of Information Studies, has been an intellectual and professional home for this work to take shape. I thank all my colleagues and students for the valuable conversations we have had, inspiring my work to reach new heights.

Some of you have been involved in giving this book the rich feedback it needed. Shane Boris, especially thank you so much—your kind and thoughtful comments and edits have given this book a polish, clarity, and quality of argumentation that allows it to straddle the public and academic worlds. Thank you, Kyle Boelte, for your philosophical musings on the meanings of technology. Rukshana Singh, thank you so much for your supportive and constructive comments on this book. Thank you Ruth Livier for your great feedback and excitement! And thank you, Dennis Shepherd, for your incredible cover design and professionalism.

Thank you to my dear friends who have talked with me about this book. You all add so much positive energy into my life.

And thank you with all my heart to all the people and communities with whom I have worked and from whom I had learned so much. You inspire what I write, how I think, and who I am. Finally, thank you to those who read this. I hope this is but the start of a conversation we will have as we think about new technologies and those whose voices they support and serve.

Introduction

The new technology revolution is neither global nor cross-cultural. It is primarily produced and shaped by powerful corporations and institutions from Europe and North America, with various collaborators across the world. Yet we treat commercial platforms such as Facebook, Twitter, or Google today as if they were public spaces and systems, ignoring that they must remain primarily accountable to their shareholders. These commercial priorities, rather than diverse publics and cultures, shape how these tools are developed and the agendas they serve. It is high time to think about how new technologies can support people across the world. What we have today is a highly *asymmetric* diffusion of digital tools and systems.

Ninety-nine percent of the world's population remains excluded from most decisions made around the future of the Internet and digital technology. Billions of people are therefore treated as passive users. Their creativity and agency is restricted to adapting, appropriating, or hacking technologies that already exist. Despite promising movements in free software and open source, even many first-world technology users are expected to comply with platforms that gather and monetize data for their creators. If these users choose not to use these systems, they may face other inequalities because so many political, economic, and social operations have moved online.

This book is concerned with what digital technologies, such as the Internet, mobile phones, or social media platforms may mean when reimagined from the perspective of diverse cultures and communities across the world. No definition of "technology" should be limited solely to digital media. Communities across the world, past and present, have always developed and crafted innovative tools, systems, and networks that shape social and cultural life.

This book focuses on digital "new media" technology due to its increased importance in shaping the economic, cultural, social, and political dynamics associated with globalization. On the whole, globalization has reinforced inequality through the way new technologies have been deployed. While new technologies increasingly shape labor, economics, and politics, they are rarely designed to reflect the perspectives of those at the bottom of these "food chains."

Digital technologies are not neutral. They are *socially constructed—* created by people within organizations, who in turn approach the design process based on a set of values and presumptions. No matter how uncomfortable it may be, we must lose the urge to universalize or naturalize new digital systems such as search algorithms, social media environments, or data storage "cloud" platforms.

We cannot simply trust our gateways to the digital world as if they were democratically designed platforms, because they are not. Instead, we can imagine alternatives that are noncommercial, public, and conscious of cultural diversity. By uncritically evangelizing language such as "cloud," "open," or "Internet freedom," we block inquiry into what may be. Across the world, we can consider alternatives around how networked technology can better support our families, communities, and cultures. I think here of the inspiring words I recently listened to from Black feminist scholar and activist Angela Davis, who described the violence of the "tyranny of the universal." In this lecture that I attended upon Davis's first visit to Chile in over forty years, she explained that many concepts we treat as universal, or perhaps "natural" or "normative," are in fact social and political constructions which block alternative ways of imagining the future. In this spirit, I would like us to avoid thinking of the Internet or new technology as universal and instead imagine alternative democratic futures for technology that serve the agendas of the traditionally marginalized and silenced.

Whose Global Village? argues for the importance of collaborations between technology developers, researchers, entrepreneurs, activists, and professionals with diverse communities, cultures, and users to reimagine how to design and deploy new technologies. Because social media, mobile, and Internet platforms are increasingly important in shaping how we communicate, it is all the more important to consider new voices as we design and develop these tools. In so doing, we can design and develop new technologies that reflect the diverse values and practices of user communities across the world.

I recognize the incredible power of the current Internet to make information available and accessible to people across the world. Many social media technologies have made transactions more efficient, improved people's ability to find information, and provided users with a feeling of "connectivity." Yet we should see newer and older technologies alike for what they are—tools created by people in particular places at particular times. In this sense, we must not think of new technology as fixed but open to voices and perspectives that otherwise remain confined to the sidelines.

The different examples I share across this book reveal the power of community-created technologies and networks. Together, they suggest the provocative possibility of an Internet that no longer is unified but instead "splintered" into distinct community spaces and systems. In the chapters that follow, I discuss the early intentions behind the Internet as a decentralized network, arguing that it would respect the autonomy of different users, presenting each with equal opportunity to share their voices and perspectives.

It is important to remember these histories to recognize that the Internet today is also a contested space. The visions of free software or antisurveillance activists remain part of our "technology conversation." Yet they also often seem to be part of an uphill battle within an environment today where the vast majority of data flows through networks and servers administered by a relatively small group of corporations.

From the monetizing of user content to make the rich richer to surveillance run rampant, today's Internet has not delivered on its decentralizing or democratizing vision. We thus live within an environment where those with little power are forced to participate in systems far removed from their control. At stake is not merely a question about equal power and voice around the design and development of technology, but the issue of whose cultural voices are included or excluded.

This does not mean, however, that fragmentation must be the path forward for the Internet. It too is dangerous. A fragmented Internet runs the risk of isolating cultures and societies from one another, making it impossible to come together around global issues such as climate change, conflict resolution, or human rights. While this book's chapters primarily stress the potential of collaboration, they also reveal what can be gained when we *balance* the local and the global in ways that respect the sovereignty of grassroots voices in informing global communication. We can think of a future where technologies serve a range of visions, values, and purposes that diverse communities hold and not just those of networked elites across the world.

Whose Internet?

In thinking about our digital future, it is important to remember the social and cultural values that make us human. This is all the more important as we move ever forward with initiatives to introduce new technologies to reach what Google cofounder Larry Page[1] and Nicholas Negroponte, founder of the MIT Media Laboratory and One Laptop Per Child project,[2] describe as the "last billion." This term homogenizes those who lack Internet and mobile phone access. Perniciously, it implies that the indigenous peoples of the Andes or the herdspeople of the Kalahari desert simply cannot wait to receive the blessings of Western technology. Why should we be so presumptuous about who these people are and what they need?

It is all the more imperative to think of alternatives as we arrive at a moment where biology and technology are synthesized. The rollout of Google glasses and Facebook's purchase of the Oculus Rift, an immersive virtual reality headpiece that covers one's eyes, are a reminder of feminist scholar Donna Haraway's argument that our bodies have long been entangled with technology.[3] It is a mistake to blindly endorse these efforts when as passive users we are left with little control and no power over our technobiological futures.

It is troubling today that we blindly embrace technologies that are constituted by databases, classification systems, and algorithms that remain opaque and invisible. They merely sort through information that has already been created rather than assist the process of creating, communicating, or reflecting.

Many conversations around the "digital revolution" reflect a *recency bias*. They focus on new tools of innovation while leaving aside questions of history and context. For example, many assume that social networks were born with Facebook, while failing to recognize that social network analysis has existed within the social sciences for decades. Similarly, we often think of Facebook as a global and universal

Figure 1.1. Facebook CEO Mark Zuckerberg lauding the powers of virtual reality at the Mobile World Congress in 2016. Source: www.popsci.com.

technology without recognizing that it was first designed for students at Harvard University.

Asked to identify a key ingredient of the web, Jonah Berger, a professor from the University of Pennsylvania's Wharton Business School stated, "What makes the Internet go around? . . . Cats!" While I share Berger's amusement at the meme of cat pictures and videos all over the Internet, it also leaves me concerned. Why have so many of our Internet-facilitated conversations devolved into activities such as cat picture sharing? What may be lost in the process? I do not mean to dismiss the power of entertainment but to question whether this should really anchor what makes the Internet "go around."

This book's concerns are not only limited to how new technologies are used and designed but also include the constraints on the visibility and accessibility of the Internet. Facebook has recently partnered with Internet.org in a seemingly benign cause devoted to bringing Internet access to the developing world through the use of unmanned drone technology. Yet what Internet is being made available to these new users? Members from sixty-seven activist groups in May 2015 signed an open letter to Facebook founder and CEO Mark Zuckerberg stating that this Internet "is improperly defining net neutrality in public statements and building a walled garden in which the world's poorest people will be only able to access a limited set of (Facebook approved) websites and services."[4] And now the government of India has joined the protest.

Facebook's free Internet provides a laudable service but it does so without supporting Internet freedom. Facebook, rather than the culturally and globally diverse populations it claims to unite, has complete power to determine what aspects of the Internet are made visible or accessible to billions of potential users. This need not be the direction by which new technology spreads across the world.

Whose Global Village?

This book's title starts with the question "Whose Global Village?" in a reference to technology theorist and futurist Marshall McLuhan. McLuhan's writing predicts a future technology that would integrate the television, computer, and database.[5] He is famous for his insight that technologies hold great meaning independent of the content they carry—made famous by the expression the "medium is the message." He foresaw a future where instantaneous electronic communication would connect people across the world, blending together space and time to make possible a "global village."

McLuhan did not advocate for such a village to only support the voices and agendas of a limited few. Yet insofar as a global village exists today, it seems to primarily support the utopic zeal of technologists to make the world transparent and governable.

The term "village" is troubling as it collapses the experiences of billions into the agendas of the few who have power and voice. There is great value in bringing the world closer around many conversations and actions such as climate change, the fight for social justice, and a host of other issues. But the ways in which this term is applied to technology assumes homogeneity instead of respecting plurality. Our world is not a global village today with respect to the Internet, nor should it be. An incorrect prediction that the world has become a global village has now come to be treated as normative, what we should be striving toward.

My goal is to reimagine the concept of "global village" so that technologies can support a range of practices, visions, priorities, and belief systems of indigenous and non-Western cultures across the world. What if we respectfully "splintered" a top-down model of technology use to consider voices from grassroots communities? What if we thought of technology design accordingly, as continuously and dynamically crafted through collaborative processes?

We could then start to visualize a world where technologies serve diverse communities rather than vice versa. Where a set of local internets could emerge and shape global conversations. Local protocols, fluid ontologies, progressive algorithms, indigenous systems of intellectual property—these conceptual terms are discussed in this book's chapters in relation to my collaborations with diverse communities. They are alternative building blocks intended to inspire technologists, scholars, activists, and the public to rethink how technologies are made and shared.

An interesting parallel to my argument can be seen around a number of nontechnological issues, despite their different histories and perspectives. One is the controversial issue of affirmative action, which proposes the inclusion of marginalized communities in hiring or admissions decisions. Like affirmative action or any other program that strives to support diversity, the inclusion of grassroots users in a conversation around technology is important. It allows different voices and perspectives to enter a debate that is otherwise limited by the homogeneity of its participants. It also empowers those outside the existing group of decision makers to gain power for themselves and their communities through their participation. Yet this alone is insufficient. The larger system may be transformed for the better only if it respects the sovereignty of its new voices. Similarly, to rethink how technologies can better serve diverse cultures and ultimately contribute to the world, we can imagine digital efforts where the voices and knowledges, or *ontologies*, of diverse communities are respected as sovereign while empowered to speak to one another. This book discusses the power of such a path, building on my collaborations with communities across the world.

Diversity and Ontology

Social scientists have argued that an alternative to the universalizing ways in which we understand new technologies can emerge if we respect cultural diversity. My treatment of diversity refers not only to demographic differences around race, gender, geography, sexuality, or disability, but also to distinctions between the beliefs and knowledges different cultures hold. I consider how diversity exists not only between but also *within* communities.

Working with diverse cultures requires respecting the different means by which communities articulate their experiences. These are revealed through actions, or practices, as well as in terms of shared values, norms, and ontologies. Yet such diversity is rarely central to the process by which technologies are designed. Based on fieldwork conducted in Southern India, chapter 2 discusses how digital storytelling can empower community voices and perspectives. Building on this, chapters 3 and 4 discuss the potential of designing networks and databases that respect community ontologies and value systems.

Many agree today that the vanishing of linguistic, cultural, and biological diversity is of major concern. Climate change has disproportionately threatened those on the margins, contributing to this loss of diversity. David Turnbull, a philosopher of science and technology, points out that "cultural diversity is, like biodiversity, facing an extinction crisis. Languages are disappearing rapidly, and in the last 100 years, agricultural diversity has also declined. Approximately 75 percent of the world's calorie consumption is now derived from only three plants (rice, maize, and wheat) Thus, we are facing the barren desert of monoculture and the possible extinction of much of life on earth, and, we have seen no limit to our drive for assemblage."[6]

Turnbull argues that the diversity crisis is worsened by the assumptions behind the technologies we use to "preserve" diversity, namely, archives and databases. Scientists and cultural heritage experts have argued about the importance of various preservation efforts. They have pushed for databases, archives, and repositories that take specimens and classify endangered flora and fauna. Yet critics ask whether diversity is being compromised rather than promoted through such efforts. The problem, Turnbull argues, is the imposition of a model that presumes it knows what collecting and preserving is, based on the legacies of laboratory culture rather than the conditions and voices of the local environment.

Like biodiversity, one could see how this issue also applies to how technologies are deployed to preserve cultural heritage. Bureaucratic and institutional approaches toward documenting, collecting, and preserving may ignore the perspectives of the people they are supposed to represent. Technologies that follow these top-down principles support the values of those in power while ignoring the voices of diverse communities.

When Turnbull references the term assemblage above, he is concerned that existing approaches toward managing and databasing knowledge significantly contrast with local customs and traditions, particularly those practiced by indigenous peoples engaging with their own environment. We must not allow ourselves to bow to the protocols of existing technology. Instead, we can reflect on how to make possible what information and media scholar Phil Agre[7] refers to as "*deep diversity,*" where knowledge is treated as a process rather than a commodity. We can think of the Internet similarly.

Techno-Inevitability

Despite their relative youth, it has become easy to assume that new technologies are here to stay and will seemingly forever be central to every aspect of life. The myth of *techno-inevitability* produced by many pundits of the digital age is dangerous because it naturalizes a belief that technologies should dictate our material and sentient experiences of being. Most insidiously, this myth transforms a set of political and philosophical agendas into words such as "neutral," "scientific," and "humane." It blocks us from questioning the agendas that shape technology production and deployment.

The global village myth sees technology as simply "technical," presuming that what is coded into a tool will inevitably come to pass. From this perspective, the mere extension of digital technology across the world transforms the world into a village. In contrast, this book attempts to de-Westernize a top-down understanding of contemporary technology by sharing stories from across the world of how digital tools have been reinvented to support grassroots aspirations, values, and cultures.

Our thinking about new technology can embrace the diversity and complexity of peoples, environments, and cultures where such tools have already migrated, considering for example the realities of rural peoples with mobile phones from a more immersive perspective. In so doing, we can think past simplistic and incomplete notions such as having "access" or being "connected," and consider how these tools may be shaped in the context of everyday life across the world.

This book describes rich examples whereby local communities have transformed new technologies to support their own agendas. Such stories remind us of the importance of creativity, forcing us to remember that innovation is not limited to technology bubbles of the Western world. From examples of how mobile phone lights are used to hunt crocodiles in New Guinea, to how credits are exchanged to make banking possible without the presence of financial institutions, the world is full of reminders that the uses of a technology are never fully determined by its designer. Yet we should not merely marvel at the creative ways in which many communities have appropriated these tools, but see this as motivation to collaborate with diverse user groups to together design technology systems and projects that respect their worldviews and aspirations.

Stories of Collaboration

This book explores Internet and social media technologies within indigenous and developing world communities and activist groups across the world. Over the next several chapters, I share stories of collaboration from rural India, Native American reservations, and revolutionary Egypt. They reveal the power of understanding new technologies in relation to places, peoples, tools, and systems.

I write this book subjectively through the use of personal anecdotes. In that sense, the observations and arguments I share are *reflexive*—they are partly about myself. Like many of the community groups with which I collaborate in this book, I too am part of multiple cultural or community identities, whether as a man of color, a South Asian, or engineer turned media studies scholar. All these are invoked at different moments throughout this book. I wish to avoid exoticizing culturally diverse or marginalized communities as "special" while labeling myself a "truth teller." My goal instead is to be mindful of my relative power and privilege, attempt to release it, and tell ethnographic stories of collaboration. I hope through this to open up a space for rethinking how technology initiatives across the world might be reimagined from the perspective of peoples otherwise seen as objectified users.

The examples this book shares reveal that technologies can be designed and developed according to the ethic of *praxis*, a collaborative approach that stresses the potential of equality and collective learning. Praxis directly contrasts with the methods adopted by projects that dictate how a community "should participate." I believe what is required is a change in understanding, which neither marvels at "what is" nor overspecifies "what should be."

My approach has been influenced by a number of scholars and activists. For example, Luke Lassiter, an anthropologist and humanities scholar, has authored a number of books and articles on the topic of *collaborative ethnography*. This approach encourages the researcher to embrace the collective process of collaboration rather than see a community as an object of study. Collaborative ethnography is a response to critiques of ethnography's positivist and naturalistic histories.[8] In the past these approaches objectified communities and cultures through quantification or exotic descriptions of them in their "natural" state. Ethnography's more recent shift toward reflexive methods forced researchers to recognize their dual roles as participants and observers in community life. Yet it did little to disrupt long-standing inequalities between academics and the communities they "studied."

Lassiter and Elizabeth Campbell, an education and development scholar, have more recently outlined a set of clear strategies by which collaboration can be consciously enacted at every stage. They defend collaborative contexts as legitimate settings for contemporary ethnographic work and argue that there are critical moral and ethical issues at play in collaborative research. They point out that field notes, interviews, and participant observation must be conducted in a manner that is consistent with the observational and descriptive practice of ethnography and the ethical principle of equality. I engage these methods actively throughout this book, while also recognizing the reflexivity in all the projects I describe—that they are partially about my own experiences and subjectivities. The projects I share attempt to push past my own biases to defer to the voices that I have heard and learned from. That said, much of my voice in this book can be seen in relation to the method of *autoethnography*,[9] relating my personal experiences to the processes of listening, learning, and cocreating the projects discussed.

This book underscores the point that the support of community-based approaches toward technology are not in themselves a panacea.

Linda Tuhiwai-Smith, an indigenous Maori woman and education scholar, critiques the community-based participatory research process, explaining that many maintain a distance from the community they study. She points out that the bodies, places, resources, and knowledges of indigenous peoples were misappropriated through processes of imperial, colonial, and neoliberal commodification, even those that claimed to include communities and cultures.

Tuhiwai-Smith points out that social justice should not be seen as anti-academic or in tension with the research process but instead as the basis of collaboration. Researchers must let go of their attachments and embrace beliefs, values, and practices that differ from their own. Perhaps most importantly, research requires caring about the agendas of one's community partners rather than paying homage to a research tradition that has harmed indigenous and non-Western peoples. This work is an important reminder that collaborative work with technology is also political.

The projects featured in this book are also influenced by action research, an approach pioneered by German psychologist Kurt Lewin and colleagues.[10] Action research rejects controlled studies to instead focus on indigenously articulated aspirations and practices. As Rory O'Brien, information studies scholar from the University of Toronto, explains,[11] this method is dedicated to linking a researcher and community within "a dual commitment . . . to study a system and concurrently to collaborate with members of the system in changing it in what is together regarded as a desirable direction. Accomplishing this twin goal requires the active collaboration of researcher and client. It stresses the importance of co-learning as a primary aspect of the research process"[12] and an ethical approach toward collaboration.[13]

Related to action research is the approach toward *praxis* that characterizes the collaborations I share within this book. Praxis is an approach that stresses collaborative learning and creation to overcome inequality. Brazilian theorist Paulo Freire, perhaps the most famous theorist of praxis, pointed out that well-intentioned "teaching" efforts might place students in subordinate positions.[14] Freire argues for the importance of initiatives inspired by the ethic of praxis.[15] Community members from this perspective are seen as active creators rather than passive recipients and subjects of research. This process conceives of the student as equal to the teacher, with both collectively engaged in a process of creating, actively listening, and committing to equality. He explains that knowledge is created through a *process* rather than by following existing protocols.

> (Traditionally) it is the people themselves who are filed away through the lack of creativity, transformation, and knowledge in this (at best) misguided system. For apart from inquiry, apart from the praxis, individuals cannot be truly human. Knowledge emerges only through invention and re-invention, through the restless, impatient, continuing.[16]

We can think of our work with technology similarly. If we apply "knowledge management" protocols toward our collaborations with diverse communities, we ignore rather than learn from one another. This book reveals my experience of attempting to work with communities while recognizing that my initial connections tended to be with elites within such groups. In fieldwork, researchers often attract members of a community similar to themselves. I often would be first introduced to male, formally educated, and wealthy members of a community.

It is important to consider multiple voices and internal inequalities *within* communities, many of which too often suppress the voices of minorities and women. We cannot simply accept the involvement of community members as a type of participation to strive toward. Communities are hardly homogeneous, and simply accepting "community" as a label does little to respect the voices of those silenced within the group. We must resist the belief that the silent presence of women or minorities in community-based projects is sufficient.[17] Without such mindfulness, community-based research introduces what development scholars Irene Gujit and Meera Kaul-Shah call a "new type of tyranny."[18] These projects, despite their use of the "community" label, perpetuate rather than combat inequality.[19]

Robert Chambers, a developmental scholar, explains that these changes in community engagement may seem subtle, but they can dramatically affect how collaboration is envisioned and enacted. As we explore a role for new technologies to serve and support community agendas worldwide, we should consider the power of "[seeing] things the other way round, to soften and flatten hierarchy . . . to change behavior, attitudes and beliefs, and to identify and implement a new agenda."[20]

A Crossroads

This book has five major chapters that work to unpack the issues I've raised thus far, presenting detailed ethnographies from the second chapter onward.

The first chapter starts with a story from my fieldwork in the heat of Egypt's Arab Spring to then transition to describe some of the major arguments around the study of global technology and media, and histories associated with digital technology and the Internet. Its contribution is to recognize how narratives influence and shape our understanding of technology, and that the history of digital media can be tied to different myths of the world and how it functions.

The second chapter builds upon the first by considering what types of new stories can be told when technologies are placed in the hands of marginalized users for active use, particularly relative to discussions around technology and economic development across the world. It discusses the problems with the concept of the digital divide and reveals through ethnographies I share from South India of what might be possible when rural and nonliterate "users" are transformed into creators using digital video cameras.

The third chapter considers how networks and databases can be reimagined through collaborations with Native American communities in remote regions of Southern California. It reveals the power of building grassroots networks within and across these communities through collaborative design processes, where community members are placed in a position of power not just to create and share content with one another but to design the very infrastructures and database that shape how such information is categorized and communicated. A key concept discussed in this chapter is that of *fluid* ontology, an approach toward classifying information developed by the community. This chapter reflects on the great potential of rethinking networks and databases "from the margins."

The fourth chapter builds on the concept of ontology introduced in the previous chapter, in the context of a multiyear collaboration with the Zuni Native American museum in remote New Mexico. The chapter tells stories that reveal how I learned to adjust to and learn from a community where knowledge, authority, and the delineation of insider versus outsider are carefully guarded and given great respect. It argues that knowledge can never be fully "represented" or "captured" through any technology, no matter how it is designed. These experiences helped convince me that in their best moments technologies support the ways we communicate and share knowledge.

The fifth and final chapter of the book reflects on the projects shared to argue for the importance of "world listening" rather than "world making." It expands upon a range of other indigenous and non-Western metaphors by which technologies can be reimagined ranging from Zapatista land in the jungles of Chiapas, Mexico, to the Navajo Native American reservation. It comes full circle to return to the story I tell in the first chapter of my recent research in Egypt, which rebuts the "Facebook Revolution" hype that dominates popular understandings of the Arab Spring. In so doing, it emphasizes what is lost when we choose to "technologize" stories of political, social, or cultural activism. This chapter closes the book by asking us to remember "Whose Global Village" we choose to support, underscoring the power of collaborating with diverse users and communities across the world to rethink the stories, representations, systems, and networks that new technology can support.

Figure 1.1. "Social Media Revolution" T-shirt purchased in Egypt's Tahrir Square.

1

Technology Myths and Histories

In June 2011, I found an interesting T-shirt in Tahrir Square, the central public space in Cairo, Egypt, that had captured the world's imagination that past January and February. Emblazoned on the T-shirt were the logos of popular social media platforms—Facebook, YouTube, and Twitter—and below them, the words "Methods of Freedom." Tahrir Square became a place of fixation for many across the world as it marked the birth of Egypt's Arab Spring uprising on January 25, 2011, which eventually forced the resignation eighteen days later of dictator Hosni Mubarak. This attention was both troubling and inspiring. The fascination I had observed with Egypt was not necessarily due to the fact that such a massive mobilization actually occurred, but it was related to the myth that such an act of democracy was primarily made possible thanks to protesters' use of Facebook, Twitter, YouTube, and other social media platforms.[1]

Purchasing the T-shirt, I walked around central Cairo for the next several hours asking people about the story that it told. "We thank Facebook for our revolution," a subsistence laborer from the nearby neighborhood of Giza commented while asking me to let Facebook know that "we need their help to organize our next government." In response to the question whether he or any in his family or neighborhood had Internet access at the time of the initial revolutionary period or even today, he simply answered "no."

Having collaboratively designed and developed digital technology with diverse populations across the world for more than a dozen years, I was alarmed by the "Facebook revolution" moniker making the rounds, recognizing that this discourse would ignore the inspirational and brave actions taken by protesters. It would simplify their creativity and agency into a story of "technology magic." This drove me to visit friends in Cairo, determined to unpack a deeper understanding of new media's role in the ongoing uprising. From 2011 to 2013, I worked actively within Egypt to explore the factors shaping the unfolding political environment.

Facebook and Twitter were accessed in fewer than 10 percent of Egyptian homes in early 2011.[2] Yet they are seen as tools that caused a revolution in a country of 85 million. Without an approach that views technology use relative to the contexts of culture and place, we continue to buy into a myth whereby Silicon Valley supplants Cairo in our understanding of political events in Egypt. We see activists and protesters outside the West as incapable of enacting change without the use of "our" transformative tools. Indeed, such a myth is so pernicious that it had even reimplanted itself on the streets of Cairo.

My fieldwork reveals that there is a story to be told that includes technology without putting it at the center. I learned that far more interesting than the fact that the Internet was used by a small fraction of activists, were the creative ways in which its use could coordinate with a range of other mechanisms of mobilizing protest and shaping activism. Many whom I met were well aware of the shortcomings of different technology platforms, yet utilized these strategically to shape international audiences and journalists while focusing on offline strategies within their nation.

The lessons I have learned from this fieldwork bring home the argument of this book, of debunking global, universal, and natural myths associated with new technology to instead pay attention to the *agency* of communities across the world. In so doing, we can recognize the potential of grassroots users to strategically employ technologies to support their voices and agendas. We can build upon this to consider how technologies can be designed and deployed through collaborations. While chapter 2 illustrates this around the theme of digital storytelling and economic development in South India, the chapters that follow consider how these insights can allow us to revisit the design of technology, to support network building amongst and within marginalized communities (chapter 3), and respect indigenous ways of describing and communicating cultural knowledge (chapter 4).

Paths and Possibilities

To consider the collaborations I describe in the upcoming chapters, it is important to recognize the paths from which the technologies we engage with today have arisen. This chapter brings to light some of the different actors, philosophies, and cultures throughout history that have shaped the digital world. In so doing, we can consider how people across the world can become creators, designers, and activators of technology rather than silent users.

As new media technologies incorporate many of the affordances and functions of "older media," at times resembling everything from the television to the telephone, it is far too easy to presume that their mere existence or use will empower democracy. Others rebut these claims by pointing to examples of technological surveillance,[3] invisible labor,[4] and the disproportional ability of the limited few to monetize data.[5] Relative to the worlds of capital-intensive older media, the decentralized use of new technology would seem to empower the voices of many, seemingly making possible what media scholar Henry Jenkins has described as a "participatory culture."[6]

It cannot be denied that digital platforms of media production, such as YouTube and Facebook, also build profit and financial value for those who control the data and monetize it through targeted advertising. Scholars of political economy, such as Robert McChesney,[7] have pointed out how media industries such as Viacom or Disney have increasingly coalesced into massive conglomerates that manage multiple content streams, thereby manipulating their audiences. It raises a similar question in terms of how we may think of social media technologies, including those who are seen as central to the "sharing economy." Are the Googles, Facebooks, or Baidus of the world monopolies in the making due to their control of how information is classified and retrieved?

One mechanism by which the protocols underlying Internet and social media technologies shape our world relates to the ubiquity and power of invisible algorithms. Media theorist Alex Galloway has argued that the very architecture of the Internet, packet-switching TCP/IP technology, is an example of how *protocol* limits the nature of participation. Protocol may be faceless, but by critically interrogating historical and contemporary examples, one can recognize how power is not just constituted through formal classifications but also through "open networks."[8] Galloway locates these design protocols within particular histories, for example, the U.S. military's Advanced Research Projects Agency's (ARPA) relationship to surveillance systems used during the Cold War. He asks us to question the assumptions built into social media platforms, considering who benefits from their design. He asks us to consider what is seemingly invisible, for example, the flow of data between environments like Facebook and the other websites, mobile phone providers, and corporations whom these technologies serve. With these systems, the protocols, algorithms, and "codes" of the technology usually remain locked, limiting the type of participation they make possible. Adding to this problem is the great trust with which algorithms are accorded, treated as supposedly neutral, truthful, and advanced instruments of knowing and ordering.[9]

Invisible, and often algorithmic, forms of ordering thus fuel the engines of labor, allowing corporations and states to develop "new" techniques for valorizing human activity. We can recognize such invisibility in action relative to many examples within today's digital "sharing" economy. Call center workers disguise their accents, names, and locations. Uber drivers are denied benefits and instead hired as contractors. Customer service has been delegated to automated bots and knowledge bases.

Tom Goodwin, senior vice president of strategy for Havas Media, recently released a compelling graphic that reveals how inventory is no longer owned but managed by lucrative digital middlemen corporations (Figure 1.2). Having power over the infrastructures of sharing presents incredibly lucrative opportunities for sharing economy corporations.

Powering new digital economies are the contributions of content producers, posting content for others to see (e.g., Facebook or Twitter), sharing photographs (e.g., Instagram), and opening up a home (AirBnB). All these forms of personal data are now available for algorithmic ordering and filtering, and in turn for targeted advertising.

Controlling information can thus be seen as the "oil" of the new digital economy. Yet instead of democratizing our world, critics argue that it has helped shape new oligopolies.[10] We may best understand new globalized technologies by looking "behind the curtain"—scrutinizing the political economies associated with a technology's design and use. We can think of alternatives whereby apps could work with labor unions, for example, rather than relying on flexible contract labor without benefits or insurance.

Search engines are an important area where such critique is needed because of the social and political choices encoded into their underlying

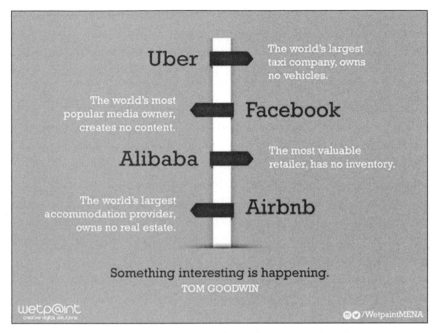

Figure 1.2. How the sharing economy shifts flows of capital to those who manage infrastructures rather than own inventory.

algorithms. These determine what information is made available (versus left untouched and invisible), how web pages are indexed, and how social concepts like relevance are technically instantiated. It is important to examine who profits and benefits by the ways in which an algorithm, or any technology for that matter, is constructed, deployed, and embedded. Users may be unaware of the values coded into technologies and of the alternatives that exist. Marketing dollars, public cache, governmental buy-in, and popular culture may lead users away from noncommercial technologies created by those without the resources or capital to exploit markets using search-engine optimization.

If we simply take the invisible, ubiquitous, and opaque algorithms that shape our digital experience for granted, even if they are designed for the "public," we may continue to objectify and subordinate those already residing in positions of disadvantage. Scholar of race and technology Safiya Noble[11] has researched the representation of black women via Google search results, revealing how the system reifies sexualized and objectified stereotypes. Simply sharing the logic behind the search results, though an important first step, is far from sufficient. The ability of the falsely represented to control and correct such search results would advance a sense of justice otherwise missing in the online experience.

It is far too easy to presume that a proprietary algorithm serves the public interest. Yet corporate slogans, rhetoric, and discourse push this myth. We are all familiar with Silicon Valley-produced phrases such as "Don't be evil" (Google) or "Think different" (Apple). We see the deification of the late Apple cofounder Steve Jobs. And we increasingly see public language being appropriated to support basic capitalist activities such as buying and selling a greater range of products. A notable example of this is introduced in Chris Anderson's "Long Tail,"[12] which argues that making more services and products available for purchase is an example of "democratization." Anderson argues that Amazon, Netflix, and other corporations support "open democracy" by allowing their users to access a greater range of information than ever before and allowing the "misses" to be sold as well as the "hits."

The dynamics I have described speak to the ambivalent and complex set of questions associated with new technology. While Facebook-provided content may provide a user with a valuable service, it can also be seen as providing free labor that provides resources to a limited number of employees (and corporate shareholders) who have created a software platform that relies on the unpaid contributions of its users. What is celebrated as a "cognitive surplus"[13] can be seen as exploitative from the perspective of labor theorists.[14] Corporate technologies can easily masquerade as public spaces without being publicly accountable.

An example of this relates to the term "Internet freedom," which is bandied about today and uncritically celebrated. We fail to consider the political agendas or philosophical underpinnings of these concepts. In his astute 2007 film, *Trap: What Happened to Our Dream of Freedom*, BBC filmmaker Adam Curtis explains how political philosophies of the early 1980s (in the United Kingdom and United States) shaped a world where politicians surrendered to the free market under the ruse of supporting individual freedom. Transcendental Western concepts such as liberty and freedom were subverted by a system that supported the protocols of elite scientists and technocrats. By blindly trusting numbers, surveys, and black-box technologies, Curtis explains how the public lost an alternative notion of freedom that trusted in the voices and perspectives of its diverse cultural constituencies. From Curtis's perspective, individualistic freedom may atomize society and in its worst cases give rise to the oligopolies recounted by psychoanalyst Eric Fromm[15] in his discussion of Weimar Germany's transformation into Nazism.

The economic, political, and social influences that shape the design of technology refer to what philosopher Andrew Feenberg calls "technical code," or "a background of cultural assumptions literally designed into the technology itself."[16] Technical codes represent invisible discourses and values that shape the design and deployment of the technological artifact and if analyzed, may reveal the ways in which tools and systems are socially, culturally, economically, and politically constructed.

A sociotechnical perspective sees technologies not simply as tools that neutrally work to accomplish particular tasks, but rather as intertwined with social processes. Societies and technologies mutually construct and shape one another from this understanding. Yet such a perspective remains uncommon in the mainstream contemporary experience of technologies. We assume the neutrality and functionality of such tools and only recognize their underlying infrastructures when they fail.[17]

Feenberg points out that technical codes are only visible when they are in flux. While these points of visibility may be easily assumed to be examples of "failure," they actually represent great moments for productive reflection where users, designers, citizens, and policy makers can observe and consider the assumptions they have taken for granted and worked to enact. They represent great opportunities to take power over technologies, shaping the destiny of those they serve. One can see, for example, the revelations of whistleblower Edward Snowden as an illustration of the failure of user privacy in today's world. While without doubt the news of the National Security Agency's PRISM project may have provoked panic and frustration, it may also inspire a rethinking of data privacy where we can move past the blank acceptance of the "cloud" as it exists.

Ambivalence and Access

Ambivalence thus seems to be an appropriate description for how one should view the shortcomings and opportunities associated with new technologies. As one peels away each human and cultural story associated with the spread of technology, another reality is revealed that complicates the understanding of what that tool may mean in practice, or what "connection" really means. For example, *Wired* magazine readers may marvel at the ability of a fisherman in India to bypass corruption by accessing real-time price information via his mobile phone. Yet they may also be concerned to learn that at the end of the day his village and his community have not made a transition out of relative economic poverty, partly because the mobile banking services the fishermen use are administered by wealthy corporations who charge high interest rates.

Similarly, citizens across the world may celebrate the innovative uses of Facebook by liberal youth activists in Egypt's Tahrir Square without recognizing that many of those who overturned power were motivated by conservative ideological tendencies, such as Muslim Brotherhood supporters. This filtered narrative also ignores that what causes many people to protest are the dire conditions they face and the social networks that bind them which often have no relation to technology. Neighborhood councils, labor unions, mosques, and other rallying points are often forgotten in a technologized narrative of social change. Yet social media technologies that are inaccessible to most, are falsely given undue credit for rallying protesters.

Viewers celebrate the power of networked technology to share the video of the Tunisian street vendor Mohammed Boazizi's self-immolation, whose 2010 protest suicide has been credited with sparking the Tunisian revolution and larger Arab Spring. Yet because of the tendency to think of technology as discontinuous, they see this immolation according to the logic of the spectacular moment rather than looking into the deeper context of Boazizi and Tunisia. Again filtered out are Boazizi's deep ties to a long-standing revolutionary labor tradition within the Arab world.

The *Wired* magazine–reading public may marvel at how the iPhone has given its users extraordinary power to gain real-time news information and yet wonder why the iPhone has so many features that also harvest and aggregate data about our every move. We wonder why our personal data is made so transparent while Apple rejects an app designed to track military drone strikes.

The question of "who wins" in an increasingly technologically connected world looms large. It's all too easy and convenient to see the spread of technologies as a "win-win" that mutually benefits corporate and political elites on the one hand and decentralized users across the world on the other. This story fails to hold up to scrutiny when one pays attention to the perspectives and practices of peoples across the world, as I describe in detail in chapter 2.

Instead of perpetuating a "good versus bad" discussion of new technology, perhaps the main question needs to be rewritten. A much more productive way forward should focus on how and in what ways technology can support visions from the perspectives of people who live on the margins, often objectified as passive beneficiaries of "innovation." The stories I share in this book can resonate not just with non-Western communities but also within the United States or Europe. As Wally Bowen, founder of Asheville, North Carolina's Mountain Area Internet network, explained in a recent interview with the Democracy Now! program, it is important to "concentrate our efforts in creating media infrastructure that is grounded in community . . . rather than beholden to Wall Street."[18]

Technology futurists and utopians have long envisioned an informational commons as a space of unity while giving less attention to the so-called "headache" of diversity. Novelist, journalist, and futurist H. G. Wells[19] described his vision for a "World Brain" that could make all the world's knowledge accessible, thus bringing greater equality, prosperity, and peace to the world. Vannevar Bush,[20] an engineer, inventor, and scientist who headed the U.S. Office of Scientific Research and Development during World War II, laid out the specifications of a technology that could convert analog objects to digital form, predicting today's "culture of the copy."

Today, with over 5 billion people having mobile phones and nearly 3 billion accessing the Internet to some degree, it is far too easy to assume that we live in the democratic "global village" that this book attempts to critique and reimagine. Indeed, Clay Shirky, a writer who analyzes the social and economic effects of Internet technologies, extols the virtues

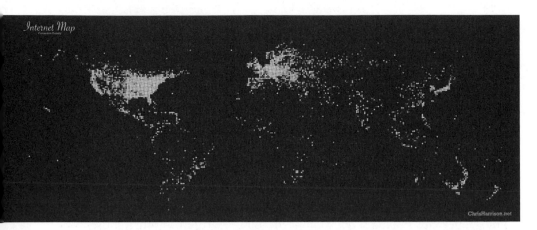

Figure 1.3. A map revealing the density of Internet connections across the world. Source: www.chrisharrison.net.

of these examples, arguing that new technologies provide "access to conversation,"[21] placing "more ideas into circulation than ever before . . . changing society."[22] No longer can an idea, document, or the "social life" of information[23] be viewed solely relative to local place; instead communities can in theory now be formed across shared interests with larger numbers of participants than ever before.

A map developed by scholar Chris Harrison that displays Internet access across the world using points of light to show connectivity, reveals geographies of inequality (Figure 1.3). Large swaths of the world from Central Asia to parts of South America and much of Africa are left in the dark, suggesting that the infrastructure of the Internet is hardly as global and flattening as usually portrayed. Mobile phones represent a growing exception to this trend, but they are also laden with their own complexities, particularly with respect to people's ability to exert a broader influence from a marginal developing world position. Bright on the map are Western Europe and North America, eastern Australia, East Asia, and urban centers across the world, particularly nations with emerging economies like India, Brazil, China, and Russia.

Access to technology has implications not only for people's ability to access information and exploit it for their own purposes, but perhaps more subtly, their ability to be an "author" in today's world. Only those

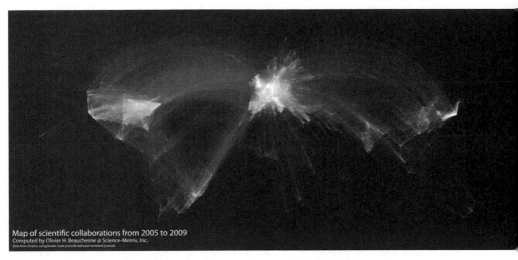

Map of scientific collaborations from 2005 to 2009
Computed by Olivier H. Beauchesne @ Science-Metrix, Inc.
Data from Scopus, using books, trade journals and peer-reviewed journals

Figure 1.4. Map of scientific collaboration. Source: http://collabo.olihb.com.

who have such tools are able to influence public and global understandings of knowledge and truth. Data scientist Olivier H. Beauchesne developed a global map of scientific publication authorship between the years of 2005 and 2009, which reveals this disparity (Figure 1.4). This map patterns what we see in Figure 1.3, but is even more skewed toward the limited regions of the world that have the infrastructures, literacies, and resources to exploit their access to technology.

Inequality is a major part of the story of today's Internet. This is the case in terms of access to technology and authorship and collaboration of scientific knowledge. These patterns are echoed by the very "nuts and bolts" of the Internet, its fiber optic cable infrastructures. By looking at a global map of fiber optic cables, we see that only three fiber optic cables connect the continent of Africa to the rest of the world, while only one connects Africa to South America (Figure 1.5).

Maps such as Figures 1.3 and 1.4 are skewed in favor of the regions of the world that have denser and higher populations. Nonetheless, it is far too easy to objectify the parts of the world that feature fewer or no "bright spots" as waiting for the blessings the Internet has to offer, instead of considering that this inequality exists partly due to a lack of access to economic resources. This is an easy and convenient perspective, yet dangerous due to what it presumes and excludes.

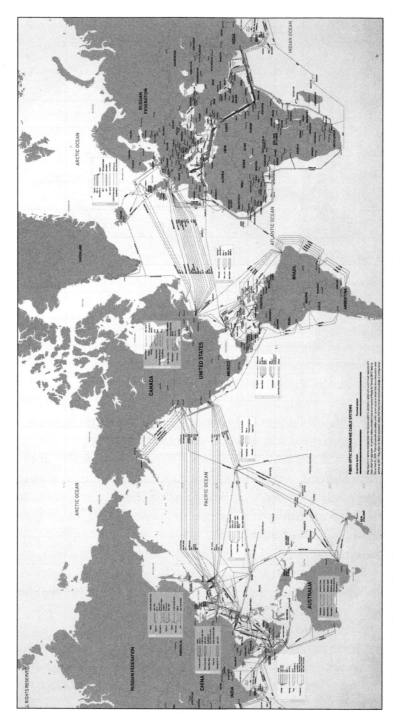

Figure 1.5. A global map of the fiber optic cables that constitute the Internet. Source: www.reddit.com.

Internet Histories

To deconstruct technology, we must pay close attention to the social and cultural practices and values that shape its design and deployment. When we critically peer into the histories and cultures surrounding technological design and creation, a range of values and practices are revealed to us.[24]

Recognizing that access to technology is neither uniform nor sufficient to overcome many layers of inequality in our world, it is important to note that the Internet and social media do not come out of a vacuum, nor are they neutral. These systems and networks, like many other digital media tools today, are the product of a range of histories, values, beliefs, and philosophies. Much of this comes out of the Western world and can be philosophically traced to precepts of the Enlightenment era around what counts as knowledge and how it is best articulated, preserved, and communicated. In this section, I share some important influences that gave rise to today's digital world. As we recognize that the contemporary digital world is socially constituted and historically contingent, we can imagine a future influenced by a number of voices that have almost always been left out of the conversation about how technologies are created and used.

Important scholarship has worked to deconstruct the myth of digital media as discontinuous and revolutionary.[25] For example, science and technology journalist Tom Staddage's recent book, *The Victorian Internet* (1998), argues that today's Internet merely builds upon earlier communication technologies by expanding the *quantity* of global communication interaction. Staddage argues that the telegraph was a more revolutionary technology than the Internet, as it marked the first intercontinental expansion of communication, making near real-time communication possible independent of distance for the first time in human history. In this regard, Staddage, like other writers, argues that new media technologies must be seen in relation to their historical precedents.

In a recent blog post anthropologist and media studies scholar Adam Fish traces the debate around who is responsible for the creation of the Internet.[26] He reviews the journalistic and academic literature to isolate four potential actors: (1) the state, (2) corporations, (3) several charismatic and brilliant individuals, and (4) Us (the public). Fish notes the considerable overlap between the four actors. For example, a combined effort that connected the state and various corporations is indicative of the neoliberal turn within much of the world that dates back to the early 1980s.

Working within governmental and commercial institutions were various individuals, ranging from Tim Berners-Lee of the European Organization for Nuclear Research (CERN) to Robert Taylor of the Advanced Research Projects Agency network (ARPAnet), who were instrumental in the early stages of the Internet. Fish's point is that in naming each of these four actors as "creators," various political discourses are perpetuated. He argues that corporate creativity and provenance can be associated with *techno-libertarianism*, while providing the state with credit is an example of *techno-progressivism*. The highlighting of the "heroic inventor" is indicative of *techno-individualism*, simplifying a complex history with a myth that gives credit to a brilliant auteur. Us, the fourth explanation, perpetuates a *techno-idealistic* ideology.

Why should such a discussion matter when such explanations and the discourses they engage in are oversimplified? It matters because the way we choose to historicize technology, most notably the Internet, shapes our beliefs and assumptions about what it can be. Creation myths shape visions of the future.

The four discourses Fish recounts speak to how the Western creation myths around the Internet dominate and limit our understanding of what it can be. They influence how most technologies are designed and deployed. Values and beliefs have always influenced the creation, design, and destiny of technology. Yet the discourses described by Fish, like any other, are partial, constructed, and circulated. It is arbitrary to think that any technology, regardless of where it was developed, should forever be limited to the values and beliefs of its creators. Instead, we can turn to collaborations with grassroots users and cultures worldwide.

My discussion thus far has focused on the ways in which first-world Western theories and philosophies have shaped the development of technology. Yet even these theories are far from unitary. Indeed, even technology innovators from the Western world have offered design perspectives that differ from Fish's simple typology. For example, the work of Alan Kay and Doug Engelbart, two early technology designers from the United States, were both influential in the development of graphical user interfaces, programming languages for youth, and other important pieces of hardware like the mouse. Their approach toward technology design was based on a shared belief in social constructionism, or the power of active construction, creation, and collaborative learning.

Kay's invention of the graphical user interface for his Dynabook[27] can be traced to theories of learning discussed by other technologists like Seymour Papert, inventor of the graphical LOGO programming language, and renowned psychologists such as Lev Vygotsky, Jerome Bruner, and Jean Piaget. Today, Kay's work focuses on Squeak, an open source software platform that allows students to create and model digital environments using graphics and multimedia.[28] His ideas can be traced to countercultures of the time that saw connections between environmentalism and technology. As he recalls:

> There was a whole 1960s thing. . . . Esalen down in Big Sur, the Whole Earth Catalog was right across the street at that time to SRI. . . . You know I am from the East Coast and I found it too confining. California was wide open, particularly during this time: anything went. . . . Basically it was a very good set-up, I think.[29]

Like Kay, fellow technology pioneer Doug Engelbart considered his efforts on Hypertext and learning interfaces as tied to the goal of improving the human condition, including his interests in supporting diversity. Scholars have described how Engelbart was inspired by the writings of linguist Benjamin Lee Whorf, who argued that human thinking was shaped by technologies and that man and machine must collectively work together to produce social good.[30] Whorf believed that the interaction between man and machine could produce emergent effects. His NLS ("Online System") presented a user with a set of connected tools designed to shape inter-user interaction and communication. This marked a contrast to an earlier model of technological interaction that focused on isolated tools. The NLS system's emphasis on conversation, communication, and interactivity rather than preservation, accumulation, and storage is a notable epistemological departure from an approach toward technology that treats knowledge as static, reclassified, and hierarchically describable.

Constructionist theory is posited on the belief that knowledge is generated through social interactions, whether between individuals or with a mediating artifact.[31] This approach toward technology design differs significantly from Enlightenment-era paradigms described later in this chapter that privilege the accumulation of facts, control of the setting where knowledge is produced (e.g., the laboratory), and the derivation of postulates and scientific facts *a priori*. These have greatly influenced the development of storage and collection technologies, and the classification systems that drive most databases.

The examples I have shared speak to a vast range of philosophies and theories. Whether we speak of political philosophies that shape the Internet's provenance and future, beliefs in learning and knowledge production theorized by psychologists, or countercultural philosophies that tie an understanding of the earth with digital media, new technologies must be seen in relation to a multiplicity of values, philosophies, peoples, and places. In that sense, the Internet and its associated range of digital media devices represent an *assemblage*, a heterogeneous collection of technologies. That being said, I next turn to describing how many contemporary systems, particularly those that store and classify information, can be traced to philosophies of the Enlightenment. I do so to explain how these philosophies have influenced contemporary paradigms of how knowledge is to be represented, stored, and communicated. By treating knowledge as a static set of objects to be managed, indexed, classified, and communicated for posterity, many technologies came to represent a far more limited set of epistemologies than what could otherwise have been.

Knowledge, Technology, and the Enlightenment

To explore the belief systems that shaped an understanding of knowledge that has long dominated the design of many technologies and especially databases, it is useful to explore some key figures within the Enlightenment. They emerged in Western Europe during the late sixteenth and seventeenth centuries when Aristotelian "natural" philosophy began to be overturned in favor of empiricism, a philosophy that rested on the belief that knowledge could be articulated through the activities of collecting, comparing, and calculating. Enlightenment thinkers were often scientific practitioners and metaphysicians, advancing the tenets of rationality and logical positivism originally introduced in ancient Greece. For philosophers of this period, scientific approaches escaped bias and represented universal truths. These truths were expected to bring society closer together, allowing it to reach a state of collective knowing and unity. The pursuit of rationality through logic and science was generally seen as the true nature of society, despite the presence of dissenters such as philosopher Jean-Jacques Rousseau who contended that scientific abstractionism and empiricism represented a rejection of nature.[32]

With the increase in literacy during this period, science was increasingly popularized and seen as every man's trade. However, certain critical histories have uncovered this plebeian discourse as a myth.[33] The period was marked by the development of a number of scientific and philosophical developments, including Newtonian physics, advances in the professional clinical sciences and physics, development of the theories and applications of electricity and magnetism, and the formalization and advancement of classification systems such as taxonomies.

Universities, societies, and academies emerged in this period and became centers for public knowledge. We now recognize that the concept of the "public" was quite limited, including males, the upper middle classes, and educated people, yet excluding others. This is a reminder that can also be applied to our contemporary thinking of technology.

The emergence of literacy and its key technology of production and dissemination, the printing press, helped science challenge the hegemony of the church. Scientific expansion occurred through the growth of specialized fields of study and organizational institutes. Historians often point out that the emergence of many new specialized terms and concepts accompanied the professionalization of the sciences.

As knowledge was formalized through these scientific fields and institutions, challenges arose around its representation and transmission. This period thus witnessed the expanded use of "information structures" such as maps, lists, and models. Each of these structures is an example of *ontology*, a means of expressing and articulating knowledge.

A range of ontologies emerged with the goal of preserving and sharing scientific knowledge, including classification systems such as the taxonomies created by botanist and zoologist Carl Linnaeus.[34] A noteworthy case is that of French philosopher, writer, and art critic Denis Diderot, whose *Encyclopedie des Arts et des Métiers* was organized and shared as a "tree of knowledge."[35] While these examples are historical, they reflect how the scientific "truths" of history shape how knowledge is classified, archived, and retrieved in technologies today.

Historian of science Steven Shapiro[36] has explained that philosophers during the Enlightenment focused on the importance of the public's access to information. Access to knowledge, from this perspective, was critical to life in a "free society." Shapiro introduces the French philosopher, Marquis De Condorcet, who in his "Sketch for a Historical Picture of the Progress of the Human Mind," explained that knowledge must be shared as a matter of nature.

Shapiro's historical deconstruction allows us to question assumptions around the ways knowledge is accessed, classified, and preserved. Our understanding of these questions, much like those of what a public was or was not then, is still critical as we reflect upon the values and principles that influence the design and deployment of technology. Instead of seeing new technologies as discontinuous, revolutionary, or unprecedented, a more critical and ethically productive reading would see such tools and systems in relation to beliefs and values that come from particular places or times. Shapiro's work encourages us to probe the relationship between terms we take for granted today around technology, such as "openness" or "access," and compare them to Enlightenment-era regimes of science and technology production.

An early philosophical tradition discussing ontology gave rise to multiple ways of working through and thinking about knowledge, specifically about God, logic, and the relationships between epistemology and the ways of expressing knowledge. Philosophers from Saint Anselm, a Benedictine monk of the eleventh century, to Gottfried Wilhelm von Leibniz, a renowned German mathematician and philosopher of the seventeenth century, have been interested in the ontological question of "being" and its relationship to God and whether God "is" or is not. This understanding of ontology, as related to the existence of divinity, is different from my use of this term in this book. In contrast, I work with the concept of ontology to consider how knowledge is articulated culturally.

Part of the preceding philosophical discussion around ontology centered around whether that which exists in the mind must also exist inherently in "reality," a concept rejected by Thomas Aquinas, the thirteenth-century Italian philosopher and theologian. He claimed that human knowledge is limited and should not be equated with the Divine.

Others have focused on this interplay between subjective and objective existence. Immanuel Kant, a German philosopher considered a central figure in European reason-based philosophy, argued in his essay, "The Critique of Pure Reason" that one could only understand the ontological concept outside the realm of "experience." From this perspective, "beingness" transcends the limitations of human perception and sensation.

Ontological inquiry can be divided into conceptual ideas on the one hand, and more structural, categorical, and *mereological* arguments on the other. Mereological arguments are concerned with connecting whole-part relations, giving rise to a variety of different claims for how to know, describe, classify, and structurally represent something. Alexius Meinong,[37] an Austrian philosopher and psychologist, extended the historical metaphysical tradition to move beyond the simple inquiry of what is possible to develop a "theory of objects," both extant and imagined. His theory holds that the part-whole relationship *orders* the larger universe, meaning that everything is a part of itself (*reflexivity*), that the part of a part of a whole is itself a part of that same whole (*transitivity*), and that two distinct entities cannot each be a part of the other (*anti-symmetry*).

Edmund Husserl, a German philosopher known as the founder of *phenomenology*, formalized this concept further to develop a "formal ontology" that created specific categories such as property, genus, species, unity, plurality, open/closed sets, boundaries, and more.[38] These operations and properties of objects and classifications became an important transformation of ontological research that moved away from Western metaphysics to the practice of the sciences. Ontologies thus became highly functional, utilitarian, and critical to the workings of both science and engineering disciplines, and therefore became useful tools for political economy and governance. This formalizing of ontology has significantly influenced work in computer science:

> To begin with we want to state that ontology should be seen only as an inter-discipline involving both philosophy and science. It is a discipline which points out the problems of the foundations of the sciences as well as the borderline questions, and which further attempts to solve these problems and questions. . . . [O]ntology derives the general structure of the world. . . . [T]he ontologist interprets and generalizes those laws and

must endeavor to establish certain of them as the most fundamental and general structures of our world.[39]

Researchers from the field of Science and Technology Studies (STS) have asked us to consider social, cultural, and contextual factors as we think about ontology. Steve Woolgar, a British sociologist of science and technology, has explained that we must look at the empirical and analytical dimensions of ontology to move past detached conceptual and autonomous thinking.[40] Woolgar's dissection questions every facet by which ontologies are constructed and wielded, including the assumed logical bases by which philosophers advance their arguments. Woolgar and other sociologists of science have argued for the importance of recognizing the fluid and unstable processes by which ontologies come into being. They explain that when we treat knowledge as fixed or "stabilized," we forget that what we experience is but the latest snapshot within a process that contains multiple actors, subjectivities, contexts, and environments.[41] Sociologist John Law and ethnographer Annamarie Mol argue that:

> Objects, entities, actors, processes—all are semiotic effects: network nodes are sets of relations; or they are sets of relations between relations. Press the logic one step further: materials are interactively constituted; outside their interactions they have no existence, no reality. . . . Endless stories about practices. About interactions. About designs. About coincidences. About sequences. About logics. About inclusions and exclusions. Endless stories about the kaleidoscope of materialities. . . . And other stories make it possible to say that we're dealing here with "different entities"; they suggest that there is material multiplicity.[42]

Consistent with this view, feminist design scholar Anne Balsamo argues that the imaginaries we have of technology, design, or innovation are based on a myth of discontinuity. It is important also to think of the contingencies and value systems associated with technologies rather than merely seeing them as devices designed from some sort of blackboxed vacuum. Just as no technology is the same, the process of design is also inherently subjective, influenced by the stories and beliefs of the designer, the community to which that person belongs, and the era within which he or she lives.

It is easy to see digital technology as unprecedented, revolutionary, and inherently positive, and to naturally assume that every technological innovation is socially beneficial. In contrast, Balsamo points out that we must remember that innovations are performative, historically constituted, subjective, emergent, and reflective of traditional cultural practices. Innovations may speak to difference rather than to an overly simplistic linear trajectory called "progress."[43]

Computation, Archiving, and Techne

How then can we read technologies in relation to the values, beliefs, and ontologies by which they are informed? Martin Heidegger, a renowned philosopher of the recent European continental tradition, has reminded us in *The Question Concerning Technology* that technologies reveal underlying ontological beliefs for how the world should be ordered.[44] The way a technology stores and classifies information, or impacts our communications, is related to the question of what counts as knowledge and how it is to be articulated. For Heidegger, the Greek term *techne*, as the root of technology, refers not only to products and tools but also to the poetics and aesthetics of the mind. *Techne* reveals the ways in which human societies make and articulate their knowledge, speaking both to social poetics and cognition. This book argues that *techne* can be interrogated and reimagined in relation to the ontologies of communities often objectified simply as users, citizens, or the public. The Heideggerian concept of *techne* can be applied to consider the diversity of ways in which human societies make and articulate knowledge, speaking to both the aesthetic and rational aspects to knowing. Consistent with this we can think of technologies more broadly, in line with the processes of making, ordering, creating, and sharing knowledge.

Historian of science and museum studies scholar Robin Boast has worked to uncover the "ghosts in the machine" of twentieth-century digital technologies. He argues that in addition to their ties to Enlightenment-era concepts, digital technologies today can be viewed in relation to a history of telecommunications that dates back to the industrial era of the nineteenth century, when data storage and the dissemination and production of documents became critical.[45]

Boast points out that by looking at the history of computers and digital media, we can see a struggle between competing discourses of computation and archiving. He argues that "computing technologies" differ from "storage technologies." The former involves the use of analog instruments to make mathematically precise measurements. This mathematical precision lends itself well to analog technology that represents actual signals rather than bit-based approximations. The technologies of today speak to the ambivalence between these distinctive value systems and practices. While the Internet supports real-time communication, it also features a number of technologies devoted to storing, indexing, and classifying massive amounts of data.

An important moment in the history of technology occurred during the 1950s when storage and preservation were preferred over computation. This followed from a philosophy that embraced collecting, accumulating, and centralizing information as a central social tenet, which in turn was tied to the colonial legacies of Western museums, archives, and libraries.[46]

In contrast, computation, according to Boast, is performative in the ways in which it works with unstructured data. In contrast to the work of archivists concerned with the preservation and identification of a document, technologies of computation view a document less as a discrete object that is preclassified and instead see it as a number of different data points and components. We thus see two destinies for technology in this period—one which treats technology as computational and process-based, and the other which sees it as a means by which information can be stored, recorded, preserved, and archived. This is an example of sociotechnical thinking in action.

Computing technology recognizes that no digital object is an original, but rather a copy, and that therefore a digital object and its components should be seen distinctively. As media theorist Lev Manovich[47] has explained, the digital object should not simply be seen as a fixed object to be stored and preserved, but rather as a complex collection of data points open to many different forms of engagement.

The experience of video, for example, depends on the hardware, software, and infrastructures that mediate its visual resolution. A video streamed to one laptop may be very different from its copy that lives on a server, or another made available on a mobile phone.

Thus while computation is certainly part of today's digital world, the values and practices that gave rise to "technologies of storage" continue to treat digital objects as fixed, classifiable, and preserved. By emphasizing storage and documentation, computers were developed to focus on the task of preserving, classifying, and retrieving documents. This goal gave rise to a certain class of algorithms and computer languages that worked with binary integers (bits) and Boolean operators, that describe entities as true or false, or "1" or "0." This European and American postindustrial thinking gave rise to hierarchical and relational databases deployed far and wide today.

I share these histories to explain that technologies are the product of complex and contested sets of values, beliefs, and ideas about how the world should be ordered and articulated. The examples I have presented demonstrate that technologies are *ontological*—they both shape and are shaped by how we know.

Histories of the Cloud

The concerns raised by Robin Boast remain today. Consider, for example, the "cloud," an increasingly popular term used today to describe the storage of data across a series of interconnected servers. The term lends itself to a sense of neutrality if not benevolence. Yet basic critical inquiry raises challenging questions, including who defines what the "cloud" is or who experiences its benefits. We have no knowledge of the places, peoples, ontologies, or political economies associated with the cloud, yet we are discouraged from asking such questions.

Media historian and scholar Wendy Chun has pointed out that we can see the cloud in relation to World War II-era military scientist and engineer Vannevar Bush's famous Memex invention, described in his 1945 essay "As We May Think." Bush wrote about the importance of recording knowledge so that it can be useful for scientific analysis. He argued for the need to replace an embodied and ephemeral technological experience with tools that process abstract and stored representations. Chun explains how technologies based on such thinking were developed:

Thus the scientific archive, rather than pointing us to the future, is trapping us in the past, making us repeat the present over and over again. Our product is burying us and the dream of linear additive progress is limiting what we may think. . . . The word [archive] may, however, also refer to an authoritarian sanction; one is given the right to think X, one may think X, in which case the authority would be the machines themselves, our supposedly loyal servants.[48]

Chun and others contend that Bush's Memex is the forefather of today's Internet, shaping the design of networked technologies to collect, manipulate, and monetize information. Like geneticist Gregor Mendel's influence on mapping and collecting genetic information,[49] the development of the Internet can be tied to Bush's vision that storing knowledge could unite the world. The Internet rests on a "belief [that] our machines are more stable and permanent and, thus, better record holders than human memory . . . [which is] at odds with the material transience of discrete information and the internet."[50]

Bush's vision rests on the belief that knowledge can live on through the ontological representations by which it is preserved. Knowledge no longer requires the "messiness" of place, person, body, or time. It need not be practiced or performed. It exists platonically and through its access can bring societies together while connecting past to present. Yet like many other examples from this chapter, this represents nothing but a myth:

Digital media is degenerative, forgetful, and erasable. This degeneration makes it both possible and impossible for it to imitate analog media. It is perhaps a history-making device, but only through its historical (or memory-less) functioning, through the ways in which it constantly transmits and regenerates text and images.[51]

As companies like IBM optimized their engineering and business models to develop systems based on the myths produced by Vannevar Bush and others, they gave little attention to the means by which information could assume different meanings as it traveled, was interpreted, and acted upon by diverse societies. This influenced the development of protocols that controlled, fixed, and stifled the sharing of information.

Technologies designed and deployed to transform knowledge into the inflexible category of "fact" or "law" do us a serious injustice. French sociologist of science and technology Bruno Latour describes such a phenomenon as "immutable mobility,"[52] a condition wherein information travels far and wide while maintaining a false aura of immutability.

What I speak of here is not mere historic analysis but a major flash point in an ongoing battle between hackers versus those who attempt to "lock down" information, such as private corporations and nation states. Idealistic, "white hat" hackers seek to open up the sharing of voices left absent within the mainstream media.[53] In this spirit, I believe we can push our thinking around how to design and deploy technology to consider the voices and perspectives of diverse grassroots users and communities across the world. This is the theme of my stories of collaboration in the book's upcoming chapters.

Relational Databases and Their Alternatives

This chapter has argued that information and knowledge are not simply abstractions,[54] but a product of infrastructures,[55] practices, and social experiences.[56] We can treat technology similarly. Scholars of science and technology studies recognize, for example, that the Atari 2600[57] or the BASIC programming language[58] are material artifacts shaped by a range of social and cultural meanings.

There is great power in applying this analysis to our thinking around databases, the primary artifact deployed to "manage" and "preserve" knowledge. Databases today continue to be dominated by the Relational Database Model, or RDBM, designed by Edgar Codd of IBM Research Laboratories in 1970.[59] The unique innovation offered by the relational database is the ability to save the schema by which information objects were or had been represented. Knowledge from the RDBM perspective exists independent of the knower, platonically separated from the messy practices of cultures and peoples.

The logic around which the relational database was derived emerged from set theory, conceptually tied to the insights of philosophers like Bertrand Russell, who posited that any natural number x can be defined as a set of members each of which have x elements. The idea that one can logically create groupings based on mathematically defined indices relates to the practice of describing knowledge according to fixed categories and their interrelationships.[60] Set theory, implemented within relational databases, thus affirms an epistemological position where technology is designed and deployed to categorize and calculate knowledge.

We can overturn these legacies in collaborations with user communities. Computer and social scientist Paul Dourish has pointed out that the database has become the normative platform for collecting and encoding social, cultural, and political life.[61] We increasingly see the world in terms of opportunities for databasing rather than seeing databases as tools to support our subjective experiences.

Dourish discusses the seminal work of the anthropologist Jack Goody who explores how modes of understanding and knowing the world, or ontologies, have been shaped over time by the ways in which such knowledge was collected and encoded. Goody has explored how information structures such as trees, lists, and tables are historically, culturally, and socially constructed. In a similar spirit, Dourish asks us to think about *how* that database can be shaped to support a set of values and practices that diverge from the static archival traditions that gave rise to the relational database. We must think of the database (or technology more generally) as coconstituted with social and cultural practice.[62]

When we do so, we recognize that the database is not a singular entity and that as a technological form, it does present different manifestations. Dourish points out that databases include three elements: First, data objects; second, the schema by which these objects are represented; and third, the software systems that manage the database. The relational database, as discussed in the context of Edgar Codd and IBM, relies on a schema of tables that fixes relationships rather than directly engaging with the data objects. In contrast, the tree database is recursively hierarchical (parent-child) yet directly describes its objects rather than relying on a relational representation table. Even less constrained are network database models. They allow for each object to specify its own set of relationships with other objects rather than remaining tethered to a particular prespecified set.

Dourish discusses a set of increasingly flexible database practices known as NoSQL, a playful rip-off of SQL (Structured Query Language), the formal language by which queries are made of relational databases. New alternative data management platforms, such as MongoDB, FlockDB, Silt, and Hyperdex, no longer fix relationships by allowing data to be flexibly communicated and described. These relationships, due to their lack of fixity, incur various transaction costs based on how they are crafted and the ways they are deployed.

Each of these different database practices must be viewed within its particular context. Overall they shape an experience of data by changing the granularity (the scale at which data are represented), associativity (how objects are clustered), multiplicity (how data objects are replicated and therefore used in different ways), and convergence of information (how the system works via an inconsistency between data objects). Each of these features shapes the experience of the data, software, hardware, and infrastructure. This reveals the power of design in shaping how information is presented.

Thinking materially and critically about the database takes us away from the myth that existing technologies represent a fixed, top-down way of representing the world. Moving past a neutral, uncritical acceptance of terms like cloud, database, or interface allows for technologies to be productively revisited and recrafted so as to shape and produce new material realities.

As I discuss in this book's following chapters, we can collaborate with communities across the world to design technologies and develop projects. For example, reflecting on the database, anthropologist Haidy Geismar, who has partnered with indigenous communities in the South Pacific Island of Vanuatu, notes:

> We need to be aware of the interaction between technology, software and programming forms and the decision-making protocols established by key actors (e.g., local communities that subvert technology) in order to move away from an understanding of the digital catalogue as merely a reification of archiving practices imported from elsewhere.[63]

Geismar, with her indigenous partners, is interested in creating a database that respects representations, values, and practices that are specific to Vanuatu. Mindful of the danger of over-essentializing any culture, she nevertheless points out that relationality rests at the core of the Vanuatu experience. Yet this relationality is far different from those written into the relational database. Within the indigenous concept of "relation" in Vanuatu, complex sets of ever-changing relations can be encoded.

This example is a reminder that technologies, like the sciences, are products of particular times, cultures, and places. A database created within Vanuatu at a particular period in history with a specific tribe might look very different from Codd's RDBM. Instead of seeing a search algorithm, mobile phone, or social media interface "as is," we can learn a great deal from "what might have been otherwise."[64]

Cultural Reimagining

Starting with an anecdote from my fieldwork in revolutionary Egypt, this chapter argued for the importance of critically reading technologies and their histories in relation to the practices and value systems associated with their creators and users. Just as we cannot see the Arab Spring as a "Facebook revolution," so too we cannot reduce our understanding of today's digital world to the direct effect of the Enlightenment. Digital technologies are truly multifaceted in their sociotechnical influences, a bricolage of histories and associated practices. With this in mind, there is great power in considering how they are used, designed, and deployed through collaborations with diverse communities and cultures across the world.

The remainder of this book turns to the possibility of rethinking the meaning of technology through collaborations with diverse communities worldwide. I examine these issues through presentations of several specific projects I have directed over the past decade. In these efforts, I explore the uses of digital technology in a variety of indigenous and non-Western cultures and how they may inspire new approaches toward design. The approaches I discuss build on the traditions from the "participatory design" field, which views design as a process that includes the voices and perspectives of all involved stakeholders. Though this field has traditionally focused on organizations and businesses,[65] it can be usefully applied to consider the voices of users across the world, including the non-Western communities I discuss in the upcoming chapters.[66]

Wired magazine founder Kevin Kelly, in a widely viewed and highly influential TED talk, argued in 2007 that the next five thousand days of the Web would unite us through our embrace of the "cloud." He argues that "what technology wants"—paraphrasing Kelly's latest book title, *The Next 5,000 Days of the Web* (2007)—should dictate who we are and what we believe in. Users must give up their data and "antiquated" notions of privacy to benefit from the services provided by an omniscient technology that has yet to truly come. Kelly himself struggles to describe what this technology would look like, be, or mean, oscillating between discussions of bacterial organisms, cerebral neurons, galaxies, and pseudo-Hindu mystical deities.

The Internet is not immersive, universal, or mystical. It is a material technology, an infrastructure created by people and therefore potentially open to human modification, creativity, and appropriation. Taking this insight to the developing world, I next examine the problematic practices of the digital divide, which rests on the mistaken assumption that passive access to technology can empower community development, particularly in the developing world. In contrast, I consider the power of storytelling, focusing on the potential of grassroots storytelling to empower community voices.

2

Digital Stories from the Developing World

The previous chapter discussed some of the histories associated with digital technology, including the treatment of knowledge as a fixed entity to be classified, stored, and retrieved. I have explained how these shifts in technology design and deployment are *sociotechnical*, that is, they shape and are shaped by values, beliefs, and the peoples and places with which they are associated. The limitations we see in many technologies today thus speak to the disproportionate voice and power of Western and first world elites in their design and deployment. Part of the problem with blindly embracing these "storage" technologies as they stand is that by doing so we limit our imagination of what they may be. We run the risk of ignoring how technologies may support the deeply human practices of communicating, sharing, expressing, and performing. This chapter discusses the potential of rethinking technology from the perspective of *storytelling*, linked to the sharing of voices within and across users and communities. Through ethnographies I share from South India, it reveals what might be possible when rural and nonliterate "users" are transformed into creators and storytellers using digital video cameras.

Digital Storytelling

Storytelling is a timeless means by which peoples and communities share their beliefs and values. The growth of digital subcultures associated with storytelling is staggering.[1] Ethnographer Mimi Ito's ethnographic study of *anime fan* cultures in Japan[2] builds on an earlier history of media appropriation and storytelling that dates back to the days of pre-Internet television that involved communities like the recognized and well-known Star Trek fans.[3] Importantly, these examples reveal the power of storytelling *within* particular communities to support local agendas.

Seen through the process of storytelling, technologies can support grassroots community voices and agendas. Today, in contrast, many social media sites take personal or community-created stories and share them far and wide, which may unfortunately misrepresent the contexts by which they were created. While global audiences can learn from specific place-based stories, it is important to recognize that storytelling has long been a means of supporting local communities.

This book shares storytelling experiences that include indigenous communities in the Americas and Australia, immigrants from Somalia, and rural communities in South India. Local communities can take technologies and shape them to support their aspirations. This term powerfully describes the potential communities have to use technology to articulate their relationships with the "modern" and global forces with which they increasingly collide.

Visual anthropologist Eric Michaels has discussed the different layers of meaning, perspective, and engagement of Australian Warlpiri aboriginal communities with whom he collaborated in their storytelling encounters with satellite television.[4] He describes how the boundaries between outside and inside worlds are navigated in such postcolonial encounters. His perspective suggests that collaborations are sensitive, complex, and dynamic. The ways a community narrates, reflects on, and shares knowledge is always incomplete and subject to change. And it should be respected as such.

While many grassroots communities may *appropriate*, or creatively use or repurpose the technologies that have entered their worlds, it remains important to not merely celebrate these acts. We can go further by thinking about how technologies themselves can be created, designed, and implemented in keeping with the voices and practices of diverse communities with which we collaborate. Most off-the-shelf systems follow precreated metadata and ontology standards and thus command how information about or for a local community is described, classified, and retrieved. This tends to favor the perpetuation of the standards of the software creator rather than support of diverse, local community-based ways of thinking and knowing. Rather than treating new technologies as fixed in stone and incapable of modification of redesign, we can rethink how they are created and deployed. We can rewrite the ways knowledge is articulated via technology, or ontology, to respect community voices and practices as they stand.

Before diving into the power of digital storytelling in supporting community development visions across the world, it is important to recognize that mere access to technology reproduces rather than combats inequality. The sobering insight that access to technology hardly remedies economic or political stratification would seem to confirm a conclusion that the spread of technology is a net-negative for marginalized communities across the world. Instead of rushing to such a conclusion, I reveal through my fieldwork within communities in rural South India in the latter half of this chapter that the destiny of technology relates to how it is crafted, appropriated, and rewritten to support local voices.

Digital Inequality

Since the 1980s, there has been discussion of the McDonaldsization of our world, where through "flexible modes of control" neoliberal partnerships between states and corporations have shaped economic and political power.[5] While many have debated whether liberal capitalism has delivered on its promise of offering greater opportunities to all, as *New York Times* political columnist Thomas Friedman claims,[6] there is little doubt that at stake is the survival of local industries and self-determined practices. We need to consider how digital technologies are implicated within this discussion. It raises questions as to whether the spread of new technology accentuates inequality despite its flattening promise.

If "global" means the exporting of Western values, then we may be ignoring diverse traditions, values, and beliefs.[7] An alternative approach toward thinking of the term "global" could be to focus on the power of place, community, and culture. This approach opens up space to think about technology from the bottom up rather than impose it from the top down.

Yet as things stand, we see evidence that mere access to new technology reinforces rather than combats inequality. The empirical work by scholars such as Manuel Castells, a sociologist who has explored the social impacts of globalization and information technology,[8] and Eszter Hargittai, a social scientist who studies how uses of the Web influence social and economic standing, have shown that on average access to the Web is far from sufficient to combat social or economic stratification.[9] This is true partially because access is hardly as simple a concept as usually portrayed. Although access may be seen as simply technical, in fact it is interwoven with related issues involving infrastructure, literacy, existing social networks, value systems, and aspirations. Certain well-intentioned professions, such as public libraries, must reflect upon their mission of spreading "access to information."

On a global level, we know that an increased number of developing world citizens have access to mobile phones, yet most have only a basic functionality that lacks access to the Internet and multimedia. To take one instance, rural India has a number of environmental and social challenges to deploying computer-based interventions: intermittent power and connectivity, long travel times, variable population density, and lack of secure places to store valuable equipment, limited education, underemployment, and limited disposable income.[10] Computing and technological literacy tends to be skewed toward the rich, urban, male, educated, and English-speaking populations, leaving a substantial portion of India's population absent from the rhetoric around "India's digital revolution."[11]

Nicole Zillien, a German Internet sociologist, and Hargittai argue that we must think past binaries such as technology user versus nonuser, and consider the range of activities by which people engage with these tools. What we do, rather than the technology itself, ultimately shapes economic and social inequality. Unsurprisingly, those with higher status in their research tend to have better technical equipment, faster connections, and stronger digital literacy,[12] defined as the skills needed to use a digital resource as one wishes and be able to do so effectively. To demonstrate how mere information access reproduces inequality, Zillien and Hargittai turned to a data set related to a heterogeneous population in Germany. They gathered data on hardware proficiency, the skills to search for and interact with information, years of use, and the level of interest.

The authors found that "status-enhancing" online activities, such as the use of economic or political websites, characterize those of higher socioeconomic status; in contrast, those of lower status more often spend their time looking at entertainment and health information. Economic and political websites can enhance one's status, for if used correctly and with ample resources they may be used to increase one's economic and political power, for example through financial investments or contributions to political campaigns. But if one does not have such resources, meaning that one is already poor, these websites have little value.

Even while controlling for infrastructure and facility with technology, Zillien and Hargittai were able to confirm these "digital inequality" findings. The rich get richer even when access, infrastructure, and technology literacy are equally distributed, which is rare in reality. The online activities that enhance political and economic power are disproportionately exploited by the already rich. Noting sociologist Everett Rogers's innovativeness-needs paradox,[13] the author write that "those with more resources—whether technical, financial, social, or cultural—end up using the web for more beneficial purposes than those who have considerably fewer assets on which to draw."[14]

These scholars show us that what people have off-line determines their ability to exploit the online. Online access is not just a one-time experience and inequality is not bridged simply by providing infrastructure and literacy. It is not overcome simply by bringing "light" to the dark regions within the two maps I have presented.

This research reveals that while access to the Web may produce occasionally positive and creative outcomes for local communities on the surface, the digital "revolution" actually makes the poor poorer. Yet is such a sobering outcome inevitable? I argue throughout this book that what needs to occur is a fundamental rethinking of technology itself. We must develop tools in accordance with the aspirations, visions, and knowledge practices of the communities whose agendas we wish to support.

Mark Warschauer, a scholar of education, technology, and learning, argues that what is missing at present amongst poorer peoples are the "skills and understandings involved in using [technologies] to locate, evaluate, and use information."[15] While his perspective likely homogenizes the poor as a single category, it is consistent with consensus amongst other scholars that access to technology is insufficient to combat inequality.

On a macroeconomic level we can see the effects of digital inequality in terms of labor patterns and the buying and selling of corporations. Technology critic and developer Jaron Lanier has pointed out that in the very month that the social media start-up Instagram—which employed thirteen people—was sold for a billion dollars to Facebook, Kodak—which employs more than a hundred and forty thousand people—went bankrupt. He thus points out that social media's "free" networks do little other than to make the rich even wealthier.

> An amazing number of people offer an amazing amount of value over networks. But the lion's share of wealth now flows to those who aggregate and route those offerings, rather than those who provide the "raw materials." A new kind of middle class, and a more genuine, growing information economy could come about if we break out of the "free information" idea and into a universal micropayment system. . . . [T]he particular way we're reorganizing our world around digital networks is not sustainable.[16]

Lanier's words are a grim reminder that the cultures and organizations that control how data flow, how technologies are used, and how information is ordered disproportionately gain from the expansion of technology, particularly within today's social media and big data climate. Whoever has the biggest computer and best processing power can manipulate "the network."

Lanier has stated in a recent interview that "even if people are created equal, computers are not."[17] To resolve this dilemma, Lanier suggests that we must think not just computationally but also culturally and ethically. The free services provided by top-down social networks not only empower economic inequality, but if left unchecked, also impose particular cultural values worldwide on peoples from diverse communities and cultures.

Despite the concerns I have shared, this chapter shall demonstrate my argument that digital inequality is not written in stone. It is useful to consider how access to technologies asymmetrically shapes connection and communication. This explains why we must understand and critique the intersections between the global spread of technology and our world today through concepts such as *network society*.

An Imagined Network Society

Network society is a term that originated in the 1980s to describe social, political, and economic changes caused by the spread of information and communication technologies. The term has also grown in popular discourse to reflect the supposed decentralization of communication infrastructures, including the spread of mobile phones. Despite the seduction of this term, as we think about the future of the Internet and digital media it is important that we maintain an awareness of the social boundaries of local place, culture, and tradition. We cannot simply fetishize technology-mediated connections and infrastructures without remembering the places, peoples, and cultures that we may implicate.

Humanities and media studies scholar Wendy Chun reminds us not to simply take this term for granted, but rather to ask why it has surfaced and proliferated. In her work "Imagining Networks,"[18] she asks her readers to consider what is gained or lost as "network society" enters the popular postmodern vernacular. In asking this question, Chun reveals the social, economic, and political choices that are made when certain terms (such as "digital divide" or "network society") are advocated. "Network society" contributes to a discourse that sees digital technology as "exceptional" or "liberatory" rather than situated or historicized.[19] Admission to the "global village" facilitated by the Internet is seen as the ideal outcome despite research that shows the many flaws with this narrative.

Extending this critique, Michael Hardt, literary theorist and political philosopher, and Antonio Negri, an Italian Marxist philosopher, argue that "network" conversations mask a reality in which the vast public has little to no power.[20] An understanding of a complex diverse public is discarded in lieu of the myth of networked connectivity. Hardt and Negri hold out the hope, however, that the diverse identities of poor peoples across the world will surface through social movements that hijack technology.

Technologies represent insightful objects for critical inquiry when viewed through the matrix of culture, context, and society. With such inquiry, we can move past blindly accepting terms such as "network society" or "digital divide," which I discuss below. Organizational theorist Wanda Orlikowski has argued that interactions with technology "will always enact other social structures . . . for example, a hierarchical authority structure within a large bureaucracy, a cooperative culture within a participative work group . . . or the dominant status of English as the primary language of the internet."[21]

While the idea of the Internet as English-dominated is increasingly unhinged by a massive parallel Chinese Internet, Orlikowski's point is well founded. We must step away from the *meta* to view technology *in situ* and recognize that if the practices associated with expanding technology access fail to challenge inequality, then technology is likely complicit with the dynamics that perpetuate stratification. One must understand the practices of local community life, place, context, and culture to rethink the practices by means of which we collaboratively design and develop new technology projects.[22]

Sociologist Manuel Castells argues that we need more deeply "utopic" thinking around the design and deployment of networked technologies.[23] I believe such utopias cannot rely solely on the abstractions of evangelizing philosophy. By collaborating respectfully and when appropriate with local communities across the world, we can more easily consider a whole range of strategies and solutions that consider how technologies can support issues that range from a lack of political agency and economic development to public health and education.

A discussion of utopic thinking must also consider the issue of profit and power in a networked society. While there have been few studies that normalize value across the different actors involved in Internet, social media, or mobile telephone-based communication, it can be sensibly argued that the outsourcing of technology provides greater value to corporations than to a developing world call center worker. Companies like Intel, Nokia, and Qualcomm have all employed ethnographers who study the uses of their technologies in the developing world. While part of this process involves seeking and understanding better ways to manufacture and sell these technologies worldwide, these ethnographers for their part must serve the financial bottom line for the corporations for whom they work.

Marginalizing the Marginalized

I have discussed the argument that the unchecked diffusion of technologies tends to reify rather than diminish inequality. Inequality cannot simply be traced to continental geographies but is also related to who extracts greater value through the networks they control and the information they can exploit. While poor citizens of the global South may remain relatively disadvantaged compared to European or North American citizens, their countries have also witnessed a dramatic increase in the number of billionaires. These individuals have extracted great power and wealth due to their advantageous position in a world of networks, whether as founders of outsourcing companies or call centers, or in other ways. Indeed, many of these networked elites may live side by side with urban slum dwellers in cities like Mumbai, India, or Lagos, Nigeria.[24] Poverty is thus no longer simply describable in terms of rural versus urban, or global North versus global South but via vocabularies of networked asymmetry or inequality.

We must not make the mistake of assuming that more wealth is being distributed to those on the lower rungs of technology labor chains and that they are somehow "better off" than before. New classes of technology workers remain at the mercy of networked time and geography. These workers tend to occupy subordinate positions in transnational, horizontally distributed companies managed by elites worldwide. Cultural studies scholar Raka Shome's discussions of call center laborers, University of Wisconsin sociologist A. Aneesh's analyses of the algorithms that dominate digital labor and obliterate normal sleep cycles (what he calls "algocracy"), and television director and producer Morgan Spurlock's *30 Days* cable program ("Outsourcing" episode, season 1) reveal the negative effects of networked globalization, all aided by the Internet and other digital technologies.[25]

From overcrowded cities and bizarre sleep cycles to increased economic inequality, critics argue that "virtual migration" and networked power have had very direct and unequal effects on the world. University of Chicago sociologist Saskia Sassen has contributed to this discussion by illustrating how new technology has transformed the "neighborhood" into part of the global city.[26] She explains that those left disadvantaged in such a world face a "democratic deficit." Despite being seen as beneficiaries of technology they are unable to voice their social, cultural, economic, and political agendas. With the dramatic increase in urbanization worldwide, if left unchecked, distance-bridging technologies concentrate economic, educational, and political opportunities into nodes of power in a global network.

New technologies only amplify such inequality due to the better position of wealthier users even before they take a seat at the "digital table."[27]

Anthropologist Arjun Appadurai describes a world of complex, globalized inequality as "a world of flows . . . [that] are not coeval, convergent, isomorphic, or spatially consistent." These flows are characterized by disjunctures of inequality or "vectors characterizing this world-in-motion that produce fundamental problems of livelihood, equity, suffering, justice, and governance."[28]

It is true that access to the information or contacts provided by networked technology tends to offer better economic opportunities than if one were completely disconnected.[29] Telecommunications scholars Rohan Samarajiva and Peter Shields point out, however, that while users and communities on the margins may gain something through this process, the overall macro effects of this deployment tend to accentuate the power of the wealthy.[30]

The sobering story I have told assumes the status quo. However, if a technological network was reconstructed to focus on "lateral connectivity" which would strengthen connections *within and between* communities, opportunities may emerge for communication and organization that could challenge an existing system of power and privilege. I consider these possibilities in the third chapter in relation to my collaborations with nineteen Native American reservation communities dispersed across the rural regions of Southern California. Along with the fourth chapter, it presents alternatives whereby technologies are designed and deployed to support communities on the margins.

Nonetheless, a bias toward deploying technologies in the image of urban elites currently persists. This occurs through projects that objectify peoples and communities on the margins, asking them to "participate" in projects envisioned and implemented by those at the top. Business Bibles like University of Michigan professor C. K. Prahalad's *Fortune at the Bottom of the Pyramid* point to the power and profit that can be made from Tier III and IV markets, populations that are poorer yet larger in number.[31] Selling more at a smaller price gives corporations and profiteers the opportunity to produce an enormous financial windfall.

Considering this position, media studies scholar Arvind Rajagopal[32] points out that we must critique the fields from which studies of technology are based. For example, Prahalad's research presumes that selling more technologies to larger numbers of users is a positive outcome.

Technology researchers who work with diverse communities must thus remain vigilant as they collaborate, analyze, and articulate their work.

Digital Divides

Chapter 1 demonstrated that technologies should not be read as neutral but in relation to a matrix of historical, epistemological, and cultural contexts. The influence of learning theories on graphical user interfaces or Enlightenment-era notions about collecting on databases is a reminder that beliefs and values shape the design of technology. Correspondingly, we can think of how a user or community may no longer be the subject of top-down research but be an active agent in shaping its own world.

A common term used in mainstream policy, academic, and professional discussions around the global spread of technology is "digital divide."[33] The term relates to the inequities between the "haves" and "have-nots" based on access to technology. It presumes that these inequalities can be overcome by spreading digital tools and Internet connectivity. Over the years, digital divide research has been discussed in the field of Information Communication Technologies and Development, or *ICTD*. Our world today features over 5 billion people who own mobile phones and approximately 3 to 4 billion with Internet access. These numbers are complicated by the reality that access is hardly as simple in practice as the word may connote. Infrastructure, digital literacy, and other existing constraints confound an oversimplified digital divide narrative. Each of these factors may compromise the ability of a given user to extract value from his or her digital access. The concept of the digital divide can be interrogated by relating it to the contexts in which users and communities engage with technology.[34] We cannot accept the hype that simply spreading digital technologies automatically empowers users and communities who are already marginalized from spaces of political and economic power.

Researchers have increasingly concluded that technology projects must carefully consider the social environment in which that technology is introduced. One cannot simply presume that technology brings about an ambiguous "developmental magic." Technology design and research must consider what these tools support *within* a community rather than

Figure 2.1. The "Hole in the Wall" TouchScreen project. Source: www.digitalcounter-revolution.co.uk.

buying into the assumption that the technology "naturally" shapes the interactions between members of a community and those outside it in ways that are positive for all involved.

A classic example of a digital divide effort is the Hole in the Wall experiment, which placed a touch-screen kiosk in a hole in walls within various urban slums in north India.[35] Evangelizers of this effort have pointed out how rapidly youth in these communities were able to make sense of this technology, using it to play games, browse the Internet, and more. Another well-known example is that of MIT Media Lab founder and technology futurist Nicholas Negroponte's One Laptop Per Child (OLPC). The OLPC effort was launched with the goal of getting a low-cost laptop into every child's hand worldwide, particularly within developing world nations. The idea behind this project was that mere access to this technology could empower learning and circumvent bureaucratic and corrupt institutions, such as schools and governments.[36]

Both the OLPC and Hole in the Wall projects have been widely critiqued for falling short of their revolutionary promises. They have been questioned on ethical grounds for clinging to the presumption that mere access to a technology, dropped from the sky, will empower learning and development. Scholars have pointed out that these types of digital divide projects fail to consider the values, practices, and protocols of community life.[37] For example, Mark Warschauer argues that simple "access-only" projects, particularly those that fail to focus on a specific issue, do little to empower community development.[38] They often fail to cultivate and work with the existing literacy practices of a given community.[39] He argues that we must recognize literacy for what it is—a cultural, local, and collective practice of encoding, decoding, expressing, and reflecting upon information.

Scale is not the only measure used to evaluate digital divide efforts. Scholars of *postcolonial computing* argue that we must consider the intentions behind technology initiatives and the ways they are framed. Women's studies scholar Kavita Philip and colleagues criticize an advertisement intended for OLPC donors, featuring African boys engrossed in laptops and urging donors to "empower" these children.[40] The advertisement implies that mere access to technology would uplift these youth from manual labor, transforming them into middle-class knowledge workers. This advertisement claims to speak to the intentions, practices, or aspirations of these youth. Yet in reality the boys are silent and invisible, only discussed insofar as they are eligible to be "saved" by the laptop. Philip and colleagues force us to confront a number of important questions, including:

> What labor conditions enable the manufacture of such an inexpensive laptop? Do these children labor to get the cash that enables the supply of Monsanto seeds, tied into land ownership, irrigation strategies, and techniques?[41]

The voices, experiences, and realities of African youth are homogenized into the category of a child needing to be "saved." Yet who decides what saving means? Or what development means? Or what access to technology *should* mean? Far too often, technology designers and funders have complete power over the project's destiny while distant users are left objectified. In contrast to this, a postcolonial computing approach asks us to recognize and respect "history, political economy, and ethnography, and specific resource, community, and technology dynamics."[42] They ask us to consider the social, economic, and cultural subtexts that accompany the introduction and distribution of any new technology. These values frame the technology's "public" meaning and command the ways in which it is designed, distributed, and embedded.

The critiques I discuss emphasize the power of context and collaboration around technology efforts. This approach is consistent with what historian Warwick Anderson describes as "semiotic formalism"[43]—a process in which the continuing absence of historical and social specificity allows Western epistemological paradigms to be applied to non-Western contexts. The problems lie not just in a myopic, Westernized reading of technology but also in the social sciences, which remain closed to the description, characterization, and ontologies that fail to fit within the Western or technocratic canon. In their treatise on postcolonial computing, Philip and colleagues argue for the importance of:

1. Characterizing "difference" (between Western and non-Western beliefs) to rethink what is creative and possible.
2. Respecting "design practices" that are culturally situated, while understanding that all translation is both linguistic and spatial.
3. Recognizing that most user-centered technology design principles perpetuate a "master-designer, God-type complex" by failing to consider the complexities of culture, economy, education, and politics.
4. Recognizing that human subjectivity has historical and social ties.

As we think about technology outside elite, urban centric contexts, it is important to reject the false binaries of colonial versus postcolonial, traditional versus scientific, or developed versus developing. We can move past these distinctions to consider collaboration and learning.

Laptop Lights

In the spirit of thinking past the creation myths of technology, we can see the power in understanding their unintended uses. For example, the One Laptop Per Child (OLPC) project can be understood not solely through its computational potential but as a source of light to be used when the sun is not accessible. As Nicholas Negroponte mentioned in a 2006 TED talk:

A little more recently I got involved [in OLPC] personally. These are two anecdotes. One was in Cambodia in a village that has no electricity, no water, no telephone, but has broadband Internet now. These kids, their first English word is Google. They only know Skype. They've never heard of telephony, they just use Skype. They go home at night, they have a broadband connection in a hut that doesn't have electricity. The parents love it because when they open up the laptop it's the brightest light source in the house.[44]

While the above discussion is driven by the belief that digital technologies "naturally" spread and benefit all, it also offers a more surprising observation, namely, that the computer laptop serves the more basic need of lighting a house in a community that lacks electricity. Thanks to its use of a hand crank the laptop can function without an infrastructure that can provide a reliable power supply. Perhaps most helpful for these communities is not the laptop as "information device" or "learning tool," but as "house light."

The juxtaposition of Negroponte's discussion of Google and Skype alongside the use of the laptop as a flashlight is striking. The first observation gives us insight into a technology creator's hope that the Internet will play a fundamental part in these youth's lives. The second reveals the villagers' unanticipated appropriation of this device to support a far more primary need.

I wonder whether there has to be such a gulf between the predictions and understandings of a technology developer and the functions it actually ends up performing in a community at the other end of the world. With this in mind, I offer a series of examples from my fieldwork throughout the rest of this book that consider technologies relative to collaborations between myself and communities from whom I have learned a great deal. This chapter focuses on stories from a multiyear partnership with two villages in Andhra Pradesh, India. It emphasizes the power of *praxis*, a collaborative process by which we move past our own privileged position as scholars who theorize "oppression" or "postcoloniality" to listen, learn, and practice humility.

Information Technology and Development

Information Communication Technologies and Development (ICTD) researchers, in their best moments, tend to recognize the marginal positions occupied by developing world communities and focus on how technologies may assist such communities in overcoming a range of barriers.[45] At one level, ICTD research focuses on moving past existing inequalities in order to have access to information. However, the field has begun to pay attention to grassroots initiatives that consider the subtleties of subcultures rather than the simple homogenization of community. These new initiatives "contest, interrogate . . . and create forms of knowledge transfer and social mobilization that proceed independently of the actions of corporate capital and the nation state system . . . on behalf of the poor that can be characterized as a 'grassroots globalization' or 'globalization from below.'"[46]

ICTD projects have ranged from providing farmers with crop prices, delivering information using different languages and subtitling,[47] developing e-governance portals, providing telemedicine advice, developing more sophisticated mobile and wireless infrastructures, sharing farmer-created videos across a distributed community,[48] and bridging gaps in understanding between citizens and governments.[49] Some efforts work to localize information in "folk-forms" as well as to cultivate voices from within a community. These projects are designed to increase awareness within communities about how they are being represented by governments and developmental organizations.

It is far too easy to place a given ICTD project on a pedestal simply on account of its engagement with a community. We must go beyond simply accepting the language of participation and scrutinize the extent to which community voices and perspectives drive the effort. Community participation can often be objectified to drive what geography scholar Frances Cleaver has described as the "development project."[50] From this perspective, the reason rural and marginalized communities are that way is because they have not effectively followed the lead of those in power. These efforts thus fail to cultivate an "open and informed debate" between development groups and technology users,[51] remaining tethered to the priorities of an NGO, academic researcher, or government official.

It is notable that some participatory efforts start with an ethnographic framework rather than solely the presumptions of a policy maker, technologist, or charity. At times these efforts may question the relevance of a technology, including the modes by which it was designed and deployed. On the other hand, participatory efforts are often critiqued for their lack of scalability and their inability to be absorbed into the logic of the state. This is unsurprising given that much of developmental funding focuses on implementing distributed, larger-scale solutions and policies.[52] Debate persists around the appropriateness of particular measurements and indicators of development, including considerations of how to think about shorter- and longer-term goals, deeper cultural and social context, the purposes of the technology, levels of observation, and the methods of approaching the data. Some argue that researchers need to reconstruct their definitions of the "divide" or the capacities they want to optimize *a priori* and then develop more incremental measurements.[53] Perhaps this debate reflects a tension between sustainability and scalability, the former related to local voices and the latter to funding and policy.

In their best moments, ICTD discussions include dialogue between engineers and technologists, social scientists, humanists, artists, and activists. These conversations may produce holistic solutions that bridge wider contexts around society and development with a more fine-tuned local understanding of culture and community. Synthesizing multiple perspectives, Ken Keniston, human development scholar from the Massachusetts Institute of Technology, and colleagues argue for the importance of recognizing four distinct digital divides between:[54]

(1) the rich and poor in every country;
(2) those who speak English or that nation's lingua franca and those who do not, including the importance of sharing and creating digital content in languages other than those dominant in a country;
(3) rich and poor nations, recognizing the power of wealthier nations to disproportionately profit from technology's global diffusion; and
(4) elites and ordinary citizens, within and between nations.

The direction ICTD projects and research should take has been the subject of significant debate. For example, a mailing list discussion occurred between researchers Kentaro Toyoma, who comes from a physics and computer science background, and Jenna Burrell, an ethnographer and qualitative sociologist. Reflecting upon their discussion, the two researchers coauthored an article entitled "What Constitutes Good ICTD Research"[55] highlighting the tensions between quantitative and macro forms of research versus qualitative and ethnographic approaches. The goal of their piece has been to bridge different kinds of research, for example, between quantitative correlations between mobile phone access and gross domestic product (GDP) in West Africa and ethnographic studies of segregation and Internet scams in the same region. Toyoma and Burrell point out the limitations of each approach. Researchers who only look at correlations may do little to explain causality or make visible the microeconomic factors that shape the mobile phone's relationship to income. Yet a study of microeconomic behaviors alone may be limited to a specific individual, family, or community. There are thus inherent epistemological differences between their ways of looking at technology research and design. Given this, Toyoma and Burrell's article focuses on points of agreement. They are interested in research that is methodologically defensible while still contributing to the goal of the field—of understanding how human and societal interaction with technologies shapes social and economic empowerment.[56]

I believe such work is important but must also consider the visions, aspirations and worldviews of peoples who often are often objectified in both types of studies. As per the argument of this book, we must embrace collaboration and as much as possible do away design and research initiatives that objectify users and communities.

The Presumption of Usability

Thus far I have discussed technology in the context of development and the ideal of information access, critiquing both concepts. I personally experienced this situation as a graduate student at the MIT Media Laboratory when I was sent to work with a number of Indian villages in Haryana, north India, as part of a joint "Media Lab Asia" initiative. As an engineer and a socially minded technologist, I assumed that the system I would design to support community knowledge-sharing across a set of villages could be easily built in the laboratory center where I was working and then "user tested" in the communities. I could gather useful statistics from villagers where I could look at user data such as how many topics were clicked, how much time was spent in a single system session, whether comments were made, and so on. All these statistics were to be built around a paradigm of use that I had taken for granted—one computer per user, basic computer literacy, and a supposed presumption by all that the technology I would develop was beneficial, natural, and useful for everyone in the village.

I soon learned of the difficulties involved in developing a set of categories to aid the villagers as they shared information. Topics such as agriculture, health, and education made no sense to the people I met. When I asked them for a better way of structuring the system, they responded with puzzled looks. Why would they need such a technology when they already spoke to one another and preserved knowledge through their traditions?

My assumption that I could "test" one user at a time was quickly confounded. The spotty electricity and my approach toward user testing did not seem to make sense to a group that wanted to use the computer collectively rather than individually. It seemed like the information I was making available, provided to me by the regional government, was of no interest to the people I was meeting. I had assumed that I could import my engineering lab training guidelines to create a meaningful technology for distant users. I quickly learned otherwise. I realized that the user statistics model by which we were taught to test technology presumed a particular scenario of interaction—one person per computer, computer-gathered statistics, and the desire to filter out any unanticipated technology uses. The idea that these users may transform our system into something altogether new, to take the technology and run with it in unpredictable directions, was a nightmare we wished to avoid at all costs. Looking back on this experience, I see it as a clear learning moment that inspires my work today and into the future.

The naïve approach I had taken is consistent with what Lucy Suchman, feminist ethnographer and designer from the University of Lancaster (U.K.), describes as "design[ing] from nowhere."[57] Without considering the power of local knowledge practices, which I articulate in my discussion of ontology in chapter 3, new technologies only maintain rather than interrupt historical patterns.[58]

Mobile Phones, Ethnography, and Grassroots Innovation

Despite my criticism of top-down efforts around understanding development and technology, it is important to note that bottom-up methods of understanding technology use have become increasingly popular. Technology corporations that produce the mobile phones available in the developing world have thus employed ethnographers. Like so many other issues, we must not simply accept the use of ethnography within technology businesses as sufficient to resolve the problems of voice and participation that motivate this book. Yet it is important to share stories of corporate ethnography to better justify my argument for the power of grassroots, community-driven digital storytelling.

Described as the "James Bond of design research" and one of business magazine *Fast Company*'s most creative people, hybrid anthropologist-designer Jan Chipchase explains how he "just came from six weeks on the road: Tokyo, London, Beirut, rural Uganda, Kenya, Barcelona, New York . . . [staying] in the Trump Towers, a $10 shack near the Sudanese border, and traveled with a Hezbollah fixer on a motorcycle."[59]

Chipchase tells ethnographically rich stories that describe the creative ways in which globally diverse communities engage with and use mobile phones. He reminds us of the power of local cultural life and creativity, explaining that we must see "peripheral" communities as active, creative, and dynamic entities rather than simply basic objects for study. On the surface this perspective seems very much in line with the arguments of this book. Such stories can be imagined not just with regard to phones but with many other digital technologies that have spread asymmetrically across the world as well.

Nonetheless, the mobile phone has been seen as a "killer app" technology by broadening information access and sharing, connecting users, and creating supposedly horizontal, democratizing networks whereby in theory any user can call any other without having to sublimate him or herself to some corporate agenda or corrupt middleman. With 4.2 billion users in 2009, mobile phones have been lauded as an effective means to improve market efficiency, particularly in agricultural markets,[60] and to foster access to health information, money, and jobs.[61]

Yet further inquiry, including within the digital inequality research I have shared, demonstrates that an unbridled "pro-mobile" narrative is not so straightforward. Much like Internet access, mobile networks tend to pattern and extend inequality based on factors such as who has better access to infrastructure, literacy, and existing social networks. Device users may be unaware of how the data gathered about them is used and also have little ability to control that process. The payments they make to buy phones or "talk minutes" end up building the profit margins for the companies that manage the larger network infrastructure.

Nonetheless, Chipchase argues that the diffusion of mobile phones has everything to do with their convenience. They allow anyone, in theory, to transcend space and time in a way that is both "personal and convenient. . . . [You] don't need to ask [for] permission to use it."[62]

We are supposed to marvel here at the powerful reach of mobile telephony and accept that an ethnographic narrative justifies the actions and assumptions of first-world technology corporations. We must focus on what technologies can make possible, rather than see the limitations and costs around how they are used. Chipchase may recognize that mobile phones are not yet in the hands of everyone, yet he seems to assume that once the access issue is remedied every user will be able to "transcend" the constraints of space and time. The exceptionalism of mobile phones is justified on the basis of concepts such as transcendence and universality. But we cannot take such language for granted and must instead identify its philosophical underpinnings and cultural biases.

Even a cursory analysis of "mobile transcendence" tells a different story. People in the developing world often lack the needed credit or "talk time" to make calls. Many use their phones only occasionally to receive calls. For example, in regions of New Guinea where I have traveled in the past it seemed that more people used their phone lights to hunt crocodiles than to speak to one another. Moreover, many such phones lack the capacity to access the Internet. The diffusion of this technology is highly asymmetric.

For many people phone plans are prepaid, such that if one has no money, making a call is impossible. In India and other parts of the world, poorer users engage in the "missed call" phenomenon, initiating the call and hanging up before it can be answered, indicating to the other party they want to be called back. While this practice reveals local creativity in action, it also speaks to an unfair dependency on those with the resources to make a phone call. It is absurd to think that a mobile phone can magically uproot users from the existing economic, political, and environmental inequalities they face.

Chipchase praises the power of "street up innovation," explaining that in the developing world people will find elegant solutions and innovate without centralized control. He presents captivating examples like Uganda's "Sente,"[63] where kiosk operators trade "talk time" credits with one another, essentially developing a system of exchange without needing to rely on a financial system or the presence of banks.

Similar to this is the Kenyan and Tanzanian M-Pesa effort, which was launched on mobile phones to engage new technology users across rural and urban regions within these East African nations. M-Pesa is an example of innovation from the grassroots, recognizing that mobile phone transactional trading is far more beneficial for communities that have long experienced an absence of formal technological and financial infrastructures. This is one of many examples whereby a technology was designed for the conditions and realities faced by communities and nations at the margins. It is an example of how we must rethink innovation, design, and ultimately what technology is or is not in accordance with the constraints and material realities that people face across the world in their everyday lives. Yet we cannot forget the political economies at play even in this effort, recognizing that it was launched by mobile provider Vodafone for major telecommunication providers Safaricom and Vodacom. In that sense, while its design is community-resonant, it may not be a venture that empowers the autonomy and sovereignty of its grassroots users.

Grassroots practices of technology appropriation, the use of a technology in creative and potentially unintended ways, speak to the ubiquity of the "informal economy" in the developing world. This economy describes those who work outside the registered formal industrial sector. They are outside the world of social security numbers and census calculations. Individuals in this economy must adapt and innovate in order to access money, food, or the services they need to survive in a volatile world. The informal economy operates within and through social networks associated with local place and community, a system of social relationships rather than relatively anonymous transactions between individuals. It is consistent with what the late anthropologist Clifford Geertz, in his poetic ethnography of Morocco, called "bazaar econo-

Figure 2.2. Photograph of an M-Pesa kiosk located in East Africa.
Source: www.samrack.com.

mies."[64] Thus, an informal economy has emerged around the mobile phone, not just at kiosks, but also in repair shops, locking/unlocking, hacking, and more. It takes nothing more than a flat table and a soldering iron to reverse engineered phones that in the Western world may head to landfills.

Chipchase concludes that we must carefully observe the ways in which local communities innovate from the grassroots and design from that perspective. What remains problematic, however, is his assumption that these practices turn every technology user into a Western, liberal, freedom-craving subject. Not only will this not occur in practice, but it is ethically problematic as it presumes the superiority of Western values, which may themselves be full of paradoxes. Technological projects that originate in the West tend to be loaded with such ideological and philosophical baggage. It is high time we did away with such assumptions and instead considered how technologies may support diverse values rather than the ones we wish to export. We can open up our understandings of innovation, creativity, and technology to listen to and learn from communities and cultures across the world.

Nonetheless, it is easy to see why we marvel at the diffusion of the mobile phone. The infrastructures used for mobile phone connectivity are far simpler to construct in remote environments than their wired telephony precedents. Yet they are not invisible—indeed, it is important to think of the numerous layers of infrastructure that went into the construction and mobility of a mobile phone tower from the ships that brought its components from China to the other infrastructures that needed to be set up to build the tower.

In many parts of the world where I have traveled, I have seen tables set up on the side of the road with hand-painted or written signs indicating that it is a mobile phone kiosk. What these kiosks mean and how the mobile phones they provide are used is a question that can only be understood by looking at place, culture, and community. In my own fieldwork worldwide, I have observed a range of creative practices on the ground in association with the mobile phone. Local communities in the developing world have found positive uses for this technology due to its cheap prices (often using Chinese-produced "knock-offs") and variable pricing systems that require no identification or routine payments. Most importantly, these phones accrue value from local appropriation and "reinvention."[65] That value could hardly have been anticipated by those outside the immediate cultural and social context.[66]

Consistent with my argument, media studies scholar from the University of California, Santa Barbara, Lisa Parks has argued that mobile telephony must be "conceptualized [within] sites of variation and studied in relation to particular socio-historical, geophysical, political, economic, and cultural conditions."[67] Parks engaged in "footprint analysis" ethnography in her study of over one hundred mobile access points, seeing how each of these points was connected to a range of other technical and social infrastructures. Parks's insights center on place, culture, and technology in interaction, and cannot be fully captured by prognostications from afar. She points out that mobile phones have now been appropriated in Mongolia in a manner that "combines the collectivist ethos of communism with aspects of digital capitalism, and reinvents nomadic practices in urban space."[68] This type of research speaks to the value of approaching media and technology "on the ground" with collaboration, integrity, and respect.

One example Parks describes is of "walking phone workers" on urban streets who provide mobile access to paying customers. They shape the traffic of phone use within an infrastructure partly owned by Mongolian companies. Mobile phone penetration, according to these and other ethnographies, defies the simple narrative of one-size-fits-all flattening and supports "variation."[69] Technology is but one small part of a wider infrastructural, cultural, and social environment.

Ethnographic research that has studied the mobile phone in the context of local environments or infrastructures reveals that like many other technologies it tends to be translated, adopted, and shaped as it moves locally and laterally. For example, Internet ethnographies in Trinidad[70] and Jamaica[71] reveal the power of local value systems and social networks in shaping the destiny of the phone. These studies consider technologies in relation to existing networks of interaction, including social networks, economies, politics, and infrastructures. Such research reflects on how classic anthropological concepts such as "kinship" are transformed as a result of the ways in which technologies are appropriated. This in turn transforms preexisting notions of time and space.[72] These dynamics occur as local communities imprint, shape, and domesticate new technologies.

Such insights indicate that the mobile phone, like other networked technologies, does not simply flatten users into passive consumers. Nor does the fact that these technologies are locally appropriated mean that people in the developing world become the equals of their first-world brethren. Researchers and technology designers must consider information environments,[73] which are "social settings or milieu in which resources, relations, and technologies undergo a structuration type process of change called informing."[74] These settings can include different forms of access, business models, infrastructures,[75] mediating institutions,[76] and already existing capacities that influence the ability of the user or community to act in ways they may desire.[77]

Innovation for Whom?

As we think about innovations and applications associated with the mobile phone, a story of ambivalence is revealed. We see powerful examples of community creativity in action, where existing tools are appropriated, hacked, and innovated upon to support peoples and places far removed from its initial technological design. We see interesting narratives of grassroots activity being circulated by corporate ethnographers. Yet we also see mistaken presumptions and conclusions, ones that seem to fit far more into a Westernized corporate narrative than one of grassroots action and mobilization. Jan Chipchase, in his TED talk titled "The Anthropology of Mobile Phones," implies that the corporations of the Western world and consumers of the developing world have entered into a mutually beneficial relationship. Such an assumption fails to consider that the reinvention of such tools may not always fit the agendas of a distant technology corporation.

We are limited by these presumptions and are supposed to accept trite expressions such as "the newly connected want to be part of the conversation." In blindly accepting such assumptions, we fail to question whether there really is a "global conversation" and if so, who defines its contours and direction. We mistakenly presume that developing world users want to connect with others across the world, rather than pay attention to empirical data that show that the vast majority of phone calls are made between people living within geographic proximity of one another.

To productively extend my discussion and introduce my research based in India, I consider two issues in the following section of this chapter. First is the theme of *political economy*, which considers the political and economic agendas underlying a technology effort, and second the theme of *grassroots voice*, which considers how technological projects can be designed collaboratively to respect the beliefs, values, and knowledges of local communities.

Voice and Political Economy

I have argued that the nature of technology use depends not just on the cultural and infrastructural factors with which it is associated, but also on the economic status of its different users and communities worldwide. We also must consider the possibility that technologies can be actively appropriated not just for the purpose of innovation, but also to shape movements or intentions that may diverge considerably from their original intended uses. This focus represents a subtle yet powerful shift in conceptualizing what technology is and the ways in which it can be engaged.

An important set of questions about technology relates to the theme of political economy—examining who controls the networks, economies, and agendas associated with a digital platform or device. We can consider different types of economic or political systems that could or should be associated with a mobile phone project. This would involve thinking about different revenue and/or profit models, considering a range of labor practices, data retention and aggregation, and business ownership. We must examine these assumptions and more if we are to truly think about technologies in the service of diverse user communities. For example, developing world users may be even less aware of what data is gathered about them than their first-world counterparts. A major question in new media studies and activism must thus focus not just on how people use technology, but what types of social, economic, and political agendas profit as a result.

As media studies scholar from Amsterdam Geert Lovink pointed out in a conversation with me, most mobile phones force developing world users to be "on call" in the sense that they are forced by existing economic systems to be unable to make calls on their own. Instead of blithely celebrating the mobile phone's existence and diffusion, we can critically examine and therefore reimagine the infrastructures by which the technology is deployed, asking important questions such as, "What values and ethical principles do we inscribe in the inner depths of the built information environment?"[78]

The projects I introduce throughout this book respect diversity at its deepest level. Feminist studies scholar Gayatri Spivak's famous essay "Can the Subaltern Speak?"[79] has long been an important catalyst for academics interested in thinking more critically about the voices of peoples on the margins of an increasingly unequal world. Yet instead of simply treating communities as "subaltern," I believe through collaborative projects we can respect the creativity and agency by which people across the world live their lives. We can reject objectifying categories such as "enlightened user" or "subjugated subaltern," choosing instead to develop respectful collaborations that challenge systems of power and oppression.

Local communities in today's world are more than capable of making choices about how they wish to engage with new technologies. Many of their choices are neither pro nor anti-technology, but instead about how these tools or systems may be appropriated. As telecommunications scholars Harmeet Sawhney and Venkata Suri point out,[80] even the supposedly luddite Amish in the United States have selectively worked with technologies in ways that support local priorities and values. The strategic choices by which communities such as these appropriate and adopt certain technologies reflect their "lateral" sensibilities, recognizing the power of values, beliefs, and knowledges as articulated at the local level. This is in contrast to the traditional central-peripheral model that dominates most technocratic thinking about technology, media, and culture. In this sense, thinking laterally represents a productive rethinking of media studies that is consistent with my repeated uses of the terms local, place, and community throughout this book.

We can confront a discourse that predicts or frames what development or technology means on the basis of values and economic objectives too far removed from local community life. Top-down presumptions saturate far too many prognostications of new technology. We see those without steady Internet access as technologically disenfranchised, in need of hand-me-downs from the West. With that access, magical transformations, whether cultural, social, economic, or political, will occur, ostensibly in ways that support Western aims. This view sees the Internet as a technological master-infrastructure that subsumes all others rather than as a tool that is coconstitutive and linked to a set of practices and processes in ways that are often surprising and fascinating.

Technology infrastructures and systems are sociotechnical—daisy-chained to place, community, and environment. In her more recent work, Lisa Parks argues that one cannot understand mobile telephony and Internet access in rural Zambia without examining how these are tied to a range of other technologies and infrastructures from hydropower to cars and gasoline.[81] Projects such as Hole in the Wall or One Laptop Per Child encounter their undoing because of the values they presume and the predictions they presuppose. They operate on the assumption that a technology designed in Massachusetts or New Delhi "transmits" values to other communities or cultures irrespective of where they are located and who they may be. Traditional structures of learning in a community are problematic, according to such technocratic perspectives, seen as inefficient roadblocks to progress. We can no longer ignore the power of praxis and collaboration, and the ways in which this may shape the design and development of technology.

Appropriation and Participation

To shift our understanding further toward the grassroots actions that communities and users across the world may take with technology, I next discuss important reflections on the concepts of technological *appropriation*, the active reshaping of a technology or text to support local uses and visions, and *participation*, the ability to share one's voice and therefore participate, through the use of a tool.

Henry Jenkins, media, communications, and film studies scholar from the University of Southern California, argues that the twenty-first century is an increasingly *participatory culture*, and that it is therefore all the more important to embrace new media literacies like play, simulation, performance, and appropriation.[82] Jenkins also recognizes the incomplete extent to which such participation has extended, and the lack of awareness of the histories of media and the inequalities produced by globalization.

Designers and scholars of media studies can engage communities as active creators and designers rather than as passive users of technology, as revealed in Figure 2.3. Each step in this diagram represents a further imprinting of a community's voice on the very texts or "codes" of a technology from the telling of a story using a technology to the recrafting of interfaces, algorithms, and databases. The ethnographies I present in this and subsequent chapters present examples of this.

This figure also asks us to interrogate the concept of participation, analyzing different components and features by which this may occur. We must ask questions about how broadly we can praise a "participatory turn" in the way people use social media and Internet technologies.[83] Revealed in the figure is the concept of appropriation. Work on appropriation considers how media and technology can be incorporated into everyday life or "domesticated."[84] Appropriation focuses on reinvention and repurposing, respecting engagements with technology that may significantly differ from its "intended use."

Appropriation studies research builds on a history that focused on television and film audiences. Despite the argument that television is

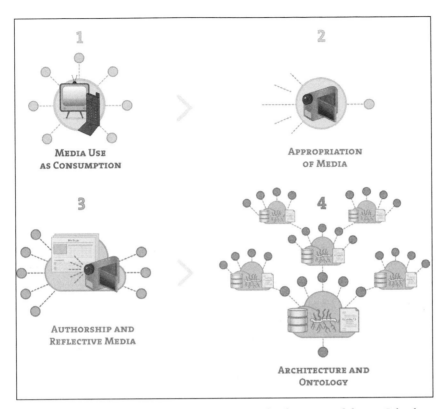

Figure 2.3. A continuum of voice and power over technology use and design. I thank Chilean media artist Diego Gomez, from UCLA's Design|Media Arts department, for his help in producing this image.

a passive medium that diminishes a community's "social capital,"[85] researchers have argued that under particular conditions an audience may actively and constructively engage with the text (whether written, audiovisual, or interactive). As Jenkins has illustrated in his earlier work on fan cultures, active television audience members may appropriate media by organizing and constructing "fan cultures," for example by creating alternative Star Trek episodes.[86] The fan is no longer a passive reader or observer in these cases, but instead a producer and creator of an alternative text, reshaping the media technology accordingly.[87] Nancy Baym,[88] communications scholar and researcher at Microsoft Research, has argued that through appropriation audiences are able to generate new social bonds and practices as they collectively move between media platforms, blur online and offline distinctions, and create and imagine new stories and futures.

While appropriation rarely engages in the task of reengineering a technology, it takes a people and community-first conversation around technology much further than typical access-oriented research. This is due to its attention to the ways in which users can locally and creatively reshape tools. In this sense appropriation represents the first important marker in the trajectory traced in Figure 2.3.

We could easily concern ourselves with simply celebrating appropriation in a way that is conceptually detached from the politics of the technology project. However, I believe if we simply accept appropriation as the trope of our times, as we see in many discussions around "participation" today, we run the risk of overly Westernizing our analysis of appropriation. We must ask whether a transmediated remake of *Harry Potter*, *Buffy the Vampire Slayer*, or *Star Trek* can shape identities and movements that have long been stifled. How emblematic are these cases of the visions and practices of peoples in the developing world?

Exemplifying this concern, Craig Watkins, a scholar of digital media and youth culture, argues for the importance of "participatory politics" by discussing hip-hop as a remix practice that takes its texts from mainstream cultures and reappropriates them within an emerging vernacular of youth culture.[89] This example stands in contrast to the long-standing debate around stereotypes in media industries whereby, for example, African Americans are presented as athletes, criminals, or sexualized beings. Social, political, and economic hierarchies can indeed be perpetuated by media industries without making such discourses visible and undermining them in every manner possible.[90] In addition to this, other media studies scholars describe the modes by which mainstream discourses may be refashioned as subcultural and intergenerational.[91]

My discussion of appropriation relates to Welsh cultural studies scholar Raymond Williams's triad of *dominant, residual,* and *emergent* concepts for understanding the ways in which culture operates.[92] Williams argues that one can understand the practice of culture by examining the interplay between the dominant, residual, and emergent. The dominant perspective is embedded in the majority of a society at a given time, yet may not be practiced or adopted by all, even at an implicit level. Within such dominant perspectives, however, are traces of the past, or residual elements, that represent the subjective means by which memory is practiced to legitimate the present, as it is reinterpreted, framed, or projected. Only when the residual and dominant discourses are in tension with one another can either of them be undermined. Finally, emergent elements of culture, which differ significantly from the dominant perspective, may also be present at any time. Williams points out that it is important to study the interplay between these three modes of practicing culture in order to understand the complexity of society and they must be considered in relation to media and technology practices.

This book's call for collaboration with and respect for diverse and often marginalized communities worldwide makes it important to consider technology appropriation with an eye toward race, ethnicity, and the legacies of colonialism. Ethnic studies scholar George Lipsitz's work on "strategic anti-essentialism" considers how a community may choose to define itself in relation to the "other."[93] Lipsitz's discussion of popular music and genre describes how majority and minority cultures strategically define themselves through the selective adoption, interpretation, and rearticulation of various cultural texts and practices.

Minorities are not alone in engaging in strategic anti-essentialism; those who hold positions of economic, political, and racial power do so as well. Lipsitz's *Footsteps in the Dark: The Hidden Histories of Popular Music* discusses a range of examples that include the seemingly contradictory practices associated with techno music subcultures amongst inner city black youth in Detroit, the articulation of multiple Latin nationalisms through mainstream music genres, and the seemingly inclusive Ken Burns Public Broadcasting Service (PBS) series.[94] In each of these examples power is shaped through the improvisations that bridge mainstream white and subaltern minority cultures. There are secret meanings at play, shaped by community and place. This explains why we cannot simply presume that a media object or text can be understood from afar or in singular terms. Instead, chains of movement and strategic practices tell a far richer story of the situated realities of inequality and power. Lipsitz's writings remind us of how important it is to interrogate profound and seemingly ever-increasing inequalities associated with race, gender, and class.

Authorship, Local Creation, and Curation

To push the conversation further and consider the activist facets of participation and appropriation, it is powerful to consider the potential of using technology to support the telling of one's story and the release of one's voice. Given this, we should ask: How can grassroots uses of technology support authorship by otherwise marginalized users and communities and promote development and mobilization from within?

Anthropologist Faye Ginsburg discusses community-driven authorship and reflection in her visual anthropology research. She argues for the power of "strategic traditionalism,"[95] her term for the creative ways in which indigenous peoples have taken hold of various media technologies:

> The cultural activists creating these new kinds of cultural forms have turned to them as a means of revivifying relationships to their lands, local languages, traditions, and histories and articulating community concerns. They also see media as a means of . . . revers[ing] processes through which aspects of their societies have been objectified, commodified, and appropriated; their media productions and writings are efforts to recuperate their histories, land rights, and knowledge bases as their own cultural property.[96]

Ginsburg's research forms the foundation of *indigenous media* studies, which is associated with an ethical shift through which ethnographers and anthropologists have turned toward collaboration and praxis and away from merely the "study of." While visual anthropology features a history of documentary and visual texts created by researchers that are supposed to be representations of culturally diverse communities, anthropologists since the 1980s have taken a "reflexive turn," recognizing that the stories they tell about others are reflections of themselves. "Scientific" and "natural" descriptions of culture have been increasingly rejected because of the ways in which they objectify communities. I argue in this book's first chapter that we must push the process even further to consider collaborative ethnography and decolonizing methodologies.

Ginsburg points out that as of 2008 only 35 percent of the world's 7 billion people were Internet users. Terms like the "digital age" or "digital revolution" therefore smuggle in a number of blanket assumptions that ignore the different parts of the world where technologies may have migrated or been reinvented.[97] The digital world must thus be explored within each specific cultural and social context to help us best understand what it means and what it can be used for in the different communities involved. While Ginsburg asks us to curb our (overly simplistic) digital enthusiasm, media anthropology demonstrates how technologies can shape storytelling to help mobilize indigenous and grassroots movements.

Media anthropologists have described their collaborations with diverse communities, and in so doing have shown how storytelling through digital technologies has shaped the social and political agendas of local communities. Important research on this topic includes, for example, the study of video in indigenous political and social movements in Brazil,[98] Inuit communities and video/television in Canada,[99] database-driven systems in Native American and Yolngu Aboriginal communities,[100] and networks of old and new media that now connect previously peripheral communities to one another.[101]

Anthropologist Terrence Turner's work with the Kayapo indigenous people of the Amazon has revealed how grassroots authorship can impact political mobilization.[102] Turner notes the political means through which stories were told with video cameras to document the negative effects of government hydroelectric dam schemes, for both local and global audiences. This video documentation was brought back to the community by the appointed storytellers and used to inform the different tribes of the impending danger. The Kayapo further found that using their cameras gave them a degree of legitimacy when they interviewed and questioned Brazilian bureaucrats and politicians, forcing the government to answer their questions, partly because of the "modern" cachet associated with such technology. This effort turned a local, place-based struggle into an international issue, allowing the Kayapo to articulate their land claims on a stage that threatened the international credibility of the Brazilian state. It is important to note that this global spectacle came up from the grassroots rather than being imposed from the top down.

Complementing the Kayapo case is the work of Eric Michaels, a pioneering media anthropologist based in the United States and Australia, and the Warlpiri Aboriginal community of Central and Western Australia. Michaels collaborated with this group to design a low-power transmitter that allowed tribespeople to produce and access locally produced television programs. Michaels argues that the predominantly oral cultures of these aboriginal communities smoothly transitioned into the electronic systems of this video infrastructure, precisely because the appropriation of the infrastructure was directed toward community-produced content and a bottom-up understanding of how the technology could support their social, cultural, and political lives. As he says: "There is no necessary translation from orality to electronics; we are instead seeing an experimental phase involving the insertion of the camera into the social organization of events."[103]

The examples of the Kayapo and Warlpiri reveal the potential of using technology to shape authorship and storytelling as a catalyst for social or political change. Accompanying these examples is the famous case of the Zapatistas of Chiapas, Mexico—an indigenous-led political movement for self-determination announced the day after the signing of NAFTA, on December 17, 1992. While this movement also involved collaborations and partnerships with nonindigenous peoples, as among the Kayapo and Warlpiri, it is notable that different groups aligned with the Zapatistas creatively appropriated various technologies to suit their own political ends, to build solidarity with indigenous, regional, and global publics. For example, while shortwave and citizens band (cb) radio supported local communities and activists dispersed across the Lacandon jungle in rural Mexico, Internet newsgroups were appropriated to build sympathy with journalists and wider audiences across the world. Harry Cleaver, a Marxist economist, has argued that the Zapatistas were able to "use electronic networks in conjunction with the more familiar tactics of solidarity movements: teach-ins, articles in the alternative press, demonstrations, the occupation of Mexican government consulates and so on."[104]

Such an "electronic fabric of struggle"[105] by different elements within the movement, including nonindigenous allies, demonstrates the clever means by which local communities can appropriate technologies to tell stories that influence their movements and agendas. The ability of the Zapatistas to become a global poster child drawing in environmentalists, human rights activists, and politically discontented citizens worldwide to support their cause, speaks to their appropriation of a wide range of technologies, including those outside the "technology research" paradigm. The creative repositioning of content to shape and influence different publics is a key to the story and remains a central theme in grassroots activist and indigenous movements today.

The examples I have given illustrate the potential of communities on the margins of political and social power to create, circulate, and benefit from indigenous information and media. Each reveals the power of authorship combined with do-it-yourself (DIY) visioning from the grassroots. These efforts point to the potential of indigenous media projects to give voice to self-determination and strategic articulation, moving past a binary described by Faye Ginsburg as a "Faustian contract or Global Village."[106] Across all these projects, communities took power as authors, producers, and storytellers, inverting a technocratic history and policy that imposes tools on local populations to support the systems and actors in power.

Sterile user statistics-focused research loses sight of the emergent and unanticipated practices that are central to each of the cases I have shared from across the world in this chapter. We must think broadly about mediation, opening ourselves to the unexpected.

Authorship and Reflection in South India

Many of the examples from across the world that I have shared throughout this chapter bring together researchers and communities in the spirit of collaboration. They reveal the power of telling one's story using technology to shape viable "participation in policy-making and shaping of environments and communities through direct action and self-reflection."[107] Many reveal the power of active *technology authorship* as opposed to passive technology use. Authoring, creating, and sharing one's story or voice allows a perspective to be shared and reflected upon.

The term *reflective practice* relates to a set of theories that argue for the importance of self- and collective awareness in the support of learning and growth.[108] It is described as "an important human activity in which people recapture their experience, think about it, mull on it, and evaluate it."[109] While most academic theories on reflection consider its meaning in relation to education research themes such as thinking and learning, the community media examples I have shared suggest that it can be a catalyst to support communities whose voices are largely ignored in technology and development projects.

Technology and development researcher Richard Heeks points out that communities are often excluded from articulating their visions for ICTD projects.[110] In my personal experiences as a volunteer and graduate student in South Asia, I too recognized that the community members I met rarely had any voice in the projects we designed. It is common in this part of the world to receive a polite yet disengaged "yes sir" to any question one may ask. At other times, there may be no response or communication at all. Although it is important to respect these moments, they speak to the challenges that block deeper communication between those who have the power to implement technology initiatives and those who remain at the sidelines.

With these thoughts in mind, as a graduate student at the MIT Media Laboratory I examined how to develop and design information systems to support refugees from Somalia who had recently immigrated to the New England region in the United States. Thanks to departmental funding I had acquired a number of video cameras that I hypothesized may assist community members who wished to share video stories with others in their community. I observed how the Somali process of video storytelling and viewing facilitated difficult conversations about topics normally considered culturally taboo, such as genital circumcision and Islamophobia. A range of issues on race, citizenship, public health, and identity became part of an internal community conversation. Honored to be invited to witness some of these conversations, I recognized the potential of seeing technology as a tool of creation and reflection.

I became interested in whether technologies could support creative and reflective practices *within a community*. This would be in contrast to most technology efforts that view local communities as passive technology users, magically edified through their exposure to information broadcast from the top down. Arjun Appadurai has argued for the power of an emancipatory "grassroots imagination" in the rethinking of technology and development efforts. He explains that "it is . . . through imagination that modern citizens are disciplined and controlled. One task of a newly alert social science is to name and analyze these mobile civil forms and to rethink the meaning of research styles and networks appropriate to this mobility."[111]

Mainstream narratives that pitch new technologies as "solutions" are far from neutral. They can be easily associated with discourses that frame what a user is and the experience he or she *should* have when given access to information or technology. These discourses come from the top-down and have long been popularized by technology corporations and development agencies. I believe they must be inverted to combat the fatalism that has afflicted many poorer communities: "More concretely, the poor are frequently in a position where they are encouraged to subscribe to norms whose social effect is to further diminish their dignity, exacerbate their inequality. . . . In the Indian case, these norms take a variety of forms: some have to do with fate."[112] Appadurai here discusses norms that reinforce inequality due to the ways in which they shape the fatalistic outlook of poor citizens. The discussion of these norms is meant to inspire transformations that come from the bottom up rather than reinforce a history of hand-me-downs that reinforce hierarchy.

Anthropological and philosophical theory that links poverty and fatalism is consistent with psychological research in India that reveals how one's unequal position in life may shape cognitive outlook.[113] Supporting aspiration and reflection from the grassroots in a way that defies pedantic projects and patronizing rhetoric is thus all the more important. All our practices of everyday life are formed through routines, actions, and modes of identity building that are both individual and social.[114] These routines, regardless of culture, community, or social strata, provide us with cognitive security. Yet in some cases cognitive patterns, cultural practices, and fatalistic attitudes may reinforce inequality. Reflection, which may interrupt habituated routine, is fundamental to the development of all peoples and communities. Yet it is a luxury rarely afforded to those who must struggle daily to survive, in part due to a lack of capital.

Appadurai writes of the "capacity to aspire."[115] He links this to work in *capacity building*, a common term used in development studies to reflect the skills or assets needed to transform one's current state. This capacity is tied to reflection and mobilization, and a concept that has rarely entered the development studies lexicon. Appadurai explains that wealthier people have this capacity "because they have a stock of available experiences of the relationship of aspirations and outcomes . . . opportunities to produce justifications, narratives, metaphors, and pathways through which bundles of goods and services are actually tied to wider social scenes and contexts."[116]

Building on what I learned from my experiences in Haryana, India, and with the Somali immigrant community that I described in this chapter, I became interested in supporting the 'new narratives' about which Appadurai speaks. Folklorists and ethnographers alike have long understood the power of stories—not solely as a medium for information sharing, but also for anchoring norms and values. Stories articulate the boundaries between sacred and profane, normative and deviant, aspirational and degraded. Not only do stories function as a medium for information sharing; they also serve as "containers" of social and cultural values. If technologies could similarly cultivate storytelling and local communities' "capacity to aspire," fueling new stories and reflections from within, a new direction for development studies and ICTD may emerge.

I contacted nongovernmental organizations (NGOs), academic colleagues, and activists far and wide to see if I could examine the potential of reflective media in South India, close to my heart given that it my own ancestral region. After several months, fortune smiled. A colleague introduced me to the Byrraju Foundation in the city of Hyderabad (Andhra Pradesh, India) in late 2005. The foundation had worked for many years to support infrastructure, education, and agricultural projects with rural communities in the Godavari region, a fourteen-hour train journey from their urban location.

As I walked into the offices of the foundation, surrounded by palatial gardens and marble staircases, I wondered how the realities of villages could be recognized and supported by those living and working in such lavish surroundings. Yet I was grateful to find a ready embrace of my interests, ideas, and experiences. The foundation leadership assured me from the start that they would be very interested in collaboration, starting with a visit to the organization to develop a project strategy. Perhaps this was due to my "status" as a new professor at UCLA, or perhaps it was due to the credibility of our mutual connection. I still do not know.

The Byrraju Foundation was created in memory of the wealthy philanthropist Satyanarayana Raju by his son Ramalinga Raju. The family

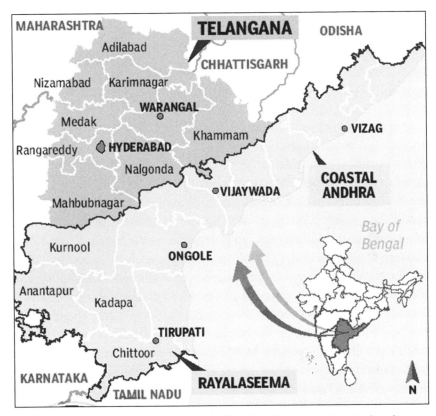

Figure 2.4. A map of the Godavari region of South India. Source: http://indpaedia.com.

is from the Godavari region of the southeast Indian province of Andhra Pradesh. Figure 2.4 shows a map of India, illuminating the Telangana and coastal Andhra provinces, which Godavari spans.

Raju is well known in India as the former CEO of Satyam Information Technology Corporation, though he resigned from the company in 2009 due to a financial scandal and was subsequently jailed for white-collar fraud. In my sole meeting with Raju in late 2007, I noted how seriously he seemed to take the mission of supporting rural development in the Godavari region. He asked me several direct questions about how technology authorship and storytelling might shape capacities, aspirations, and socioeconomic outcomes in the villages where I might collaborate. His questions were driven by a sense of technical skepticism, but I appreciated how they forced me to speak to my own intuitions about reflective media and the ethical principles that would motivate my effort. Even more hands-on, Raju's wife Nandhini attended our periodic brainstorming sessions and strategically advised the Foundation directors, most of whom came from the Indian Information Technology (IT) industry.

India's middle class boom is often lauded as an outcome of the growth of the IT industry. While macroeconomic data have revealed a significant growth in the percentage of the middle class relative to the overall national population, it is noteworthy that many estimates put the overall numbers at under 25 percent of the overall population, with approximately 20 percent living below the poverty line. Indeed, some studies indicate that India has the largest number of people in the world below the poverty line, approximately 360 million of the nearly 1.2 billion population. While it is not fully accurate to attribute Indian middle class growth solely to the IT industry, many leaders of Indian software corporations are widely viewed as heroes, new fathers of the nation who have taken their country to a place of greater global visibility and power. Deregulation of these industries and the support of the private sector has become a platform on which the current national government, led by Prime Minister Narendra Modi, operates. The common narrative in India today is that it is only a matter of time before the rest of the population will learn from the stories of the nation's fathers of Information Technology.

Implicated in contemporary global urbanization across the world are questions about technology's diffusion and use. Many technologists, bureaucrats, and scholars in India have freely shared their opinions on the future of rural life across the nation. Some, including Narayana Murthy, billionaire founder of India's Infosys Corporation, have argued that urbanization is inevitable and necessary given that it is in cities that jobs may be found. The prevailing narrative is that the only way the rural poor can hope to find employment and earn an income is by migrating to the cities.[117] Some disagree, arguing that these dynamics only exist because the villages have not been effectively incorporated into these development plans and thus urban flight has been the logical result. But what remains unchallenged is the assumption that a neoliberal IT-outsourcing industry is the positive path forward for all.

This perspective toward the rural population as needy of "transformation" contrasts with that of the father of the modern Indian state,

Mahatma Gandhi, who argued for sustainable, self-supported, grass-roots "village industries" driven by local self-determination. Discourses about development and technology in modern India seem to assume that the only choices are to either end rural life completely or better connect rural communities to outsourcing opportunities. In either case, the urban dominates the rural and the voices across village communities remain largely silent. "Subalternity," to reference cultural and literary studies scholar Gayatri Spivak's writings on those left out by Western epistemologies, runs into trouble when deployed to see rural and poor people as objects of study rather than active agents of change and mobilization.

It was thus unsurprising for me to enter a posh foundation led by former IT managers who claimed to be dedicated to the theme of "uplifting" rural peoples in their province. Nonetheless, the pragmatism of my goal of supporting grassroots community reflection and aspiration resonated with the Foundation leadership. At the same time, I was asked several tough questions, including: Why was I not interested in simply providing a service and measuring its outcome on development? Were reflective media and storytelling not too open-ended and ambiguous?

The Byrraju Foundation, like many other Indian organizations wedded to the IT industry, was interested in infrastructure, access, and resource provision—each seen as technical tasks rather than subject to the type of social and technical complexity I describe throughout this book. Many Foundation activities involved exporting services to communities—meaning more schools, Internet access, call centers for business outsourcing, community tourism, or health care access. These are the types of projects often supported by development organizations, private foundations, and governments. It is notable that what brings these together is the mistaken belief and assumption of what effective development should be. *New York Times* journalist Thomas Friedman, an outspoken proponent of global trade, had recently visited the Foundation and praised its efforts to "flatten" the relationship between its constituent villages and domestic industries.

My goal was to find an alternative to this conversation, both ethically and reflectively. I approached the Foundation in order to explore the power of collaboration, praxis, and media storytelling to shape collaboration with the communities that the Foundation "served." I had become increasingly drawn to exploring low-cost video technology to shape my effort based on these conversations. Creating simple videos could be done with little to no training and I hoped it would help catalyze reflection and action in the villages in which we would collaborate.

The Byrraju leaders explained that they had developed a "vision protocol," a document over ten pages long that asked villagers dozens of questions about education, technology, health, agriculture, and more. The questions and categories to be assessed in this survey reflected the assumptions of the Byrraju administrators. The goal was to allocate services based on the data collected. Yet the answers they received were more likely related to the questions asked rather than an awareness of the context in which they were asked.

A leading agricultural scientist from the Foundation anonymously explained to me that "these people would not know how to come up with visions on their own—they should trust us in the foundation to make choices for them." Rural people in his view were too "traditional," too conditioned by their traditions and families to make such choices about development. In contrast, my project was dedicated to inspiring reflection and dialogue from the communities with which I would collaborate. I wished to respect existing traditions and practices while recognizing that they had partly been shaped by the dynamics of marginalization.

My challenge was to convince a group of technologists and urban development specialists to consider an alternate vision—one that rejected the myths of rural obsolescence and top-down development studies. I asked for patience and assured my partners at the Foundation that even if what we learned took us far away from our previous "development map," we may arrive at a place far richer.

Stories from Godavari: Meetings and Coconut Trees

It is mid-September in 2006. The Byrraju Foundation has asked TLS Bhaskar, a sociologist and ethnographer, to support our efforts in the Godavari region in Andhra Pradesh, South India. After a night of uneven sleep, I pull open the window and see multicolored homes, rice paddy fields, and coconut trees, all illuminated by bright sunlight. The land has a rich dark colored soil and seems to support dense green natural vegetation and farming. Bhaskar was the only social scientist I had met in my initial three-day visit to the Foundation's headquarters. He voiced his unbridled enthusiasm for every idea I proposed. His usual work at the Foundation involved survey deployment and collection, which he felt had disengaged him from the communities he wished to support and learn from. The Foundation had dismissed ethnographic practice, as it did not provide data that could be quantified or compared.

Bhaskar was an excellent field collaborator given that I could only come to India during the periodic breaks offered by my home institution, UCLA. He appeared open to unlearning his own assumptions about fieldwork, which I challenged whenever he made sweeping statements about the village communities we would be visiting. All researchers have hypotheses and assumptions about the communities they study, but Bhaskar's seemed particularly rooted in the language I had sometimes heard at Byrraju. It was a form of unintentional paternalism. Initially he said, "[The villagers] won't know what do [with a reflective media project]—we must tell them how to learn from this project." Leaving ourselves open to the unexpected was a challenge indeed, but one that I hoped in our time together in these communities to overcome.

The Godavari region is notable not only for its agricultural fertility and prawn farming, but also its intense heat. Stepping out of an air-conditioned train compartment at 8 a.m. was an intense sensory experience. For field researchers and practitioners, however, it is always important, although rarely discussed, to maintain our own vitality and health under such conditions. Our abilities as researchers to listen and collaborate are contingent on our own health and personal presence, which could very easily be threatened by scorching heat.

That morning, Bhaskar and I visited the Byrraju district office in the city of Bhimavaram before heading to two villages where the Foundation had done little work. The Foundation leadership had set up "hub" district offices in small cities close to hundreds of surrounding villages so as to better structure and organize its operations. I had been granted permission for our team. By this time, Bhaskar and two assistant field researchers had joined the project. We asked for permission to collaborate with two villages with which the Foundation had only minimal contact. I preferred to do it this way so as to avoid any biases about the Foundation as we began our collaboration. I also recognized the value of collaborating with two communities that had little interaction with one another. This would allow us to learn from each one while minimally affecting our efforts in the other community.

In addition, I chose to collaborate with two villages with similar overall demographics in terms of economic status, male-female breakdown, and religious and occupational diversity. I recognized the power and pitfalls of such statistical information—yet also knew that as long as I held such data at arm's length it could help orient me in my fieldwork. Our team's goal was to collaborate with each village to explore how technologies we may introduce could shape reflection, mobilization, and development.

Bhaskar and the Foundation leadership recommended that we visit the villages of Kesavaram and Ardhavaram. Located near the coast in the West Godavari district of Andhra Pradesh, Ardhavaram and Kesavaram are approximately fifteen kilometers, or a little more than nine miles, from each other yet from what we had learned they had little contact with one another. Both are prawn farming and agricultural communities and have basic schools that educate students to the eighth grade. For further schooling, villagers have to leave the villages and (often) the Godavari region as well. Because employment tends not to be available outside the agricultural and occasionally the construction sector, younger and more highly educated villagers have begun to move to cities in the province, many heading to Hyderabad, the provincial capital of Andhra Pradesh, 425 kilometers, or about 260 miles, away.

Both villages had robust electricity and television infrastructure, and mobile phones had begun to circulate in each one, although with uneven access and coverage. For services and everyday necessities, the villagers had to travel to Bhimavaram, the main city in the district where the Foundation hub was located. Both also faced similar challenges, according to Foundation surveys. Consistent with what we later learned ethnographically, the dynamics that affected the communities included inadequate medical facilities (public health), public sanitation, job availability, dissatisfaction with local politicians, and divisions between castes, genders, and across religious lines (both villages were approximately 80 percent Hindu and 20 percent Christian). The sections that follow briefly introduce each village and describe our initial visits to each.

Kesavaram

Kesavaram is a small village with a population of approximately 1,200 (as of 2006 when the last "census" statistics were collected). It is primarily agricultural although it also engages in small-scale prawn farming with basic mechanical labor and services. It is relatively diverse in terms of caste and gender breakdown with the traditionally "lower" castes, or Dalits, representing approximately 75 percent of the total population. Divisions in caste, while unfortunate and the residue of history, still tend to shape Indians' lives in cities and villages.

Family homes in Kesavaram are stratified by caste, a division common across the region and nation. Very few families have the resources to develop any physical infrastructure in the village, such as roads, electricity, or plumbing. Byrraju survey data indicated at the time that approximately 65 percent of the community's households had access to electricity, and most field estimates have concluded that the community has about 50 percent overall textual literacy, with this number highly skewed toward those from higher castes or with greater economic resources.

Figure 2.5. The fertile lands in the vicinity of Kesavaram village.

Bhaskar and I arrived in Kesavaram and were greeted by the village community leadership council (in Sanskrit called "Gram Vikas Sammidhi"). An elderly man, who had been a upper-caste schoolteacher in the community, presented me with a small bouquet of flowers as a welcome. While honored, I was mindful of the formal nature of this greeting. Formality and respect for visitors is a widely practiced norm throughout rural India. While I certainly appreciated this, I recognized it could also work to distance me from the people I would meet.

My goal was to approach the Kesavaram community without specifying a project, although I was excited by the idea of working with video creation and reflection. I did not wish to enter the community as a voyeur and recognized that my introductions would have to come from our field researchers who had visited the community in the past. I found it inappropriate to think I could easily absorb myself into the community's everyday life, given that I was a visitor. Instead, my goal was to be honest without imposing the reflective media project I had imagined. I described my interest in using whatever resources I could muster to support local goals and visions, and spent most of my time speaking with people in the community about their own lives to the extent they were willing to share. At the same time, I shared my own stories, including my connections to the neighboring province of Tamil Nadu. I visited several local farming fields, local businesses, and local schools. It was important for the council to bless my visit and our relationship through a *darshan*, or religious blessing ceremony, that would occur at the local Hindu temple by day's end. A respectful and collaborative effort could only come about when I made myself personally, ethically, and intellectually transparent.

Although women comprised half of the leadership council, it was mainly men who interacted directly with me in Kesavaram. The women who did speak to me directly were either my age or older. Many women in rural Godavari marry under the age of twenty, but these young newlyweds were generally very shy in their direct interactions with me.

Every culture and community maintains practices, values, and protocols that are specific and local. That said, my visit to Kesavaram reminded me of my other ethnographic experiences working with communities around the world. At the same time, I recognize that this sense of similarity was rooted in my own experience of self rather than that of the community. Those with whom I initially interacted were people similar to myself—relatively more educated and more affluent males who had political and social capital in their community. I attempted to be mindful of the shortcomings of these elite voices to which I was initially exposed. It was clear that to move past a "curated" experience of Kesavaram, many future visits would be needed. Our team needed to actively reach out to those who tended to remain silent while respecting the choices they might make to continue to distance themselves from us.

Bhaskar would later detail in his field notes that Kesavaram had a greater sense of cohesion and communication between castes than Ardhavaram, which I will next introduce. People born into the higher castes in Kesavaram would often reach out to others lower than themselves, understanding that together they could develop and support the village's collective goals. While we observed that the upper castes traditionally initiated this relationship, Bhaskar and I wondered whether a two-way dialogue could surface over time.

Ardhavaram

Ardhavaram is somewhat larger than Kesavaram, with a total population of 3,500 during our initial visit in 2006. It resembled Kesavaram in terms of its demographic profile with respect to gender, religion, caste, profession, and economic class. Like Kesavaram, Ardhavaram's past involvement with the Byrraju Foundation had been minimal, while the infrastructural challenges it faced were similar to those of Kesavaram, according to Foundation reports. Survey data described water access, electricity access, sanitation, and employment as challenges, and estimated that literacy was at approximately 50 percent, although these numbers tended to be higher for women in both villages.

Ardhavaram had one Internet center in 2006, as did Kesavaram. It is on the outskirts of the village, where some villagers (approximately 50 in total) work in "Business Process Outsourcing" (BPO) centers. Here villagers use Skype connections to answer calls outsourced from call center hubs located in urban Indian metropoles such as Bangalore, Hyderabad, and Pune. The Byrraju Foundation had supported the development of this center. This extension of call center labor to the villages is consistent with the neoliberal outsourcing model that animates many projects that explore the role of technology in shaping development. Not only do call centers expand out of wealthier nations to poorer ones, but they were now also shifting from the city to the rural village. Information technologies in Ardhavaram were thus deployed to "network" villagers to urban-centric political and economic models. Such a dependency-oriented configuration of technology creates a network that places the rich and powerful at the center while all others are positioned to support architectures of inequality and hierarchy. The project I was attempting to develop was designed to support an opposite outcome by cultivating practices of reflection and grassroots development.

While our visit to Kesavaram was highly formal, it was notable for the rich, vibrant communication initiated with the villagers I met. Perhaps this was simply a performance designed to impress an outsider. That said, I was struck by how every villager I met—a group that included different castes, both genders, and even those who were shy—seemed to radiate confidence when speaking and communicating with one another.

Figure 2.6. Ardhavaram village and its contaminated tank.

Our visit to Ardhavaram was in direct contrast to this. I experienced far less eye contact and a great deal of silence. This was so not just when villagers spoke with me but also with other community members. I had a sense that a two-way conversation about any issue would be close to impossible. I was concerned that I was "talking at" the community rather than listening, and collaborating in the spirit of praxis and collaboration. Wary of Brazilian philosopher and educator Paulo Freire's critiques of a "banking education"[118] which disempowers the process of learning and maintains injustice, I nervously sensed that our well-intentioned visit would do nothing but perpetuate the subordination experienced by this community. Bhaskar explained to me that because of the relatively large population of Ardhavaram fewer resources were available for distribution to those less well off in the community. To his mind, this was responsible for the sense of strife and distance that we felt between villagers.

A Tale of Two Villages

Our initial visits to the two villages gave us many insights. Despite their similar developmental survey results, our ethnographic experiences were quite different. Villagers in Kesavaram seemed open to the reflective media project I had envisioned. In contrast, Ardhavaram community members seemed burdened by divisiveness and fragmentation. This made it all the more interesting to see whether over time Ardhavaram, the village to which we would ultimately choose to introduce video, would engage in the types of reflective practice about which I have written. However, this intervention would only begin after several introductory months of meetings.

Many of our initial insights associated with both villages were confirmed in the sustained, longitudinal ethnographies we undertook over the following twenty-four months. I visited the villages every three months. In the meantime, Bhaskar and his assistant Raju would either live in the communities, visit them biweekly, or live in the neighboring city of Bhimavaram. Our primary challenge was to foster a collaboration that could support the voices and perspectives of community members.

My interest in exploring reflective media and storytelling was partly motivated by the partial absence of written literacy in each village while recognizing that literacy is hardly uniform or singular. Although prior measurements by the Byrraju partners had found that both Ardhavaram and Kesavaram were 45–50 percent "textually literate," we recognized that these statistics needed to be critically interrogated rather than blindly accepted.

I also recognized the potential of these interviews, ethnographies, and surveys to shape my deeper understanding and respect for both villages. If we could explore the impact of the process of creating and sharing video on the actions and aspirations of community members, this could support a decolonized agenda of thinking about technology where grassroots community priorities were at its center rather than seen as unintended effects. We wished to compare the effect of video authorship and sharing with the traditional, "control" process wherein development conversations occur in villages in India by simply speaking about goals and visions without any tools being used to facilitate that dialogue. Over a twenty-four-month period, we would thus better understand the effects of one intervention (reflective media) versus the standard one (focus group discussions). Given the higher level of openness we found in Kesavaram, we decided to choose it as our control, where meetings would focus on in-person discussions. Ardhavaram would be where our reflective media intervention could then occur. We recognized that "control" could be an objectifying and inflexible term.

In view of the greater divisiveness we sensed in Ardhavaram, we decided to observe how these dynamics might change over time. We anticipated that what would occur would be likely unpredictable. Training field researchers to work with communities without overspecifying their roles or activities is often a challenge for development organizations. However, over the course of a three-day workshop, Bhaskar and I trained our lead field researcher Raju and his assistant Vimal. They would both maintain an ongoing presence in both communities to the extent that Raju was welcome on account of his support of existing education, health, and infrastructure projects. Via this entree into the community, we hoped to learn what issues were important the villagers with whom we could collaborate. Then we could form focus groups to study the relative effects of collective video creation and viewing.

Ethnographic methods are useful when they step away from presuming what should be "collected" and focus instead on the technique of *par-*

ticipant observation.[119] Our ethnographic discussions occurred through twelve to fifteen person focus groups that convened on a monthly basis over the two-year period. Yet because these discussions tended to favor those who were more vocal, confident, or socially empowered, we also conducted individual ethnographic interviews with focus group members every two months. This allowed us to separate what we learned at the individual and group levels. We also asked each of the community members with whom we were able to collaborate a set of general questions to learn about the villagers' satisfaction, aspirations, cohesion, and community spirit in each community. We believed such general questions could be asked in both villages while also remaining open to modifying our approach over time.

Our team worked with one focus group per village, each of which had twelve to fifteen members. Bhaskar and Raju explained that the themes of gender, caste, village geography, and political affiliation were important to the group in Kesavaram. Our team saw these as salient social factors based on our initial ethnographies. In Ardhavaram, we found that economic class, gender, and caste were most relevant, and thus we recruited our focus group accordingly.

The following three months of fieldwork allowed us to identify key commonalities that shaped life in both villages. We found that economic class was more divisive and therefore more pronounced in Ardhavaram. While caste shaped social life and identity in both villages, economic class was less pronounced in Kesavaram. One dynamic that persisted throughout the entire project, however, was that changes in economic class failed to combat the importance of caste as a form of stratification. Though it originally spoke to the economic division of labor, caste also played a huge social and cultural role in the lives of both sets of villagers.

Listening as Decolonization

Much of my discussion throughout this chapter has reviewed theories and applied case studies and my previous experiences to explore the role of technology in supporting community appropriation and authorship. Part of the personal and reflexive experience of collaboration in community-based work involves examining one's existing assumptions and moving past them. Our collaboration in Ardhavaram and

Kesavaram brought this lesson home. It reminded me that even the most well intentioned global technology researchers, professionals, and activists are often puzzled by their first encounter with diverse communities.

"How have the information kiosks in your village shaped your life? Do you believe in the power of such technology?" "Yes, sir." Such a pattern of question and answer often characterizes community-based research in parts of the world where researchers and practitioners assume and enact their privilege—everything that I was attempting to avoid. Indeed, we witnessed some of this in our initial visits to these communities.

Two weeks after our first visit, when Bhaskar and I visited Kesavaram and Ardhavaram again, we noticed several changes in the way we were treated and received. This was consistent with my experience of the importance of putting in "face time" in collaborative projects. Many community-based projects, despite the ethos of participation after which they are labeled, are often implemented in turnkey fashion with the lead researcher rarely being physically present, and research goals being prespecified without consideration of community voices. Despite my full-time employment at the University of California Los Angeles (UCLA), I was determined to avoid this. Over the two-year project, I managed to attend meetings in each village at least once every three months and far more often during both summers, when I lived in the Godavari region.

The significant change I found on our second visit was the openness of villagers in Kesavaram to speaking with Bhaskar, Raju, Vimal, and myself when out of earshot of the village council members. Either their openness was the result of the council's public endorsement of our efforts, or simply the fact that they saw our faces again. We were invited to have tea in various homes, present our stories at local schools, and partake in a tour of local farms. In contrast, in Ardhavaram the villagers would speak with me and open up their workplaces and homes, but only when no one else was present, particularly people from different caste or class groups.

In both cases, I noted how my own South Asian, specifically my Tamil South Indian background, allowed me to converse with community members in a rough version of their own Telugu language, though many spoke local dialects of their own. The rural landscapes where my mother had grown up, which I had visited several times as a child, reminded me of these communities, with their fertile land and the mostly agricultural labor they performed. Both villages featured Hindu temples with deities. As a Carnatic music-trained singer myself, I was able to perform short songs in each holy place, much to the delight of our hosts. I began to feel familiar and confident in these surroundings.

It was remarkable to see how quickly we developed an informal and open relationship with community members in Kesavaram on just our second visit. While our first visit was marked by important initial rituals such as the offering of garlands and a visit to the local temple, our second visit featured cups of chai, visits to the schools and fields where community members worked, and long, casual discussions during which stories were shared. But there was no such lack of formality in Ardhavaram. We continued to hear privately from individuals about their problems with others in their community. This was fascinating, given the demographic similarities between the communities, and evidence that demographics are but one way of understanding culture or community and that like any other they may be flawed.

Despite the willingness of the village councils in each case, our sense of ease and informality could not have been more different. This remained the case throughout the next several months of our work. Yet eventually the story would change dramatically.

Video Visions

The goal of our work was to stop seeing new technologies as externally removed from community life. By exploring the potential of video to release and share the voices within Godavari, Bhaskar and I hoped to support the visions and aspirations that might emerge.

In each of our monthly meetings in both villages, we moderated a discussion with the focus group around the possibilities and themes of "development." The focus groups would discuss their visions of development based on a set of questions that they had developed and iterated upon. These questions were designed to elicit visions, goals, and experiences from fellow community members. Either Bhaskar, Raju, or I would ask the group to discuss successes and shortcomings they had experienced in their personal lives as well as the larger community, recognizing that trust and rapport would only come over time. We encouraged the participants to look at the present as well as the past as they reflected on community life.

We anticipated that the focus group meeting notes might be biased in favor of those who were more vocal. Thus individualized interviews and survey data were also collected and maintained separately from the larger focus groups to encourage open sharing by all individual participants. Survey and interview questions measured the level of connectivity experienced by participants within the larger village, the level of positivity felt toward the village and the focus group, their sense of knowledge about development, the level of agency toward decision making that impacted each person's life, and the aspirations each person had for the village's future. Our research thus gathered focus group transcripts, ethnographic field notes, individual interview notes, and surveys.

This qualitative data was analyzed using the *thematic analysis* technique, a multi-step model that finds categories within ethnographic data.[120] These patterns were subject to change over the course of the study and were iteratively created and modified. The gathered longitudinal data, bridging both qualitative and quantitative data sources, applied the technique of triangulation to uncover shared insights.[121]

Our ethnographic and focus group experiences raised a number of interesting questions about the role of video making, reflecting on, and sharing development projects within the village. We were curious whether and how over time this would impact mobilization and consensus building within the community, and more philosophically how our effort might have interrupted existing forms of fatalism and aspiration.

Apart from these research questions, our goal was to learn from the communities in an open-ended manner. Altogether, the focus groups, surveys, and interviews asked participants:

To discuss their lives, families, and occupations to the degree they felt comfortable.

To reflect on their participation and engagement with village life.

To reflect upon ongoing, planned, or past development projects in their village.

To discuss what development meant to them and their village.

To reflect on the relationship between certain subgroups in the village versus others, as well as the village relative to its rural and urban counterparts.

Our effort was notable for its roadblocks as well as its epiphanies. Indeed, in just three months our focus group in Kesavaram surprisingly reached a level of stagnation in terms of the discussions and the dynamics of communication it featured. Larger village dynamics related to caste issues reared their head in the focus groups. The standard protocols around who should or should not speak seemed to have continued rather than been interrupted by our intervention.

In his field notes, Bhaskar described the situation as the continuation of an "invisible dialogue" wherein community members with less political or economic capital would describe their community as incapable of change. Collaboration, communication, and imagination seemed to be insurmountable goals. This was surprising, given the excitement and openness with which we were initially received in Kesavaram. However, just a few months into our work our progress stalled.

In contrast, despite deep-rooted divisions over economic class, we were fascinated by how the social dynamics became unhinged in Ardhavaram over the course of these two years. In this village focus group members were given two video cameras to share with one another. Subgroups from the focus group would create and share different video stories at each meeting. To minimize the chances of our team influencing the focus groups in the making and theme of the videos, we abstained from providing them with any production or editing training. Ardhavaram participants were only shown how to turn the camera on and off, "zoom" and "pan," and recharge the battery. This method contrasted with our approach in Kesavaram, where the focus group member meetings were structured around oral conversations without any use of technology or video cameras.

While initial video pieces in Ardhavaram were created without any deep knowledge of the camera's functionality, our team was struck by what was recorded and how it impacted focus group conversations and the interviews we gathered from individuals. For example, an initial piece showed footage of the local school, a brief interview with the school administrator, and a tour of Ardhavaram's main street. None of these topics was surprising to us. Indeed, they reflected the practice of everyday life in the village. Yet we were struck by the five-second snippet in the middle of the video featuring a contaminated local water source at a pond located between the school and other small buildings on the main road.

This snippet activated the focus group in a way that we could never have anticipated. Those who had always been much quieter in our monthly sessions challenged the reign of more vocal focus group members. This surprised us, given that it was only the fourth month of the project. J. Lalitha, a farm laborer from the Dalit (poorest) caste, took charge of the video camera in this moment, rewinding, fast forwarding, pausing, and manipulating the video piece so that we could repeatedly analyze the contaminated water source. Our sense was that taking power over this technology made possible a conversation over a topic with which the entire village felt a connection. The focus group was debating a theme that had previously been an internalized source of frustration. Instructed to pause the video, focus group members animatedly asked one another a number of questions, including:

How was the contaminated water source affecting the school?
Could the school advocate for cleaning the water source?
Was the water source positively or negatively affecting the "spiritual cleanliness" of the temple?
Could classes in the school move from the classroom to other parts of the village, including inside the temple?
Were there ways to bring more attention to the school and its priorities to the larger village through the temple?

The release of such questions resonate with what Amartya Sen calls the "capacity" of voice.[122] Voice in this case lay not just in the aspiration of ridding the village of contaminated water, but also in the technical decoding of this issue into actions, practices, and strategies that continued after the sharing of the video and in the discussion we observed. Voice also relates to collective reflection, which we observed in action in this moment. This reflection was not made possible through passive access to Foundation information or the provision of data from a government database, but through the collaborative process of using a technology to create and share stories *within* the community. As Bhaskar later e-mailed me:

[Community members of Ardhavaram] represent voice. They are starting to believe that they can be newsmakers in the village regardless of their place in life. . . . Villagers encourage them to actively participate in whatever they do . . . There are also villagers who discourage the whole video activity, come in the way and try to obstruct etc. Yet they are being stopped. Another line of gossip is about people who are given the charge of taking care of videos. I have selected two people to keep the whole equipment with them. I think many NGOs or development work really did not "involve" them, and the approach always was top-down or give-take, donate-accept models. Here in the current project, it's not about money, it's not about any program that benefits instantly, and it's all about coming together and talking about village, their needs. It is like a discourse that is taking various routes each time. (January 15, 2007)

Bhaskar's words speak to the potential of *media authorship and reflection* as a catalyst for community action. This is in direct contrast from most research focused on the "study of" a focus group. Bhaskar points to the "disruptions" that occur when aspiration and reflection are unlocked. The power to imagine, hope, and act can be cultivated from within. And technology can have a role in catalyzing this process.

Our experience in this fourth month was but the first domino to fall. Indeed, we found that in almost every month from that point onward either an entire video or a snippet in it would inspire conversation, debate, and proposals for change.

I discuss these insights in relation to four themes in the following sections: Viral media; agency; prioritization and aspiration; assets as capacity; and collective action.

Viral Media Practices

From the fourth month of our collaboration, instead of simply following our limited instructions the focus group in Ardhavaram developed an internal system of sharing the video cameras, using rotating teams of authors, producers, and collaborators. Our research team steered clear of advocating any single set of "rules" about collaboration. Instead, we observed and learned from a process whereby the camera migrated from being a focus group tool of conversation to a catalyst for a larger village-level conversation. This migration speaks to our first insight, that of *virality*.

We were unsurprised that interest in the video cameras was initially high. One often finds both seduction and excitement in new tools. What surprised us was that this interest did not plateau a few months after this fourth-month episode; on the contrary, it increased over the nearly two years we worked with the Ardhavaram community. Communications scholar Everett Rogers's writings on innovations[123] and their modes of diffusion were of interest to us in our own study. While his writings have primarily influenced corporate marketing and sales, our project remained intent on appropriating the concept to consider grassroots media practices.

Recognizing that the video effort was directed at the community itself, villagers shifted the stories they created to cover events in the larger village. They created videos around internal issues such as local marriages, discussions of urban migration, their political relationship with the district government, and rural outsourcing projects. Thus we saw new themes emerge as stories as focus group members grew increasingly confident about the video making and sharing process. The videos also shifted from specific topics to engage strategic and imaginative themes. Thus, the women in the focus group created a video that imagined a community where women were truly equal. Videos were created that examined longer-term strategies toward development, questions about power and authority, and reflections on cultural histories and values. At times, these videos challenged the role of external organizations, including the Foundation with which they were collaborating!

After eight months, we noticed how the camera had begun to move outside the focus group into the hands of villagers across social and demographic strata. By the end of the project's first year, videos were being produced in higher frequency by a greater number of villagers. The cameras were thus being treated as mobile, rugged devices—moving between families, occupations, genders, castes, and economic classes. Not only was the technology moving, but so too was the content it produced. Videos were screened in homes across the village, during community meetings, and at events such as religious festivals or marriages at the local temple.

Villagers asked our field researchers whether they could show these videos on the local television network, and one villager even asked whether videos that documented undelivered promises from the government could be placed on YouTube to attract more attention. This emergent interest in *social documentation*[124] surprised both Raju and Bhaskar, as our team had never planned to use video in this way.

The video camera followed paths and practices that resisted the scope of a narrowly defined project. As the camera moved into new hands, it became a tool to support the reflection and imagination of a wider number of Ardhavaram villagers. No longer could we simply understand our project as the study of a focus group. Instead it became a catalyst to shape aspirations and reflection on a larger scale. What we learned took us off the predicted and planned "research map" to consider not just our preconceived assumptions and hypotheses, but also the unexpected and emergent.

The Power of Agency

Creating, reflecting upon, and sharing narratives unlocked conversations within the focus group and over time in the larger village. We observed how *agency*, a sense of the capacity to collectively act and transform lives, took hold in Ardhavaram just months into our collaboration. After the sixth month, focus group participants demonstrated greater confidence in sharing their individual and collective reflections in the monthly meetings, perhaps because they had already seen and discussed the videos they had made throughout the village. The process of reflection defied individualistic constraints. Reflection seemed to occur collectively, via discussions and dialogue that occurred as the technology and the stories it was used to create traveled across the village.

Despite common issues faced in both communities surrounding sanitation, literacy, public health, political corruption, and more, the sense of ownership over our collaboration differed significantly over time between these two villages. In Ardhavaram, the focus group identified its own ability to develop and act on solutions for the community. In contrast, while Kesavaram focus group members developed significant comfort in discussing development topics, over time they failed to identify their own roles in resolving these issues in a strategic and proactive manner. This distinction speaks to a second attribute of agency, that of believing that one's actions can produce effects and outcomes.

At first, the focus groups in both communities echoed a fatalistic attitude. The future was beyond their power to control. Nongovernmental organizations, businesses, and governments were sources of both strife and hope. The fatalism came from the recognition that these outside institutions were far removed from life in the village.

Once they began creating and viewing their own videos, however, Ardhavaram participants identified an internal capacity to resolve the issues they faced and to further their goals for the village. A number of members began to see themselves as partially responsible for the problems the village faced. They identified personal roles for resolving issues around public sanitation, education, and village-level decision-making. According to both our ethnographic and individual insights, the videos functioned to shape and strengthen focus group members' personal connections with the content they and others had recorded.

In contrast, in Kesavaram the group's finger remained firmly pointed toward the local government (*panchayat*), with focus group members repeatedly expressing their desire for a better government, more money, or the blessings of God. They saw their efforts as meaningless—removed from the forces behind development. Kesavaram participant, V. Suryakanthan, a local teacher, explained to us that "development is not in our hands." Participant Suryakumari, a housewife, expressed a similar connection between future activities and those already undertaken in the village, stating, "The important activities taken up in the past just need to be continued." Our team observed a sense of resignation, a feeling that an unsatisfactory history would likely carry on into the future and that change could only come from outside.

Prioritization and Aspiration

At the start of our collaboration, both communities identified general developmental goals though neither expressed confidence in their ability to develop and promote realistic visions for their community. These visions included the goals of making more money, harvesting more crops, and supporting political transparency. Over the course of two years, a key distinction between the two surfaced—participants working with video began to see their priorities as positively aligned with those of others in the focus group and larger village. I have described how focus group members within Ardhavaram began to think less specifically about themselves, as they shifted their concern to the larger village. Part of this change involved an increased belief in the intertwined nature of personal and village-level priorities. In contrast, throughout our collaboration Kesavaram participants argued that their own goals were more important than those of others in the village. This included the feeling that other group members' priorities were counterproductive to their own well being. Though these individuals attended twenty-four focus group meetings, their attitudes toward development and one another remained mostly unchanged.

Creating, reflecting upon, and sharing media in Ardhavaram seemed to reduce the fatalism that we had observed in the community. This was demonstrated when villagers began to strategize and develop their own initiatives in specific ways. We noted a confidence and pragmatism from within for enacting change. Their goals included increasing literacy within the community. Community members began to critique and question existing top-down meanings of literacy and consider how to "indigenize" literacy as a community practice. Some participants even recognized that the media literacy they were developing through our collaboration could shape the development of economic, social, and political objectives.

Focus group members selected video topics based on their sense of what would appeal to the larger group. Ardhavaram focus group member V. Sujatha, who had initially been skeptical of video, explained during the eighth focus group: "Our village is [now] progressing in the right direction as all of us discuss and exchange each other's ideas about village development [in specific, practical, and longer term ways]."

Capacity Building—Assets, Not Needs

Creating, sharing, and collectively reflecting upon videos shaped aspiration and a sense of connectedness with others. Yet there was little discussion in either focus group about what the community already had in terms of skills and resources, and how it could build upon this. This changed in Ardhavaram as our sixth focus group came to an end. From this point onward, we found that discussion focused more than before on the capacities and assets[125] of the community as a starting point from which to mobilize and strategize. An asset can be understood as a resource or capacity that can be exchanged, supported, or transformed into a positive outcome for its holder. Whereas earlier the conversation in Ardhvaram had been "need"-based, that is, the community would speak about what it lacked rather than what it already had, now there was a remarkable shift in tone, approach, and outlook. This shift accompanied some of the perspectives on *agency* mentioned earlier in this chapter.

Ardhavaram focus group members, soon followed by others in the larger village, viewed themselves as *already* possessing the skills and resources by which their world could be positively transformed. They began to see their community as resource-rich rather than deficient. This realization became the basis for them to advocate and fight for developmental goals for their larger community.

Much of development studies literature identifies marginalized communities as groups with needs that can or should be resolved from the outside. The shift away from "need" to "asset" speaks to the potential of aspiration, which moral philosophers have long argued is important to peoples of all cultures and communities.[126] Certainly this is even more substantially the case when it comes to communities patronizingly labeled as being in need of assistance or being saved.

Looking closely at the power of exchanging and sharing assets in a community speaks to the potential of collaborating *within* a community, in lieu of seeing one's fellow villagers as competitors for limited resources in a world of scarcity. Researchers have argued that a vibrant intra-community exchange of assets can benefit not only those involved in the transaction, but also others in the larger village, city, or social unit.[127] Free expression, central to all forms of democracy, is central to the project of grassroots development. In this regard, asset sharing can become an important first step toward the collective development of any community. This form of development is not legislated from outside but fought for by those living in the community.

Videos were increasingly created on the basis of innovative concepts and strategies devised by focus group members in Ardhavaram. We viewed video pieces that revealed innovative farming practices, ceremonies that bridged caste and gender in the temple, and Information Technology business models. All of them built upon existing possibilities, resources, and people in the community. They discussed community members' ability to positively shape a collective economic, educational, and social future.

Collective Action

I have described the process by which the authorship and sharing of videos expanded outside a small focus group to recruit authors and viewers across the village and thus inspire larger scale conversations. Yet what did this change mean other than cultivating dialogue? Did it inspire action rather than simply conversation?

Over the last six months of our effort, Ardhavaram members began to strategize an approach toward sharing the videos externally as a means of influencing wider publics such as the regional government. One villager was placed in charge of contacting local television networks that reached over a hundred and fifty villages in the region, with the goal of sharing a video based on the unique practices of prawn farming in the village. They hoped that this in turn would increase economic activity and call attention to local farmers. Another group decided to submit several videos to YouTube, using newfound Internet connections. These videos focused on the undelivered promises made by the regional government and nongovernmental organizations (NGO). The goal was to put pressure on these institutions by documenting the grievances expressed by the villagers.

Ardhavaram participant and farmer Bangar Raju explained in our seventh month of collaboration that in his everyday life there was already "a significant change in the entire village." When we tracked the responses of local laborer member P. Ramesh our findings confirmed this longitudinal shift. While initial interviews with this participant emphasized the unfulfilled promises of NGOs and the panchayat government, stating that "little has been initiated," his later focus group comments noted the "significant effect that the development activities [our community has begun] has had on our collective life."

These new developments speak to the potential of community-created video as a catalyst for collective action in Ardhavaram. Community members were able to create and share their experiences regardless of their level of literacy and education. All that was required, and easily adopted, was the pressing of an on or off switch and an eye behind a camera lens. The collective viewing of these pieces sparked discussion and reflection on topics that were part of the community's collective *habitus*, or its habituated patterns and experiences. The ease with which a video camera could be shared between villagers allowed it to support collaboration and conversation between people from different families and social groups.

Villagers in Ardhavaram began to adopt what philosopher John Searle has described as "we-intentions" (rather than I-intentions).[128] A "we-intention" comes into being when a group maintains an openness to an outcome that is independent of the biases or preconceptions of any given individual.[129] We-intentions came into being as villagers reflected and communicated about the video stories that had brought them together.

In contrast, the focus group in Kesavaram exhibited little such behavior, as their discussions remained largely confined to the initial group. Focus group member VV Sharma, a wealthier landowner, stated throughout our collaboration that there was little that his focus group could do to resolve developmental issues, which would just depend "on hope and time."

For collective action to emerge from the grassroots rather than the objectifying imagination of an NGO or a researcher, our team learned about the power of aspiration and agency. Our work in India speaks to the importance of not taking the codes or texts of technology for granted, not assuming that a video camera is the magic bullet to all developmental problems, though it may facilitate a grassroots process that uses this technology creatively and reflectively.

Exit and Voice

My experiences in South India and the insights I have shared throughout this chapter remind me of the importance of economist and development scholar Albert Hirschman's writings on *exit* and *voice*.[130] Hirschman considers the question as to whether a social group should accept the deterioration of the life it may face, particularly when it is caused by a more politically powerful entity such as the nation-state, an NGO, or a corporation. He argues that the two responses available in such a situation are "exit," where the community withdraws from the relationship, or "voice," where the group communicates and collectively acts to achieve the needed social change. Hirschman concludes that it is voice that empowers, as only through voice does one acquire the ability to articulate grievances and rally around their eradication.

I find Hirschman's formulation fascinating in a time when technologies are increasingly interwoven into questions about development. As I have demonstrated in this chapter, it is difficult to see a possibility for "exit" in the case of development, technology and global communities. Technologies are here to stay and they seem permanently ensconced within questions of development. Although communities may choose to exit from these circumstances, it is far from easy to do so.

In contrast, my collaborations in Ardhavaram and Kesavaram reveal the power of voice. Voice is not merely an academic fetish or a philosophical theory. It is tied to the beliefs people have and their confidence in enacting change on their terms. Voice is intertwined with agency— the capacity to aspire and act. A technology that allows a user to receive information is not in itself voice producing. However, when we focus on the cultural and social practices that empower voice, we can transform our thinking about technology accordingly.

Remembering Scale, Sustainability, and Impact

This chapter has rejected the passive embrace of technologies as they stand to instead consider how they may support the voices and agendas of grassroots communities and users across the world. I have focused on the power of rethinking technology from the perspective of storytelling, authorship, and reflection. I hope that reflecting on my stories of collaboration in South India in the latter half of this chapter helps us rethink information technology and development (ICTD) research in ways that start and end with local communities and emerging users.

Richard Heeks, a development and technology scholar, has argued that in the ICTD field three agendas remain.[131] These are *sustainability*, *scalability*, and *impact*. Sustainability considers the long-term potential of a project and how it may generally support appropriation, voice, reflection, and authorship. Scalability considers economic policy making and viral outreach. And impact considers appropriate indicators or measurements of development that can be articulated to investors and funders.

Heeks argues that little has been done to explore how communities can use ICTs to reflect upon, articulate, and mobilize around their own ideas, visions, and strategic agendas. A new, more "productive view" would humanize the technology and development conversation to see a community as a group that has the potential to create, share, and mobilize. This is in contrast to research that sees rural or poorer technology users as passive beneficiaries, waiting and hoping for resources to be given to them by the wealthy and powerful.

It is in this sense that this chapter presents a path forward. I have argued for the need to consider how technologies may be reimagined in the service of local voice. My goal in so doing is to rid us of objectified and immutable understandings of community or technology, and do away once and for all with a myth that takes *storage technologies* as inevitable and for granted. While the research I have shared in this chapter has focused on two neighboring small villages in South India, I want examples such as this to contribute to collaborative research and practice across the world that considers how increasingly globalized technologies can be reimagined to support local communities and cultures.

I end this discussion with a keynote lecture I attended in Doha, Qatar, in 2008 at the international technology and development (ICTD) conference. The location was just a few miles from the headquarters of Al Jazeera, an emerging but still quite small television network. The billionaire speaker, Bill Gates, founder of Microsoft and one of the world's wealthiest men, dissected the many challenges that face the ICTD field, explaining the important roadblocks to health, education, and democracy that ICTs may help overcome. Gates went on to present projects funded by Microsoft and the Gates Foundation he cofounded. One of them was Digital Green,[132] which provides farmers with multimedia tools to help them share their best practices with one another. It was striking that Gates also mentioned how technology and development projects often fall far short of their lofty transformative goals, at best failing to resonate with communities and at worst becoming imposing and paternalistic.

As I listened to this talk, I kept reflecting on my experiences in Ardhavaram and Kesavaram. When the time came for questions and answers, I asked Gates about the inherent challenges of thinking about sustainability and scale. Foundations, agencies, and governments tend to fund large-scale initiatives. This is because they must provide comparative and longitudinal data to justify their investments, and such data can be easily generated through the use of large "big data" projects. Yet I believe that such a thirst for data ignores the ethical and philosophical bases on which development studies should be grounded.

Gates suggested in his answer to me that promoting local ownership, entrepreneurialism, and appropriation represented an ethical and sustainable way forward. He seemed to recognize the need to bridge the agendas that drive funding and research agencies with voices and outcomes on the ground. Scalable models must have enough flexibility to support local practices of appropriation, authorship, and reflection. Models of change must consider how community-based practices can expand and virally grow to shape emergent forms of collective action.

As with many of the ethnographic moments I narrate in this chapter and throughout this book, this moment was inspiring. It reminds us of the importance of doing away with master myths of the "global village" that leave so many silent and lead to technology initiatives that do little but mirror the misguided agendas of a limited few. I consider this approach further in the chapters that follow, turning next to the question of how we must intervene in the very languages or codes by which technologies are designed to respect the values and knowledges, or ontologies, of indigenous and other marginalized user communities across the world.

3

Native Americans, Networks, and Technology

Having discussed the power of storytelling in relation to technology and its potential to shape and empower community voices across the world, I turn now to the challenge of rethinking the very languages, or codes, by which technologies are designed. This chapter considers how networks and databases can be reimagined through collaborations with Native American communities in remote regions of Southern California. It argues that technology-facilitated networks can be formed and created from the grassroots. Communities themselves can take hold of digital technologies to build connections with others to empower shared economic, cultural, and political objectives. This is in contrast with a history in which technologies have been deployed to maintain a reliance on institutions of power and privilege. The story I share in this chapter relates to the importance of developing collaborations that support *community ontologies*, or the shared values, beliefs, and ways of knowing that are central to the cultural and social lives of grassroots users.[1] This must be the case even when such ontologies fail to correspond or fit neatly with beliefs and values that originate from Western intellectual and professional traditions.

The previous chapter considered the power of using technology to tell one's story. This chapter takes that theme further to intervene in the "ghost in the machine." We can reconsider the design principles we employ when we develop databases and network infrastructures based on community ontologies.

This book's first chapter explained how many of the ontologies that populate the digital world emerged from the Enlightenment-era histories of cultural institutions such as museums and libraries. Anthropologist of science and technology Lucy Suchman has coined the term "detached intimacy" to describe a troubled world in which technologies resemble the image of their creators rather than those they claim to serve.[2] Starting a conversation about how we create and design digital ontologies

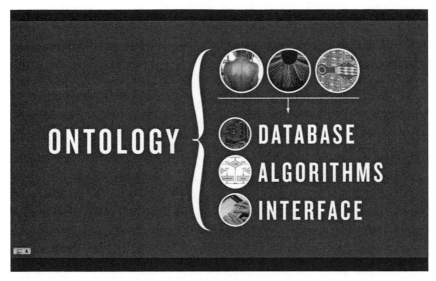

Figure 3.1. The theme of ontology influencing different components of technology.

provides an opportunity to rewrite the structures and languages of technology to support the initiatives, voices, and understandings of communities left invisible and objectified. An interest in ontology advances this book's argument that we must transform our thinking about technology to support collaborative community-based projects. Not only must the support of diverse ontologies shape projects concerned with preserving or archiving knowledge, but it must also inspire collaborations and design efforts that invert long-standing relationships of power and inequality between cultural "professionals" and culturally diverse peoples on the margins. I discuss the possibility of transforming the networks and databases of technology in relation to a multiyear collaboration with nineteen Native American tribes dispersed across San Diego County in Southern California. To best introduce this effort, I first discuss what is lost when the belief systems and ontologies of Native Americans are objectified or ignored.

Auctioning the Sacred

It seems that every couple of years a controversy breaks out that juxtaposes assumptions of the "modern" Western world with the beliefs and values of indigenous and developing world communities. The current controversy about which I write involves the selling of Hopi and Zuni (Native American tribes from the American Southwest) sacred items and masks at an auction in Paris, France.[3] Indigenous items have historically entered the hands of art collectors and cultural institutions via ambiguous and unethical histories that date back to the times of their theft from the lands and the peoples from which they came. The "routes" these objects have traveled, often over centuries, speak to a range of political, economic, social, and cultural histories, the vast majority of which are conveniently forgotten.[4]

Conversation around the power of preservation or "archive fever" has emerged as a response to histories of exploitation.[5] This approach argues for the importance of preserving these objects so they can be maintained for "posterity" or "society." Yet these approaches toward archiving, including the implicit belief in preservation they espouse, are rooted in the epistemologies of those with power and privilege, which have the power to define what preservation or archiving may mean. This can be seen to be the case even with the current interest in "community archives," which turns over the archival task to community institutions without questioning the epistemologies of "saving" that underlie the larger archival project. Much like sociologist of science David Turnbull's criticism of the contradiction that one can "collect" biodiversity, indigenous beliefs and values are often dismissed and demeaned whether we speak of colonial auctions or cultural heritage projects.

As discussed in the previous chapter on my work in Andhra Pradesh, the auction I describe in Paris speaks to the challenge of respecting a community's rights and the power of collaboration and praxis. Not only is collaboration that starts with the voices of a community the correct and ethical choice, but it also holds the possibility of supporting a world where diverse voices, priorities, and practices of knowing are respected and shared when appropriate. This support of diversity must not be based on the panoptic, cosmopolitan gaze of knowing the "other," but on the respect of traditions by which culturally diverse or indigenous communities share and pass on their knowledge.

With respect to the auction in Paris, both the Hopi and the Zuni tribes claim their items entered Western and foreign hands through illegitimate channels and now they wish that they be returned. These objects represent the spirits of ancestors that have passed on. The items are thus integrally connected to rituals, people's lives and families, mythologies and stories, and most importantly the sacredness of land and geography. To break any of these connections without proper sanction by the tribe itself represents a type of cultural "violence."[6] This is related to the concept of "structural violence," which refers to institutionalized relationships that structurally increase inequality and harm the life chances of a subordinate group.[7]

Philosopher and social theorist Michel Foucault has argued that such forms of violence are enacted and normalized through seemingly innocuous institutions and practices.[8] This occurs by having the power to define, for example, what is considered sick versus healthy, or achievement versus failure in medical and educational institutions. Foucault describes the "rarefaction" of discourse,[9] whereby commentary and dialogue are made possible relative to existing definitions, but only insofar as they accept assumptions about what is normative and acceptable. These assumptions are created by elites and perpetuated through historical inertia and bureaucratic structures. Foucault points out that cultural violence is perpetuated through seemingly inclusive systems, what one today may describe as liberal or neoliberal. These systems appear democratic, yet in practice they subordinate beliefs and practices not in line with those who manufacture discourse and manipulate media and technology systems to maintain their power and privilege.

Consistent with this, the liberal nature of collecting and preserving that accompany institutions such as the Paris auction may effectively silence the voices of the Hopi and Zuni. "Educational" projects that make cultural objects widely available to the public, as positive as they may seem from one perspective, may work to silence, devalue, and disrespect indigenous or community-specific approaches that seek to guard and protect information.

The Paris auction chooses values of commodification and exhibition while violating indigenous spiritual principles. The Hopi and Zuni see the auctioning of such items as harmful to their own community and the wider world; indeed community members have pointed out both in conversation with me and in published literature that they see themselves as stewards to these objects whose duty is to ensure that their spirits remain beneficial to the world.[10] When a spirit is wrongfully treated, as with this auction or any other process of wrongful collecting, tribal leaders believe it can create great harm for all beings by interrupting the harmony of the complete cycle of life.

Indigenous peoples have responded to the troubling museum and archival practices of collecting and preserving tribal objects by developing their own cultural institutions, whose inward focus differs dramatically from that of their Western counterparts. These organizations are dedicated to serving their own communities rather than the larger public. Objects in such institutions are preserved insofar as they are woven into the lived experience of community life. The idea of separating an object from its "source community" is considered profane in such institutions. These organizations thus represent what some tribal leaders have described as a "middle place" by upholding their community's sovereignty while recognizing the external world for what it is.

Taking this perspective, Jim Enote, Director of the A:shiwi A:wan Museum and Heritage Center at Zuni wrote a memo to journalists, institutions, and diplomats, imploring them to boycott and stop the Paris auction. He argued:

> In the late 1800s and early 1900s ethnographers, anthropologists, and associates of museums and private collectors were dispatched to Zuni to collect items that represented the ceremonial and ritualistic aspects of our culture. This was no simple and painless undertaking because items ceremonially made and used in our religious ceremonies are never to be sold and traded. . . . If the shameless business of dealing in sacred and ceremonial antiquities and bad karma that goes with it isn't enough, I must say buyer beware because the only way to absolutely authenticate a Zuni ceremonial object is to see the truth at the source by having Zuni people . . . inspect the object. . . . Let's bid farewell to the deceptions, plundering and pain brought on by this exploitative and unethical trade in sacred objects.[11]

Enote's remarks focus on the question of "authenticity" as Western colonial cultural institutions grapple with troubled histories. His reference to the "source," or the originating community from which an object comes, is important to consider in today's digital world. This is because the "source" is often forgotten when what counts as knowledge depends on the output of various crowdsourcing algorithms. The importance of the source is compromised when what counts as knowledge is that most voted upon or most highly estimated by the crowd.

The belief systems, values, and perspectives of source communities are threatened in the digital world, where terms such as openness or participation are evangelized without scrutiny. We cannot simply develop systems, technological or otherwise, that just "average" everyone's opinion. These support mass participation rather than diverse knowledge. The perspectives and ways of knowing held by diverse communities must be considered sovereign, autonomous, and worthy of respect.

It is interesting to consider the idea of *source* in a world where the effects of climate change are proving increasingly disastrous. Indigenous peoples as a whole represent the largest mobilization against projects such as gasoline pipelines and mines that threaten the natural environments in which they live. In cases such as climate change, it is all the more important to think about the power of source—of regional, local, and community ontologies and of how they can inform movements for change and justice.

Just as everyone should not be given an equal voice in discussing the destiny of objects sacred to the Zuni, perhaps it is time to think more carefully, ethically, and respectfully about the overall sovereignty of local knowledge. Yet unfortunately we seem to be headed in the opposite direction. Gilles Neret-Minet writes: "I am also very concerned about the Hopi's sadness, but you cannot break property law . . . as these are in [private] collections in Europe: they are no longer sacred. When objects are in private collections, even in the United States, they are de-sacralized."[12]

In the above passage, French auctioneer Gilles Neret-Minet states that indigenous objects are tradable, "public" commodities. In so doing, he dismisses the practices and beliefs of the indigenous communities from which these objects came. Ethical notions of sacredness, heritage, and history are discarded in favor of stated "values" that treat an indigenous object as a public commodity. Neret-Minet's words speak to the continued reign of inequality in a global cultural economy where images, finance, objects, and peoples asymmetrically move from local context to global spectacle. Cultural anthropologist Arjun Appadurai describes this phenomenon by the term "scape," which he defines as fluid, ever-changing factors that contribute to cultural, political, and economic inequality.[13] In this mirage of equality and access, one voice matters far more than another, even in cases where the "other" has a deeply personal and spiritual relationship to the object at hand. My analysis exposes the discourses that empower corporate and colonial interests at the expense of indigenous and subaltern peoples.

I wish to build on this example throughout the remainder of this book to consider the supposedly democratic and participatory digital world in which we live. Can we acknowledge different knowledges as sovereign even when they fail to neatly "fit" together in our newfound digital age? To do so, we must rethink how we design databases, networks, and other "codes" of technology.

Databasing Cultures

How have technologies been used to preserve cultural and biological knowledge? A classic response in scientific and cultural institutions has been to create a database. Sociologist of science David Turnbull elaborates upon this:

> Hardly a month goes by without the announcement of a new database, some massive assemblage of information. . . . But at the same time, we are facing in classic postmodern fashion, a profoundly challenging conjecture in modernity . . . the possible wipe-out of most life on earth including ourselves. . . . With the recognition of the need for a global biodiversity database has come a rather belated acknowledgement that biodiversity does not exist in isolation, biodiversity is inseparably linked to cultural diversity, to indigenous knowledge.[14]

Turnbull's point is that despite potentially benign intentions, most databasing efforts perpetuate the misguided oxymoron of "collecting" diversity. Historically the accumulation of these objects and materials occurred via the use of analog databases, employing lists, indices, and categories as organizing tools. As chapter 1 has described, it is dangerous to place blind faith in "storage technologies" such as databases as they stand, as thus runs the risk of treating a social or political technology as neutral and universal. Similarly, we must probe the languages and ontologies by which databases are created. From this perspective, we should not see a database as truth, but as a container or structure by which information is stored and classified.

Digital technologies are increasingly implicated in conversations about climate change and the loss of diversity today. These crises have only magnified public calls to collect and preserve species that may soon be lost to extinction. What is often left undiscussed are the epistemologies behind collecting. It is assumed that knowledge is preserved despite the displacement of an entity from its original environment. For critics like Turnbull, knowledge is erased rather than enhanced through such practices because the conditions that make such diversity possible are conveniently ignored. We have become so obsessed with managing "knowledge" that our efforts have focused on managing data rather than understanding the processes and contexts by which we actually know!

National Geographic anthropologist and TED talk luminary Wade Davis has described linguistic and cultural diversity as an *ethnosphere*. He points out that in the last generation alone half the world's languages have been eradicated. Davis argues that "it's not change or technology that threatens the ethnosphere. It's power."[15] His point is only partially true. While technologies in a vacuum, if that were to ever exist, are not at fault, it is their deployment in line with the ontologies of the powerful that threatens diversity.

Technologies that claim to "collect" or "connect" may in fact ignore the profound differences between the cultural traditions, perspectives, and knowledges that they attempt to "preserve." In this spirit, we can see how the biodiversity archives Turnbull critiques may fail to "preserve" knowledge because of their mistaken belief that one can work with a single classification system to integrate objects and knowledge that come from different places, peoples, and times:

> Assemblage of cultural diversity is an oxymoron. To coordinate commensurability, to order according to a common standard or measure, to make uniform, is to deny, suppress, and stifle diversity. It sublimates different into [a singular] identity. Assemblage and diversity are in contradiction with one another, so we have little alternative except to find ways of working with incommensurability and contradiction . . . if we are attempting the assemblage of knowledge of complex, multiplicitous, interactive phe-

nomena we need a complete rethink of all the components and ontologies involved. We need to rethink the very ideas of assemblage and of diversity, which implies rethinking our understandings of science and knowledge and of the enlightenment project itself.[16]

Most scientific and cultural archives take specific actions, events, and practices and abstract these into indexable, comparative data. In the process, they filter out that which fails to "fit" with existing classification protocols. Lost in this transaction are the voices, values, and practices of communities on the ground. The microprocess is transformed into the stable and quantifiable entity. The "noise" of culture is ignored. Knowledge, through this process, is mistakenly seen as a specimen or commodity to be managed rather than a phenomenon that emerges from a complex range of peoples, places, and landscapes.

A powerful illustration of the articulation of diverse ontologies is through maps. Maps, created by diverse cultures and communities in distinct places and times, speak to the power of thinking through multiple ontologies. An example of this may be seen in maps created by aboriginal peoples.

The *dhulan*, or indigenous map, illustrated in Figure 3.2, is based on the "dreamtime" of the Yolngu, an aboriginal tribe based in North Arnhemland in Australia. In contrast to the linear longitude-latitude system that anchors Western Cartesian maps, the Yolngu map is *experiential*. It relates the embodied experience of walking on the land and represents a memory of this experience through *dreamtime*, or songline, stories. Both this and a Cartesian map are expressions of different ways of knowing, different ontologies, neither of which can be fully described by the other. We can apply this example to how we think more broadly about the design, deployment, and meaning of technology.

The Paris auction case discussed earlier in this chapter is a particularly egregious example of what happens when a complex cultural or social knowledge system is objectified within an ontology that treats knowledge as a fixed specimen. Blindly assuming that one can transform an indigenous object into a commodity to be sold or a specimen to be exhibited ignores the practices of peoples for whom such objects may have profound local, cultural, and spiritual meaning. Folding such objects into existing technical systems of classification or ordering can

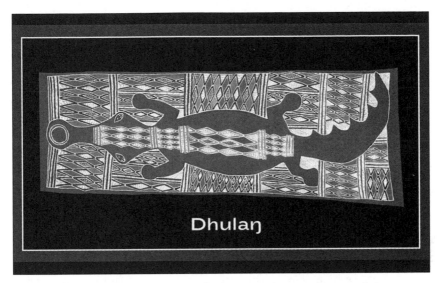

Figure 3.2. An aboriginal map in light of indigenous concepts of space and time.

violate the perspectives and voices behind the object, precisely because these systems of ranking or classification were developed with little consideration of the knowledge practices that gave birth to the object.

An alternative approach could support the sovereignty of multiple ontologies, or the knowledge traditions and practices of diverse communities. Such technologies could support the sovereignty of different ways of knowing. Yet sadly, today we seem to uncritically embrace technologies that subsume, filter, absorb, and misrepresent diverse community ontologies. When we maintain this unfortunate status quo, we silence rather than support diversity. We must do away with the types of user-centered design or appropriate technology projects that give all the power to an engineer or creator far removed from the project's communities of users. We can complicate and open up our understandings of what makes up a technology, whether we speak of an indigenous map or an Internet infrastructure:

> [New media technology is] forged of connections made up of secretaries, semiconductor manufacturing workers, railroad systems, data centers, trade agreements, arms dealers and other hybrids. These appear as background to the heroic actors (programmers, marketers and users). . . .

> [T]he origin stories of the standing reserves of nature and labor are part of the narratives one must unravel in postcolonial computing.[17]

Much like the need to criticize terms such as "user," we must also rid ourselves of the myth that knowledge is fixed or static. Essential to this is the treatment and respect of culturally diverse knowledge as sovereign, autonomous, and incommensurable. Instead of seeing diversity as a problem of "lack of fit," we can respect and embrace difference. We can think of technology similarly.

Postcolonial Moments—Stories from Aboriginal Australia

Our cultural diversities neither can nor should be translated into one another—they can be respected for their differences. To illustrate this point, I share historian, anthropologist, and philosopher of science Helen Verran's discussion of a meeting between an aboriginal tribal community and environmental scientists in the early 2000s.[18] Her ethnographies describe the motivations of scientists seeking to learn from the Yolngu aboriginal people of Australia's Northern Territory. These scientists came to the meeting interested in learning from the indigenous practice of "land burning," a process where fires are deliberately started on the land to assist its fertility. Despite their acknowledgment that the outcome of this process has contributed positively to the land, Verran explains that environmental scientists remain biased toward the sciences. This comes into play in the "postcolonial moment" of this meeting where

> disparate knowledge traditions abut and abrade, enmeshed, indeed often stuck fast, in power relations characteristic of colonizing, where sciences usually line up on the side of the rich and powerful. Postcolonial moments interrupt those power relations, redistributing authority in [the] hope of transformed contests for the exercise of power.[19]

This story juxtaposes distinct ontologies. On the one hand we have the Yolngu aboriginal practice of *worrk*, the process of setting fire to the brush. On the other is the scientific practice of a *prescribed burn*, which follows protocols from the environmental sciences on land management. While knowledge of *worrk* is passed down through oral and performative traditions, the prescribed burn exports its traditions via videos, procedures, films, and books.

Verran analyzed these two practices ethnographically over the duration of the collaborative workshop. She points out that *worrk* builds on a metaphysics that combines people and place (people-place or clan-land). In contrast, seen from the perspective of environmental science, they are distinct. For Yolngu, however, people and place cannot be seen as distinct—place gives birth to people and people tend to place. They are better understood as integrated and interwoven. For there to be harmony between the two, it is thus critical to reject the distinction between them. Yolngu knowledge builds on specific relationships between families, lands, and practices. They are activated through practices, performances, and rituals associated with the ontology of *worrk*. In contrast, the prescribed burn for the sciences abstracts these practices into sets of steps and guidelines that can be enacted theoretically anywhere, independent of the specific scientist or landscape. The connected vector of *people to land* is absent in this scientific ontology.

Both *worrk* and the prescribed burn represent different ways of knowing and are thus examples of distinct ontologies. Although both relate to the collective memory associated with their traditions—articulated through performance and ritual on the one hand, and scientific rules on the other—they do not neatly fit with one another. Neither can be fully captured or defined by the other. The scientific ontology filters out contextual, personal, and environmental information, which it sees as nonessential to the prescribed burn and fails to fit within its preexisting ontology. Specific people, places, and performances are removed from the equation. Yet in the indigenous case, these specificities and materialities are essential. In this sense, the two ways of knowing are ontologically incommensurable.

Verran's story reveals the scientists' inability to translate or absorb the knowledge of the Yolngu into the canon of environmental science. She points out that the fact that Yolngu knowledge and environmental science fail to neatly fit with one another is an opportunity rather than a problem. Incommensurability presents an opportunity to appreciate rather than dismiss diversity. Sadly, what tends to occur in contrast is the misrepresentation of local knowledge into the supposedly stable and omniscient ontology of the sciences. During this process, local knowledge is filtered and cleansed so it can be inserted quickly and easily into existing databases of scientific knowledge or cultural heritage. Ironically, these knowledge management systems may be seen as advanced because of their objectification rather than appreciation of such diverse knowledge.

Within any postcolonial moment, such as the meeting Verran describes, lies an invaluable opportunity to "open up and loosen" our treatment of difference and diversity. We can make more explicit the means by which we understand that which differs from ourselves and use this as a point of departure to reimagine how we may choose to design communication technologies. The possibility of moving past one's own ways of knowing requires an awareness of existing biases. The scientists are unlikely to ever become full-fledged members of the Yolngu, and while the converse may occur, it is unlikely that a Yolngu member would be seen as a traditional scientist. What offers the most hope is the possibility of having a new conversation based on the appreciation of difference. Verran thus argues that working with multiple ontologies, respecting the sovereignty and autonomy of each, can be exceedingly valuable. She gives an example from the Yolngu meeting:

> [The scientists] worried that the decision about the site might be made solely on the basis of what they saw as "Yolngu politics." . . . [S]ome of the scientists had begun to feel that too few people knew what was going on, or what would happen next. Perhaps some began to sense that the proceedings were the almost arbitrary decisions on the part of just one man. While scientists might be content to trust a scientific expert, it seemed much harder to trust the expertise of this old clan leader. . . . One of the scientists expressed anxiety over his perception that people were just blindly doing "what they had always done" without appropriate consideration and planning. There seemed to be no general understandings of habitat, and without that how could any evaluation be made? . . . . And further, while the talk of "mother fires" and "child fires" was romantic, how could that metaphorical language be taken seriously?[20]

Verran's story ends as a failed opportunity. She argues that this failure is due to the scientists' refusal to give up power and control in terms of how they wish to learn from the Yolngu. The scientists failed to "loosen" their understanding of how the world is ordered and how the land should be understood, maintaining what feminist philosopher Donna Haraway describes as the "biopolitical narratives" by which they configured their studies. Haraway describes the means by which scientists polish "an animal mirror to look at ourselves," a form of narcissism that persists alongside the claim to learn from the "other."[21]

Verran's ethnography points to the contrasts between the *performances* of the Yolngu and the *abstractions* of the scientists. What may bring all these actions together, however, is an underlying *sameness*—they speak to what makes us all human, our ways of knowing. There is a deeper underlying humanism that connects us all, but it must not be embraced at the cost of disrespecting diversity or maintaining historical misrepresentations. We live in a world where different ways of knowing are not treated equally. We must not embrace sameness without confronting the continuing asymmetries of power and voice.

That said, we cannot respect diverse ontologies without recognizing how the knowledges of those at the margins tend to be plundered by existing systems of political economy. Simply stating our respect for difference is thus insufficient—we must also guard against the usurping of the other. Philosopher of science Arun Agrawal has argued that non-Western knowledge practices are often commodified and plundered through the use of science and technology.[22] What is "included" is in reality captured, objectified, and misrepresented. One example of this is bureaucratic repositories that collect and manage exotic, indigenous knowledge. Yet they cling to political and social agendas exported by their creators.

Classifying Knowledge

Consistent with the turn I describe in chapter 1 toward "storage technologies" that took technological development and design hostage, we must consider the implications of archiving knowledge according to the fixed ontologies of the sciences. Historian of science and technology Geoffrey Bowker describes the birth of the scientific archive as an attempt to take control over the *commencement* and *commandment* of knowledge.[23] This involves taking power over both "creation stories" and the political economies that shape the respect for different forms of knowledge.

Systems of *discourse*, or the presumed conceptual generalizations that govern and shape many aspects of social and political life, are far from neutral. Like many of the technologies that populate our world, they are constructed and communicated by those with power and privilege. One mechanism by which these forms of knowledge are developed and transmitted is through *classification*, a key "knowledge practice" that demarcates the distance between deviance and acceptability, between what is invisible and visible.

Bowker and feminist sociologist Susan Leigh-Star's important text, *Sorting Things Out: Classification Systems and Their Consequences*,[24] describes the power of classification through historical and cross-cultural examples. The authors explain how the "noise" of knowledge is filtered into 'stable" categories through 'black-boxing." Black-boxing includes social, political, and cultural arrangements that govern many aspects of our world. These only become visible when their normal "behind the surface" functioning ceases. Black-boxing has a type of "casual magic" so invisible and "normal" that it tends to go unnoticed. This works to silence controversy, the presence of dissenting opinions, and the possibility of accepting fundamentally diverse knowledges on their own terms.[25] As information and classification scholar Jonathan Furner points out:

> The presence of standardized classification systems allows the organization to work with a variety of different types of "knowledge objects," compare these, perform generalizable and repeatable operations, yet ultimately privilege a particular type of memory, which actually involves forgetting the ultimate singular, commanding architecture by which the classification system was created. The classification scheme is then "an objective representation of a subjective point of view—that of its human constructors, who share the perspectives and ideologies of those populations with which they identify."[26]

Classification takes the subjective and makes it objective, transforming the specific into a science. In doing so, contradicting narratives, those that fail to be neatly translated, are erased and forgotten. One of Bowker and Star's prime examples is medical classification, specifically the International Classification of Diseases (ICD). The authors describe the multiple meanings left invisible by this classification. They further discuss other systems, including the Nursing Interventions Classification (NIC), the classification of viruses and tuberculosis, and race in apartheid South Africa.

Bowker and Star point out that the use of these classifications by medical institutions speaks to how discourse operates. Their presence in seemingly neutral and public institutions helps them be uncritically accepted. This is due to their acceptance by supposedly "beneficial" and "scientific" institutions. Yet in reality many of these classifications ignored the diversity of South African tribal cultures and treated their traditions as savage or unworthy of acknowledgment. In so doing, the classification systems represented a key pillar of a racist regime.

Activists, scholars, and others can transform and disrupt these systems of classification. From this perspective, systems can be reimagined to support the *boundary objects* that reconcile different ways of knowing and classifying data.[27] Star had long used field-based, observational methods and feminist critiques to study the infrastructures of information and technology.[28] She argued that what is seen as marginal is most critical because it may reflect an inflection point through which "layers of control and access" are produced.[29] In this sense, power and marginality are dialectical—each produces and shapes the another.

The concept of boundary object, now a central tool of deconstruction and critique used by sociologists of technology, identifies the central role of objects to serve as a pivot between different ways of knowing, linking community-specific and shared meanings.[30] This theoretical term is insightful as it speaks to any entity that can be connected to multiple perspectives, opinions, or knowledge practices. Examples of a boundary object could include maps, field notes, specimens, museum objects, or any entity that can be tied to multiple understandings or perspectives.

Boundary objects are dynamic and can have different meanings for different communities. They can become discursively commanding at times, particularly when tied to the agendas of those with power and privilege. As they become more powerful they "move and change into infrastructure, into standards . . . [and] other processes."[31] One can subvert the reign of elite meanings around boundary objects by designing systems that unlock the multiple ways by which these objects are understood and worked with.

One must deconstruct and interrogate the practices that create technology-facilitated facts, realities, standards, and classifications. The library and information science field (LIS) has contributed greatly to the intellectual study of classification, as it has long looked at how classification "standards" are formed and has considered different methods by which they are reconceptualized.[32] Primarily, LIS scholarship has focused on libraries, archives, and museum institutions. Yet in theory these approaches can be applied to the critique and design of any system that claims to preserve or share knowledge.

Information studies scholar Barbara Kwasnik has written about a wide range of classification systems, arguing that ordering and categorizing powerfully shapes one's experience with information. She asks us to reflect on how classification systems may enable or constrain the process of knowing, including the context behind the information one may access:

> Classification is the meaningful clustering of experience. The process of classification can be used in a formative way and is thus useful during the preliminary stages of inquiry as a heuristic tool in discovery, analysis, and theorizing. . . . A good classification functions in much the same way that a theory does, connecting concepts in a useful structure. If successful, it is, like a theory, descriptive, explanatory, heuristic, fruitful, and perhaps also elegant, parsimonious, and robust.[33]

Kwasnik discusses a set of different classification structures commonly used by information professionals and scholars to model the informational objects, referred to in the LIS field as "documents," that they wish to share, preserve, or enable for access.[34] She argues that "hierarchies" have become a standard for information classification based on their use of "parent-child" relationships. Hierarchies carry rules of attribute inheritance, meaning that every feature of the parent is transmitted to the child. She also mentions other models, including (a) *trees*, where information maintains a partial, but incomplete, inheritance from its parent/s; (b) *paradigms*, where pieces of information are connected on the basis of an intersecting relationship between two different categories; and (c) *facets*, where pieces of information are placed in more open-ended relationships which themselves may shift over time.

Much like Bowker and Star's African apartheid example, the vast majority of classification systems follow hierarchies and standards developed by those with political and social power. With this critique in mind, feminist LIS scholars have discussed the means by which standards maintain the power of elites. Feminist studies scholar Hope Olson's analysis of the Library of Congress Subject Headings (LCSH) notes the absence of any discussion of women and non-Christian religions within this supposedly neutral and public system. Olson argues that such standards perpetuate an Aristotelian project that privileges hierarchy by treating their various categories as discrete, fixed, and endowed with "watertight" boundaries.[35] These logics must be challenged and rewritten.

Olson reminds us that the "philosophical traditions of the West have delineated a concept of reason that is exclusive of women and other oppressed groups."[36] One can thus say that classification systems tend to reflect the biases and ontologies of those with the power and privilege to design and circulate such systems. We must consider this in relation to databases, algorithms, and other "codes" of technology.

Classification decisions shape the standards that govern how cultural knowledge is preserved and shared, particularly in information institutions like libraries, archives, and museums. In short, they form the basis for managing knowledge. Yet these standards are often in tension with the very processes by which knowledge is created. For example, the CIDOC CRM standards model[37] has been applied to a wide variety of cultural objects that originate in diverse communities worldwide. Yet it filters out the stories, practices, and experiences associated with these objects. Within this ontology places are seen as distinct from peoples and communities, and time and space are seen as unrelated. Certainly there are ways of knowing the world that are inconsistent with such assumptions.

Standards, much like classification systems, allow data to be interoperable, or cleanly comparable and computable.[38] Data can therefore be calculated, quantified, and processed to supposedly inform policy and decision making. Yet they encounter a problem when they misrepresent the experiences and realities of the communities from whom the information they gather originates. Inflexible standards, classification systems, and database architectures can thus block alternative approaches toward thinking about design and communication, invoking a classic problem with the history of science whereby an overreliance on computational models obscures other possible realities.[39]

Much like my discussion of databases, standards, and classifications, the ontological questions this book asks can be viewed in relation to the *algorithm*, a set of rules acted upon by an automated system, particularly a computer. Algorithms increasingly shape our technological experience as they present information to users on the basis of the rules by which they are programmed. Google.com, the world's most popular website, owes its popularity in part to its famous search algorithm. This and other sites and mobile platforms have begun to "push" information onto users on account of the choices encoded into the algorithms by which they have been programmed. As algorithms shape our experience of what counts as knowledge and how it should be presented and ordered, they must be critiqued, questioned, and reimagined.

A cross-cultural awareness reveals that algorithms, repetitive and formulaic patterns of abstract thought, have been articulated in societies in the Arab world as far back as Mesopotamia.[40] Sociologist Ted Striphas in his book *Algorithmic Culture*, and communications scholar Tarleton Gillespie have written about the cross-cultural origins of algorithms and the ways in which they increasingly shape many facets of contemporary life.

We must consider who writes and is influenced by algorithms in relation to our current moment of *algorithmic personalization*. Eli Pariser, CEO of Upworthy and cofounder of MoveOn.org, has argued in his book *The Filter Bubble* that personalization is increasingly part of the everyday lives of users of networked, digital communication systems.[41] His critique is that the invisibility of algorithms, such as those that generate the Facebook news feed, are opaque to most users and may privilege the trivial and agreeable rather than introducing perspectives about which we may disagree. Even if our "friends" on such systems tend to be similar to ourselves this invisible algorithm performs a civic injustice.

Despite this important critique, our discussions of algorithms and classification systems ignore the grassroots perspectives of communities and cultures that have little power over the destinies of public politics and business.[42] We must change this as we think about collaboratively designing and deploying technology to support the ontologies of diverse communities and users.

The Community Ontologies of a Refugee Community

To provide some background on my work with ontologies, I share an early experience I had working with Somali immigrants in the Boston area while a graduate student at the Massachusetts Institute of Technology (MIT) Media Laboratory. At the time, my thinking about knowledge and how it is represented in computational systems was influenced by my professor, renowned MIT computer scientist Marvin Minsky.[43] In his courses, I learned about the concept of ontology from the perspective of the computer sciences, focusing on the design of databases, algorithms, and computational models according to Western-derived precepts of logic and rationality. The computer sciences have thus created ontologies in the design of knowledge management systems, which model knowledge "objects" according to predefined semantic sets of terms, rules, and relationships. While computer science ontology projects differ substantially from one another, they are united by the common assumption that knowledge can be formally described, mapped, and expressed through logical categories and relationships.[44]

At this time, I had also become interested in electronic publishing and community technologies. Our research group at MIT had developed software and web-based platforms for diverse community groups to publish their stories and even develop their own electronic newspapers. We had even begun to explore the possibility of building web-based templates for the simple publishing of user-created content. While some of us found this amusing given our geeky knowhow of the HTML scripting language, we quickly realized that in these distributed publishing models lay great promise. We eventually recognized that the software we designed helped give birth to today's blogosphere!

Entering MIT, I was interested in exploring the theme of electronic publishing and community technology in collaboration with peoples of diverse cultures and ethnicities. Thanks to the advice of a friend I had begun to volunteer at a local Somali community center. I noted how the Somali community in New England consisted of mostly recent immigrants from a part of East Africa that could not simply be defined based on race, religion, or geography but instead as a deeply diverse group. My volunteer work had focused on working with youth on schoolwork. In that process I had noticed stark differences related to gender and clan between the different kids I would meet. While I learned about such significant diversity within this community, I also recognized a commonality of experience amongst those I met. The vast majority of Somalis attending the center were refugees fleeing a civil war as Sunni Muslims in a post 9/11 America.

Given the absence of immigrant-oriented projects at the Media Lab at the time, I saw great opportunity in exploring how to collaboratively design a system to support my new friends. Community leaders from the refugee center had expressed to me their concern with the digital divide they were facing. Their concern was focused less on access to technology and more with the inability to use digital tools to support the many challenges the faced around housing, legal rights, employment, heritage, Islamophobia, and racism. Thus, together we embarked on a project that we called "Village Voice."

I had recently been introduced to ethnographic methods and was convinced of their value in supporting my relationship with the Somali community of the Boston area. Engaging with the methods of participant observation, an ethnographic approach that bridges descriptive observation with engagement, many interesting insights began to come my way. For example, I observed the importance of Friday visits to the mosque, not simply for religious reasons but for the social capital, or civic meaning, for those attending these events. The Friday meals served political, social, and cultural purposes, and the patterns of eating and conversation provided a powerful glimpse into the cultural process of navigating between traditional and contemporary subjects of importance to community members. Could I design a technology that supported community-based practices such as these Friday meetings? An approach that presumed what the Somali community's values or "needs" were would likely misrepresent these ethnographic experiences. If I designed a database or digital archive that understood the Friday mosque visits solely as "religious," I would lose sight of the multiplicity of other meanings related to the events of this important day. The ontology that influenced how the system classified different pieces of information would objectify and stifle a dynamic cultural practice. I would also have to carefully distance myself from technocratic tendencies by presuming that the technology itself would empower the community.

I learned to respect what I learned from collaborating with this community rather than remaining attached to the computational models designed in our laboratories. With such a spirit of praxis, we could collaboratively develop technologies to support community-based values, practices, and ways of knowing. Over several months, we developed "Village Voice," used by the Somali community center in Boston and at home by various community members over the next five years.

Fluid Ontologies

How then can we change the ways in which we design technologies to better work with the communities with whom we collaborate? With that challenge in mind and many frustrations behind me, I developed the concept of "fluid ontology" dating back to my collaborations in 2001 with the Somali refugees in the Boston area, described above. Fluid ontologies represent a methodology by which classifications, descriptions, values, and the priorities of communities can influence the design of digital systems. Later in this chapter, I describe how I applied this approach in my collaboration with tribal members across nineteen Native American reservations in San Diego County.

A fluid ontology is created through community-driven consensus. It works with a select focus group placed in charge of reflecting on the collective traditions, practices, values, priorities, and epistemologies of their community. In light of these reflections, the group designs maps of key topics and themes in the life of the community. These maps must do more than simply list topics; they should describe the relationships between different elements.[45] The fluidity of this method relates to the importance of it being seen dynamically rather than being a static map of community life. Community members are thus requested to iteratively design and reflect on the ontology they create over time. It is also important to see the fluid ontology as more than a statement of areas of agreement. Thus, the design of this ontology may also include themes that have provoked disagreement and dissension, such as the politically loaded questions of sovereignty and casinos among Native Americans. This method is thus employed as a way of transforming the technical codes of a new media technology to support what is salient in community life. Algorithms, interfaces, and databases can thus all represent points of intervention through the use of this method. It is inspired by the belief that we must design and mold technology to serve our communities rather than the opposite way around.

My development of this method was influenced by psychoanalytic philosopher Michel de Certeau's writings on *tactics*.[46] In contrast to top-down *strategies* that exert control and maintain power, de Certeau explains that tactics are the "means designed by people to circumvent or negotiate strategies towards their own objectives and desires. . . . [T]actics broaden the scope of who participates, how, and in what contexts." In particular, I was inspired by the design tactic of tracing, which exposes the origins of an issue and its subsequent evolution.[47] Tracing is a type of "mark-making" where data are collected to record changes that occur over time. It relates to the idea of fluid ontologies because of its interest in designing systems to support the values and ontologies of otherwise silent user communities.

In contrast to these approaches, the majority of human computer interaction research (HCI) focuses on developing easily usable interfaces, limiting its attention to the front-end experience of a user. This makes sense, given that most design research explores how to "efficiently" communicate information to users. This approach can be revisited in light of our recognition that the goal of efficient information sharing may not be quite as neutral as it may seem. The fluid ontology approach moves past the limitations of a "user" to embrace the diverse knowledge systems, values, and protocols that are part of community life. Communities are no longer simply users in this approach—they are the masters, and the system becomes the servant. Yet researchers must be mindful that the concept of "community" itself can serve as a homogenized construct. Often community-based initiatives merely privilege the voices of those who have the power to "speak" within that community.[48]

Fluid ontologies are thus "flexible knowledge structures that evolve and adapt to communities' interests based on contextual information articulated by human contributors, curators, and viewers."[49] Cultivating such an ontology involves considering the following:

(a) *Gathering a set of representative digital media objects*: This recognizes that not all knowledge can be represented through an image, audio, or video object, and that even these representations are partial and incomplete. Different types of media objects have different capacities built into them, and what they may mean to different community members depends on the information being shared within a database.

(b) *Community-driven practice*: As with any larger project, the sharing and communication of knowledge must be motivated and led directly by community members rather than solely by the researcher.

(c) *Back-end as a blank slate*: Designers and engineers, much like ethnographers, tend to have preexisting assumptions. For designers, these often relate to their ideas about how systems should be designed and what represents a well-designed database architecture or classification system. While recognizing the inherent reflexivity in any collaboration, developing fluid ontologies requires stepping as far away from these biases as possible.

(d) *Ontology emerges through collective reflection, based on values, ethics, and knowledge practices*: This most challenging element of the fluid ontology process is also the most satisfying and enriching. A fluid ontology is emergent, not preconstructed, and its emergence is a function of collective dialogue and reflection. What ends up being included in an ontology may involve objects, actions, times, symbols, concepts, experiences, or anything else agreed upon by community partners A fluid ontology represents a way of demarcating a digital community space. It is important that this "map" be created on the basis of the choices made through the messiness of reflection and dialogue. This is facilitated by community members themselves, who rotate in terms of helping to streamline group conversations.

(e) *Recognizing that a fluid ontology is partial*: Simply because an ontology is generated by a group of community members does not mean that their choices completely reflect others in the community who they may claim to represent, or even represent themselves fully. All communities are diverse and multifaceted. Instead of this being an obstacle, this complexity can be embraced by the humble recognition that no ontology is totalizing. Thus, fluid ontology is a subjective, ever-changing, representation of choices led by a group of community members in their attempt to take command over a technology that stores and communicates information.

(f) *The embrace of adaptivity and instability*: Many technologies are designed on the precepts of persistence and predictability. In contrast, fluid ontologies view instability as a virtue rather than an obstacle to be eradicated. Indeed, the form of a fluid ontology should never be predetermined.

One can apply the fluid ontology approach to consider nondigital environments as well. One area of intervention could be in information institutions such as museums, libraries, and archives. These institutions have long been criticized for misrepresentation, partly due to their support of objectives detached from the peoples they claim to represent. Today museums, archives, and libraries are confronting these histories and attempting to rethink their practices of representation and ownership. Particularly important is the growth of community-based approaches toward assembling, appraising, and managing archival records and collections, a potential game changer from the practice of objectification and inequality.[50] This may force a radical requestioning and rejection of principles of preservation or memory, to adopt a worldview that rejects Western principles of accumulation, storage, and classification.

We must rethink the building blocks of new technology, including interfaces, databases, and algorithms, to support collaborations with diverse cultures and communities. Chilean engineer, entrepreneur, and politician Fernando Flores and his colleagues have pointed out insightfully that "technology is not the design of physical things. It is the design of practices and possibilities."[51] With these insights in mind, I turn now to the Tribal Peace technology initiative, a multiyear collaboration I had with a group of Native American reservation communities.

The Tribal Technologies of the Kumeyaay

For three years I collaborated with a remarkable project involving nineteen Native American communities living on fragmented reservations across San Diego County. The project, called the Tribal Digital Village,[52] provided access to wireless Internet technology and supported the design of a digital environment that voiced the perspectives, aspirations, and ontologies of disenfranchised indigenous peoples.

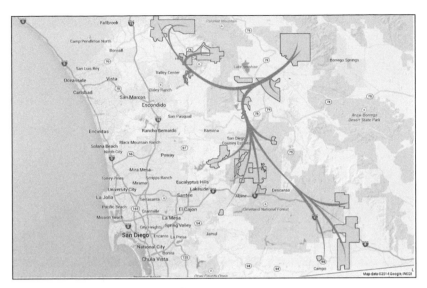

Figure 3.3. The Tribal Peace network.

The Tribal Digital Village was a partnership between UC San Diego, a group of tribal reservations in San Diego County, and Hewlett-Packard (HP). I was initially invited to join the project by a revered family friend, Srinivas Sukumar. He had worked for HP for many years with the intention of serving communities outside the company's normal consumer profile. The goal of this partnership was to set up wireless Internet infrastructures to serve marginalized Native American communities who lived in highly mountainous, dry, windy, and inhospitable regions north and east of San Diego. The intention was to support a group of nineteen Native American reservations of Cupeno, Luiseno, Kumeyaay, and Cahuilla tribal ancestry.

Knowing of my work with Somali refugees and my interests as a graduate student at Harvard's Graduate School of Design, Sukumar and his team invited me to consider how the infrastructure could create a digital space that would serve these communities, in contrast to the vast majority of digital networks that reinforced inequality. The project would later be named "Tribal Peace." The existing team invited me to attend project meetings with tribal leaders to see if there was interest in collaboration. I soon moved to the region and ultimately to the reservations with the goal of supporting a vision articulated by cultural and political leaders

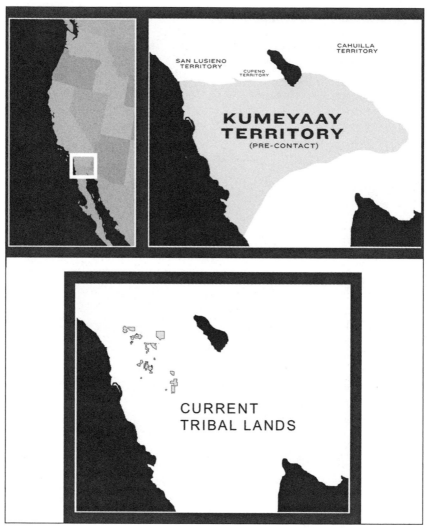

Figures 3.4 and 3.5. Maps of traditional and current lands inhabited by the Native American communities of San Diego County, California.

from the nineteen reservations. They hoped that this environment could energize their "ways of knowing," threatened heavily by many years of violence and disenfranchisement. After building positive relationships with them over some time, I later lived on the reservations for a period of three years.

By combining the different reservations in this project, Sukumar and his colleagues were creating a type of "metacommunity" across a set of nations whose cultural histories were significantly different from one another, and who had sometimes taken opposite sides in past conflicts. The reservations were dispersed over a hundred-plus mile radius in East San Diego County that differed topographically, with some communities located in fertile valleys while others were on more remote and mountainous terrain. Some of the reservations featured a checker-board geography that broke up the contiguity of shared tribal land. As Christian Sandvig, a communications scholar who has spent some time in these reservations studying technology infrastructures, has pointed out, "The only common feature of the reservations in this area may be that they were lands that no one white wanted."[53] The Spanish, Mexicans, and finally Americans had forcibly stolen the most fertile lands, including those with coastal access. These tribes were "pushed into the rocks" and placed on arid desert mountainsides.[54]

The reservations were disconnected not only in terms of space but also in terms of infrastructure. The distances between communities cannot simply be measured "as the crow flies" but must also take into account their access to physical infrastructures, for example, to roads and public utilities. For example, while two reservations may have been only fifty miles apart, to travel between them could take several hours. Additionally, the violence of the national border nearby added to the disconnection experienced by tribal members, given that their ancestral lands straddled the border between the United States and Mexico.[55]

During my time with these communities I witnessed many forms of fragmentation. Communities experience a disconnection not just from one another, but also from the common threads of their history and culture. Tribal historians and scholars of ethnic studies have pointed out that the tribes' shared seafaring and agricultural traditions were lost as their lands and identities were attacked over centuries of colonization.[56] All that seemed to remain was the annual journey taken by reservation youth to their ancestral homes next to the sea. Over the years of my collaboration with these communities I accompanied groups on this pilgrimage. The sight of a group of tribal youth singing and dancing on the beaches against the massive backdrop of the La Jolla-based mansion of former presidential candidate Mitt Romney brought a sad feeling to my heart.

The tribes had long been disconnected from their historical threads of identity, memory, and economy. Indeed, over three years of fieldwork from 2002 to 2005, I observed a stunning absence of access to resources and infrastructure, history, memory, language, and identity. Over multiple years, I met fewer than ten tribal members who spoke their traditional languages and only three elders who were respected as medicine people and carriers of knowledge and tradition. While I am mindful of the need to avoid exoticizing a connection to tradition as a panacea, my ethnographic experience seemed to me a cultural extension of what sociologist Emile Durkheim conceptualized as "anomie,"[57] a condition of placelessness, fragmentation of identity, and dissolution of social bonds.

This was the context in which the Tribal Digital Village infrastructure was introduced as an intervention to empower local and cultural connectivity within and across the reservations. Yet as with many other digital divide "solutions" that I have critiqued throughout this book, this infrastructure too was mistakenly seen as a technical obstacle to be overcome rather than an opportunity to develop a sociotechnical approach in collaboration with communities that remain alive today. Indeed, there are over 50,000 Native American people living in San Diego County today, though there were only 8,000 on the nineteen reservations where I lived and worked. The nineteen reservations together represent approximately 15 percent of the overall county's Native population. Studies have repeatedly shown that urban Natives fare far worse than those on reservations in terms of educational, economic, and health attainment.[58] Moreover, these reservations represent only the statistics calculated in the United States. A large number of indigenous peoples of Kumeyaay, Luiseno, and Cupeno descent live in greater poverty just miles away from their counterparts on the southern side of the U.S.-Mexican border.

We often assume that the decreased cost of communications and storage technologies makes possible greater connectivity between rural and urban communities. Yet the private corporations that provide the infrastructure for communication tend to be disinterested in providing information and communication technology resources to these communities, given the lack of easy returns on that investment. Native Americans' lack of financial resources, combined with their lack of population density, means there is "too much space and not enough bodies,"[59] which contributes little to no capital investment in initiatives that directly serve the Native American communities.

The lack of a robust infrastructure, whether one is speaking of water, power, or telecommunications, is the residue of an undelivered promise whereby tribes historically had exchanged land for infrastructure and subsidies. Native communities across the United States have long been the ethnic groups most digitally disconnected from broadband infrastructures.[60] Sadly, they are also the most disadvantaged communities in the entire nation in terms of economic well-being, education, and health.[61] Communications scholar Christian Sandvig points out that the Native reservations of San Diego County are often seen as "rural . . . [with] drugs, [with) alcoholism, (with) different types of abuse, the poverty . . . just the whole thing."[62]

The issues are not just infrastructural but also interwoven with the presumptions of use and sharing that drive most Internet and social media technologies, according to Craig Howe, a Lakota scholar: The Internet's "universalistic and individualistic foundation [must be] restructured to incorporate spatial, social, spiritual and experiential dimensions that particularize its application[. Without this,] cyberspace is no place for tribalism."[63] Overcoming these barriers was a challenge that involved thinking about technology and infrastructure in relation to the material conditions of place and the ontological experiences of culture. Indeed, the Tribal Digital Village project designed and deployed a digital infrastructure on a physically harsh topography and landscape, navigating winds over a hundred miles per hour, intense amounts of dust and dirt, steep mountains, heat, light, and the ever-present risk of earthquakes and landslides.

Yet such a project would not have been possible without the local knowledge of the communities living on this land. As Sandvig explains:

> While one might think of the corporate engineers that developed and sold these towers, antennas, and radios as the experts on them, in fact the user of a device who is intimately familiar with its operation in their

local context often has far more information about its performance characteristics and uses. . . . [T]heir approach provided some innovative engineering.[64]

It is rare for urban scientists and engineers to think of infrastructure as local or place-specific. Much like new technology or the Internet more generally, infrastructures are far too often viewed in a top-down manner. Produced by intelligent and well-intentioned scientists, mere access is mythologized as bringing about empowerment. At most, scientists think about usability, of manipulating local conditions to make the tool "fit." Sadly, space is seldom provided for the voices of "users' to shape the design or deployment of infrastructure.

Consistent with this, the history of the Tribal Digital Village started as a conversation that excluded the communities that were to be "connected." The idea originally emerged from conversations between elite technical institutions, including the UC San Diego Supercomputer Center scientists, the National Science Foundation, and Hewlett-Packard. As scientist Hans-Werner Braun, a research scientist at the supercomputer center and one of the technical designers of the Tribal Digital Village wireless infrastructure, put it, "I wanted astronomy stuff and ecology stuff. . . . [S]omehow I got the thought, for no good reason, wouldn't it be cool to involve Native Americans? And I put it into the proposal, but had no idea how to do it."[65] The specifics of community and place were afterthoughts.

Despite his perhaps benign intentions, Braun's perspective represents the common teleology of the heroic scientist or engineer. The dogma associated with a "technical solution" is far too easily imposed on "needy" rural, immigrant, and indigenous communities worldwide. What remains notably absent is the agency of the local community. Indeed, such efforts fail to consider the ethical approaches toward collaborative ethnography and praxis described in chapter 2, and the importance of respecting local ontologies. It is for these reasons that indigenous communities often see such technological and scientific developments as misguided, intrusive, and worse still, as culturally imperialistic.[66]

My first connection with the nineteen reservations in San Diego County was through their governing "Southern California Tribal Chairmen's Association." This was the institution that enacted the Tribal Digital Village (TDV). Having been invited to join the effort and help the team think about a digital space to serve the communities, which we ended up naming Tribal PEACE (acronym: Preserving Education and Cultural Expression), I became interested in working with the existing dynamics and networks in and across the nineteen communities. I was fascinated by sociologist of technology Madeleine Akrich's rich ethnographies from Cote d'Ivoire, which describe the different ways in which lighting kits were hacked and modified to suit the community goals of watching television rather than the "developmental goals" delivered by the French NGOs.[67] While my initial introductions were to tribal cultural and political leaders through the TDV effort, I was determined to collaborate and learn from a far wider range of community members.

My goal was to collaborate with tribal members to develop a technology that respected shared local ontologies, keeping in mind the lessons around praxis discussed in chapter 2 in relation to my work in India. During my fieldwork I noticed that some technologies lend themselves more easily to "modification" than other devices, practices, and infrastructures. This flexibility, described by scholars as *generativity*, can be an important precept in design thinking about technology.[68] While the TDV effort was based on the idea of "appropriation toward parity,"[69] I was interested in designing a technology in the image of the voices, ontologies, and priorities of tribal members across the reservations.

I reflected on stories I had read about the introduction of plumbing in the 1980s in the villages in India where my parents grew up. Despite the promise of this infrastructure to make life easier and empower the community, in many ways it supported civic disconnection. The community no longer met and communicated at the local water well, making the latter obsolescent as a public space. I was concerned that TDV could have a similarly anti-civic effect that magnified existing cultural disconnections. From this perspective, the TDV could threaten local organizing and communication. In the next section of this chapter, I describe further ethnographies of peoples and places that shaped the development of our Tribal Peace project.

Listening and Learning

Just five months after my initial meetings with tribal leaders, it is October 2003 and Ross Frank, UC San Diego (UCSD) professor of Ethnic

Studies, and I had driven two hours into the deserts of East San Diego County. After traversing several windy roads, we arrived at the Campo Reservation. Campo is one of the nineteen reservations located in San Diego County. According to Frank, it was similar to several others in terms of the health and education challenges it faced.

Upon arrival, tribal members explained to us that there was an absence of physicians with knowledge about traditional Native American health. Diabetes, obesity, and alcoholism were rampant across the reservations. Visiting primary and secondary schools on this reservation was even more distressing. I observed students studying their own histories via textbooks written in New York and London.[70] According to those I met on this reservation, this perpetuated a sense among the youth that their culture was no longer vibrant. They lacked the agency to write their own histories. Indeed, I met no one at Campo who was conversant in traditional languages, songs, dances, and rituals. Power over the past, present, and future lay elsewhere.

Nonetheless Campo's tribal leaders expressed their desire to reclaim the sovereign identity from which they felt disenfranchised. Understanding that my role was to listen and be of service, I was interested in how I could support the reclamation of community identity through the design and appropriation of technology. I noted that this community would have to be "imagined,"[71] as the tribal communities of Southern California had been in conflict with one another through much of their recent history. Just as we must guard against homogenizing the world through the use of terms like "global village," as I have argued in this book, I recognized the dangers of homogenizing a tribal or indigenous community. There was great conceptual value in the idea of "imagined community," however, as it could assist us in our collective effort to counter systems that have shaped inequality and poverty.

Communities like Campo are rarely the recipients of substantial technology infrastructure grants. Now I was being invited to understand and design a project for Campo and several other reservations. I listened, learned, and looked for opportunities to support the goals and visions that would emerge from the conversations I would have with a range of community members. In my first three months of fieldwork I visited every tribal leader possible across the nineteen reservations. My most fortunate encounter was that with Shonta Chaloux, a young visionary leader from the San Pasqual Reservation. Shonta was a former football star and local hero who had decided to return to his community in order to transform the educational deficit and loss of cultural knowledge among the youth. Shonta was widely respected in his community, and respected by its different subgroups as well.

It was far easier in these early days to develop connections with tribal elites, given the ways in which I had been introduced to the field. My initial contacts were with the Tribal Chairmen's Association and the Tribal Digital Village project. Navigating this challenge represents a delicate balancing act for those of us who work with ethnographic methods, for while we respect our contacts we realize that they may not represent the voices of others in their community. I recognized that I would need to *lateralize* my outreach efforts and ethnographies, reaching out to as wide a range of community members as possible to develop the types of partnerships that would make our Tribal Peace project more radically inclusive.[72]

Shonta had laid out his vision for developing technologies that could reconnect his people to their cultural, educational, and political priorities. Wanting to build on the work of Anthony Pico, the Viejas Band leader, and Leonard Peltier, a famous Native American revolutionary who has been incarcerated since 1977, Shonta argued that we could design a system devoted to the issue of political sovereignty on the basis of the principles of action research and praxis. This system could serve as a space for communication and dialogue that leveraged the TDV infrastructure.

I had envisioned designing a system to empower conversation and community building around a wider range of issues, rather than simply that of sovereignty. Nonetheless, I noted the importance of following the perspective of leaders like Shonta. My initial experiences across the reservations led me to believe that the theme of sovereignty could become an important bridge to a range of other conversations. For example, in Native American politics tribal sovereignty is connected with education, cultural customs, and gaming. While education speaks to the reclamation of history, cultural customs speak to practices that reveal the distinct and original rights of Native Americans as early sovereign nations within the United States of America. Casino gaming, according to other leaders, is critical although controversial, as it may provide the needed resources to allow reservations to operate their own educational, political, and social institutions.

In the months that followed, I learned how important it was to learn from and listen to the gatekeepers I encountered. This built upon a sense of comfort I had developed after six months of living on different reservations and meeting a range of political, educational, and cultural leaders. With the familiarity tribal members had developed with me, I was invited to share my background and interests at an intertribal culture and education meeting. In February 2003, I spoke of my previous projects at MIT that were based in India and with Somali refugees. Reflecting on these experiences, I shared my belief that we could leverage the Tribal Digital Village infrastructure to design a technology that respected the local ontologies across the reservations.

As my presentation concluded, I was introduced to Linda Locklear, professor of Native American Studies at Palomar Community College and a member of the Nambi Nation of North Carolina, who had relocated many years before to the San Diego County region to work with the Kumeyaay and Luiseno reservations. Shonta mentioned that I should meet Linda as she could help me better understand the dynamics of the local tribal communities. Linda had conducted language training and video interviews with different Native members in the region for local cable access television programming, and was interested in seeing how some of these initiatives could also be applied to digital media projects.

After a polite introduction, Linda asked me about my motives for conducting this project and whether I was planning to profit from my work with the Native American communities in any way. She asked whether as a graduate student I had tried to iterate upon and replicate a model from which to craft an academic or professional career. Noting that research productivity is an academic currency, Linda pointed out that her Native American friends were not interested in being studied or framed as an object of curiosity from afar. This conversation was my first direct critical encounter with a Native American community member during my first months of fieldwork. I had been warned that when working with Native American communities I would face mistrust and suspicion and have to deal with it. The projects that succeed are the ones that recognize and respect such cultural and social tensions.

It was thus important to respond to Linda with both openness and understanding. I explained to Linda that like many graduate students I was indeed investigating a thesis, but my motives behind my work were activist and humanist. I believe deeply in being of service and doing what I can where welcome to support the social, cultural, and political empowerment of the communities involved. My research would focus on the process of collaboration and design around technology rather than an exoticized objectification of the communities. In many ways my ethnographies would focus on stories of self. If invited to do so, I believed our collaboration would help us create a technology that could be a resource for community members in the nineteen reservations. It would be the property of the Tribal Chairmen's Association, and live on the Tribal Digital Village servers.

In response Linda expressed further doubts, asking whether I had read Edward Said's *Orientalism*,[73] and stating that she knew the true motives of graduate students and outsiders from institutions like Harvard and MIT. As a self-proclaimed "mother hen" of the Native peoples, her role was to protect their interests and say what others were too afraid to say. She even asked if I knew whether Shonta was an enrolled tribal member of San Pasqual, given the blood quantum rules that governed enrollment. I responded with my personal reassurance that she would be helping to oversee and critique the project on an ongoing basis. I had signed a nondisclosure agreement and property transfer to the Tribal Digital Village administration, and I gave her my word that I would not try to market or make any personal profit off my experiences with the native communities.

I left this interaction feeling I had learned an important lesson about how an outsider could be perceived in tribal communities. I also learned that despite the distressing poverty such communities face, they have agency and a spirited determination to fight back against those who perpetrate oppression. Linda's justified concerns spring from a long history whereby anthropologists have "studied" native communities, masking malevolent intentions through the use of deceitful language and performance.

Over the next several months, my collaborations with Shonta and others in the reservations allowed me to learn from the important criticisms raised by Linda. I realized, however, that Shonta was not the key point of reference for most of the people I was meeting. He was better known at San Pasqual and its neighboring reservations than in others that were further away. Because of the time he spent off the reservations and his relative youth he was not universally identified as a key interlocutor across the communities. In my initial months of fieldwork, I noted that to design a technology to support local practices of knowledge sharing and communication, I had to *work with rather than ignore* the networks that already existed.

Over the next three months, I tried to understand how the Tribal Peace system could harmoniously build on existing connections. This in turn forced me to grapple with important questions related to the larger one, including: How were people in the communities connecting with one another presently? What types of networks were influencing the existing elements of identity, economy, culture, and politics? I realized it was neither technologies nor institutions that connected the people I had met. Instead, the very few threads of kinship I noted were related to revered individuals, regarded by most with collective respect and as a source of inspiration.

Tribal members would often mention the name of Anthony Pico, chairman of the Viejas Reservation. Not only was Viejas self-administering a successful casino, but Pico's government had also reinvested the revenue it had acquired into supporting community health and educational programs. Pico had channeled his leadership position into becoming a major national advocate for political sovereignty at both the state and federal levels. He wanted to eliminate dependence on government programs, which had provided poor services and infrastructure that contributed to their poverty.

After attempting to meet Pico for several months, I was given a thirty-minute audience to present our project and listen to his perspectives on the technology that we could then work to design. Pico referred me to a number of his most successful teachers and aspiring entrepreneurs. He advised me to recruit a demographically inclusive group of tribal members across the reservations to lead the effort. Some months later, with the first release of the Tribal Peace system, Pico recorded a greeting video for users who logged in. He also created several video pieces based on conversations with me and other youth. These were then circulated via the system. As a popular political and educational leader, Pico became a key bridge for the project, whose networks could be supported and augmented by the Tribal Peace system.

The only name I heard more often than Pico's as I traveled and lived on the reservations was that of Jane Dumas. She was from the Jamul Reservation and had grown up in a small hut, learning Kumeyaay and Spanish before English. Many tribal members saw Dumas, who has now passed on, as the last living link to a shared cultural memory. She had witnessed the fall into poverty of many reservations and was determined to support cultural and linguistic revitalization. She had learned a great deal about tribal plants and medicinal traditions that were specific to the region from her parents, particularly her mother who was a revered medicine woman in the late 1800s and early 1900s. Thus, as one of the few traditional speakers of the Kumeyaay language and as a practitioner of tribal medicine, she was a bridge between tribal heritage identity, collective action, and aspiration.

When I met Dumas, I went with sage and tobacco in hand, token offerings in recognition of her status as a powerful spiritual teacher. My offering of these sacred herbs was accompanied by an introduction of my own background as a South Indian Hindu, helping to create a shared and intuitive space of kinship, respect, and mutual understanding. As we sat together, I reflected upon my own beliefs and values, while showing her my familiarity with her people. I explained my goal of designing a digital technology that could support the sharing of local ontologies and the building of social networks across the reservations. We visited nearby Lake Crenshaw, a sacred landscape that Dumas suggested would be appropriate for our first meeting. She first recited a prayer to the four directions, blessing our collaboration. Explaining the potential to "recover so much that we have lost," Dumas explained that new technologies could only support community building and cultural revitalization if they were built upon existing values, knowledge systems, and beliefs. Despite the changes in climate, the region had retained its beauty, Jane said, so all was not lost. The land inspired her tribe to recover its political and cultural identity. As long as the land survived, the tribe could hope for a rebirth.

It was time to face the challenge of creating and mobilizing grassroots networks across the reservations. As most technologies had misrepresented Jane Dumas's community historically, whether through book or video, our meeting convinced us that our collaboration gave us a unique opportunity to challenge the dehumanizing effects of colonization. I recognized that Dumas's blessing of the project could shape its destiny within the community. She could connect us with her extensive social networks while serving as a spiritual and cultural guide.

Cultural knowledge had long been shared between the communities of San Diego County through performances and oral traditions such as songs, dances, and storytelling. These were now being lost at an increasing pace. It was important for us to design a technology that could reactivate these traditions as a catalyst toward the future. I recognized the potential of multimedia elements such as sound and video to assist us in this goal, allowing people to speak as they chose to share places and images with fellow community members. Supporting these local ontologies would require us to recognize that a video in a database, even if it was classified according to tribal categories, was hardly sufficient in and of itself to speak to this performativity. Instead, it was how the communities engaged with such objects that would make all the difference. In this sense, a sociotechnical crafting of our system would need to consider how it could fluidly represent the practices of the reservations, actively engaging peoples to transcend passive spectatorship. We recognized that we would have to design a technology that facilitated rapid feedback, thereby empowering conversational elements important to native life and identity. While the practice of sharing and viewing video or songs is not the same as being present in person at a ritual, as I note in chapter 2, I believed certain elements of the oral culture could be experienced through the rapid sharing of video, promoting the interactive practice of digital storytelling.[74]

Over my first eight months of fieldwork, it was my time with Anthony Pico, Jane Dumas, and Shonta Chaloux that shaped my consciousness and the design and development of Tribal Peace. These introductions and partnerships became part of my larger effort to visit as many educational, political, cultural, and economic institutions as possible across the nineteen reservations. I visited schools, libraries, tribal government offices, health clinics, housing groups, technology offices (for the TDV), youth association programs, and local businesses. At times I walked across the public lands of the reservations, sitting, reflecting, and contemplating.

I recognized that the system's appropriation by these organizations needed to be understood in ways that went beyond mere user statistics. Our goal should not be to fixate on how many people would "use" the system but on *who* these users were, and how the system could support their diverse practices, aspirations, and agendas. I thus began to build connections with educational resource centers on the reservations, tribal government offices, tribal libraries and museums, and employees at local clinics and schools. If even one political leader were to leverage this system in support of a struggle for sovereignty, my vision of supporting the causes of these communities would be realized, even if the user statistics told a different story. Rather than how many, I was most interested in the who's and how's.

Fluid Ontologies and Tribal Peace

As I became better known across the reservations, people from different reservations began to express an interest in working with Shonta and me. We were able to form a focus group of community members that included men and women, and a range of occupations and ages. Our first design workshop in January 2004 brought together seventeen tribal members from thirteen of the nineteen reservations.

It became clear that it would take time to build the trust that would increase collaboration and representation across the tribes. Many of the attendees were unfamiliar and uneasy with new computer technologies, but still brave and curious enough to attend the workshop. They ranged between the ages of 28 and 65 and were involved in teaching and education programs on different reservations. It was our hope that after they learned the techniques of multimedia storytelling, the attendees would be inspired to share these techniques with others on their reservations. In this workshop, each attendee presented an example of what he or she felt was an inspiring story from his or her reservation, focusing on elements of community life. Each attendee then created a video of his or her own based on his or her personal vision. Shonta and I assisted with editing or storyboarding questions.

"This was created by your own people, your children, and grandchildren," I explained, "and without any knowledge of technology beforehand. And today you too can create rich visual stories of your own." This was an important first step in engaging community members to share and reflect on their own stories, given my experiences just two years before of collaborating with Somali community members in Massachusetts. A rapport was established, especially between class attendees. We ended the meeting by asking the attendees to create one or two pieces on their own time to present at our second meeting, which would focus on designing the initial version of Tribal Peace based on the fluid ontology method described earlier in this chapter. This method dynamically engages community members to reflect on shared themes and concepts to shape the underlying architecture by which a system can be designed.

Our second meeting occurred six weeks later. In between these meetings, Shonta and I traveled to different reservations, hoping to publicize the project and recruit more members to join our committee. With some success, we were able to recruit members from seventeen of the nineteen reservations to the fluid ontology design meeting. This time powerful conversations began to surface after the participants had watched the different video stories. One provocative piece that warrants discussion came from a teenage student from the Pala Reservation.

In this video, the student interviewed fellow students and a local tribal leader about the jobs available on the reservation. As the video was playing, several members of our design committee objected to the arguments presented. An attendee from Viejas, where Anthony Pico was chairman, argued that reservation members at Pala were not embracing casinos in the "correct way." This stance was immediately countered by another committee member who explained that casinos often represented a gateway to alcoholism and the plundering of her people by wealthy corporations from Las Vegas. A third member, from a reservation that had no casinos but was closely aligned with Viejas, added his perspective. Casinos could have value, he argued, if they were brought into the communities in "the right way."

Instead of viewing these disagreements as forms of weakness to be ignored or filtered out of the technology design, the fluid ontology approach recognizes the great power of debate and discussion. Indeed, themes in tribal life that heightened people's passions and inspired differences of opinion were privileged in Tribal Peace's initial fluid ontology. For example, there was a great deal of debate in our meetings around "gaming," or the influence of casinos on tribal life. Some participants argued that this reflected a sustainable and robust form of income. It could support their peoples, given all that they had lost in a history of fragmentation, displacement, genocide, and depression. Others, however, saw the presence of casinos as the "gateway drug" that afflicted tribal members. Casinos, if administered by an external company such as Harrahs from Las Vegas, would be given power to influence tribal life and force the dependency of community members. Some participants argued that casinos stymied alternative possibilities—their presence cultivated a detachment from entrepreneurial, activist, and public forms of organizing that empowered self-determination and sustainability from the bottom up.

Such debates must be welcomed rather than dismissed when we think about technology and community life. Including the theme of "gaming and casinos" in our fluid ontology is an example of how the classifications and databases of our system could be organized around the boundary objects theory described earlier that brings together multiple forms of interpretation that fail to "fit" with one another. The design of this ontology could support what scholars of information, social life, and education John Seely Brown and Paul Duguid describe as the "social life of information."[75] This idea argues that shared interpretations about information have great social and cultural impact. Our goal was to design Tribal Peace's fluid ontology accordingly, recognizing that over time this ontology would shift as social life and interpretations themselves took their own turns. We would thus continue to design and modify the fluid ontology for Tribal Peace over several meetings.

Casinos and gaming were but two of several themes that emerged from the first focus group meeting. Several other topics were raised, including political sovereignty, youth education, the U.S.-Mexico border, and more. As political writer and commentator Walter Lippman famously observed, publics are ever in the making. Accordingly, we considered our design meetings part of a process rather than a naïve statement of truth or empiricism. The fluid ontology we would develop would be revisited and redesigned over time via periodic committee meetings reservations in line with shifting social, political, and cultural life across the communities.

Designed over three focus group meetings in the end of 2003, approximately nine months after I had made my first visit to the reservations of San Diego County, Figure 3.6 illustrates our first fluid ontology. It was important for the committee to design this ontology in the shape of a tree. Trees hold powerful metaphorical and symbolic allure for people in the reservations. Over our two years of collaboration, community members often spoke to me about the importance of the Manzanita tree, in particular as a collective symbol of rebirth. They thus saw a relationship between this tree and our collaboration. Both could serve as catalysts for collective action and thus a rebirth of sorts in the communities.

The fluid ontology was not just a list of categories and their relationships, but a visual articulation of imagination, memory, and aspiration. We can see how the roots of this tree diagram display the San Diego County native reservations, while its branches are divided by major themes and their subtopics. The tree has a depth of two levels: Roots, six major branches, and their sub-branches. Each of these represented careful design choices that came out of our meetings and were revisited in later design workshops, which produced new structures and classifications.

Critical to this or any ontology are the selection of topics and the ways they are grouped together. Figure 3.6 contains branches labeled "Medicine People," "Order," "Ocean," and "Darkness and Light." These topics were identified on the basis of conversations between focus group members. They also relate to collective memory and meaning. "Darkness and Light" was a carefully chosen term used to reflect the recurring theme of negative and positive energies by which community members experienced the living and nonliving worlds, based on threatened spiritual practices. "Ocean" is a powerful term for the Native Americans of San Diego County because of their historic proximity to the ocean and their ancestral practices of fishing and being coastal people. The category "Medicine People" describes the ancestors and communities of their past (Jane Dumas is one of the last survivors), following the traditional approaches toward health and plants that were at the core of indigenous life.

It is notable that this ontology weaves together terms as distinct as Culture, Imagery, Community Development, Leadership, Education, and Technology. With these major themes, the past, present, and future can be articulated within an integrated, yet fluid, architecture. In line with the goal of maintaining fluidity, the focus group could choose to remove, rename, or reclassify a topic as they wished.

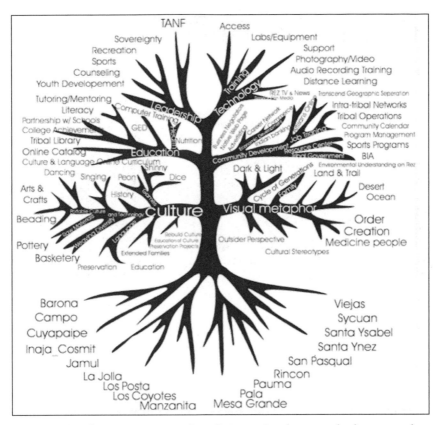

Figure 3.6. Our first community ontology, listing topics, themes, and values across the nineteen native reservations.

The decision to designate "Culture" and "Education" as top-level categories speaks to their central importance in the eyes of the committee. Additionally, the decision on where to assign a given sub-branch speaks to the community's unique means of understanding itself. That choice also raises other interesting questions, such as: Why is the category "online library," for example, placed under Education rather than under Technology? These types of choices can inspire valuable reflection.

The first interface of the Tribal Peace system is depicted in Figure 3.7. The system was designed to allow community members to share content with one another based on the themes from the fluid ontology. Community members could share, view, and comment on video, text, or photos between the nineteen communities. Any tribal member could select one

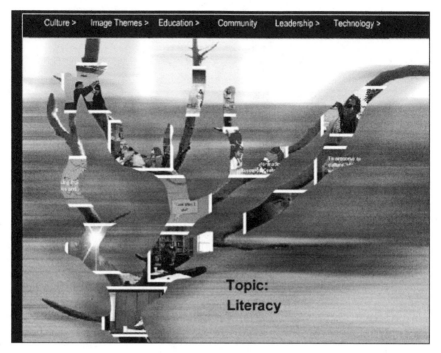

Figure 3.7. The Tribal Peace system interface.

or multiple topics from the ontology through our interface. The system would then retrieve image, audio, or video pieces that would be grafted onto the branches of the above Manzanita tree interface. Thus, while a tree interface supported the front-end experience of system use, another tree structure represented the fluid ontology that structured how pieces of content could be categorized or retrieved.

Our initial focus group meetings paved the way for the recrafting of further fluid ontologies, to be held every three months from that point onward. In these meetings, the committee would reflect on content shared via the system by users in all nineteen reservations, and craft or modify the fluid ontology. The essence of fluidity lay in the ability to adapt, evolve, and recombine the codes of the system based on ever-changing perspectives coming from the community. The Tribal Peace system ontology was thus continuously revisited and recrafted. To this day, it remains accessible to the reservations and is maintained and lives on the TDV servers.

Ritual Communication

This chapter has focused on the power of intervening in some of the codes of digital technology, whether we mean by this databases, interfaces, or algorithms, to support the values, knowledge practices, and aspirations of local communities. My collaborative efforts with the tribes of San Diego County and the stories I have shared of Tribal Peace represent an example of how we may strive to design technologies collaboratively to respect the voices and ontologies of local communities.

The system we designed has been incorporated into the Tribal Digital Village technical infrastructure. While it continues to be used by schools and cultural institutions on the reservations, its technical and design maintenance remains a challenge. This speaks to the reality that a technology cannot be understood in an isolated vacuum. It is interwoven with a range of places, peoples, values, and other infrastructures. Without robust educational and economic systems, even more community-centric technology efforts such as Tribal Peace may be unsustainable.

As I argue in my critique of user statistics, this project is meant to respond to what philosopher and social theorist Michel Foucault has called the "triumph of quantification."[76] Standard metrics that measure numbers of users can be set aside in favor of more deeply intuitive insights focused on design processes, representations, and supporting appropriation by existing community networks and institutions. All these challenges speak to the complexity of working with technology to support local communities in a world where their voices remain mostly silent.

Our effort was inspired by the goal of supporting *lateral networks*— activating connections between peoples living on the margins. This is consistent with communications scholar and theorist James Carey's insights on "ritual communication,"[77] which describes the power of grassroots knowledge sharing. In this communication process, no singular technology design blueprint can have all the power. In contrast to the ritual model, Carey argues that the transmission model, which treats users as passive and the designer as omnipotent, is a tragedy of our times. Supporting ritual communication must include a consideration of the codes by which such communication systems are written. For Carey, the tragedy of the transmission model has long-standing precedents dating back to the time of the telegraph. This model is obsessed with social elites while treating the rest of society as passive consumers or users.

When we step away from a myopic model of design, policy, or system development we open up a wide space of possibilities within the framework of what telecommunications and policy scholars Harmeet Sawhney and Venkat Suri describe as "liminal."[78] They argue that "what is especially interesting about Tribal Peace is that it goes way beyond solving problems or puzzles, and tries to generate indigenous ontologies. . . . [I]t is the 'fluid' of fluid ontologies, enabled by lateral networks that make the whole effort so special."[79]

It is at the margins or peripheries of first world-centric thinking that technologies and networks can be reimagined. For example, media studies scholar Anita Chan's recent book *Networking Peripheries* describes how the grassroots digital cultures of Peru may shape practices, strategies, and material realities that diverge from the universalizing imaginaries of Silicon Valley.[80] Consistent with this, scholar of social informatics and computing Eden Medina's writings on "cybernetic revolutionaries" present a Chile-specific set of narratives that influenced the CyberSyn system in the context of Allende's democratic, socialist government of the 1970s.[81]

The many examples I have shared throughout this chapter reveal that the stories, codes, and infrastructures associated with digital technologies have the potential to represent powerful means for ethical reimagining. We are beginning to see interesting examples along these lines today, for example via the video game "Never Alone," designed collaboratively by Inuit Alaskan indigenous peoples with a game designer. This game follows scripts that are consistent with community values and ontologies.[82]

As my involvement with the Tribal Peace project came to a close in 2005, I reflected on what I had learned through this collaboration. I had to rethink the ways I designed technology, approached communities, learned to listen, and opened myself up to the unexpected. My goal remained the same—to consider "life-worlds, livelihoods, life systems, lifestyles and life cycles"[83] that shape renewed thinking about technology and whose voices it can represent and support.

Chapter 4 builds upon this extensively by recognizing that ontology is much more than the technical expression of a community. Rather it is a way of *performing knowledge* that supersedes technology. It reveals that in their best moments technologies support the things we do—the actions and practices by which we know and communicate.

4

Multiple Voices

Performing Technology and Knowledge

The previous chapters have revealed how the technologies that we take for granted, both old and new, are *socially constructed*. They are created by and in the image of particular peoples, in particular places, and at particular times. The values, beliefs, and ways of knowing, or ontologies, practiced by those who create technology naturally influence its design and the ways in which it is deployed. Yet we perpetuate a myth that treats these tools as sacrosanct and untouchable. We therefore lose the opportunity to reimagine what they may be in relation to the voices of users and communities otherwise left silent.

Through stories of my collaboration with the Zuni Native American tribe, this chapter reveals the lesson I learned that our work with technology should never rest on the myth that cultural knowledge can be fully "represented" or "captured" through any system, no matter how it may be designed. It discusses the power of creating technology to work with the people, places, and "actors" that shape cultural life. Technology, in this sense, is but one part of a wider assemblage that shapes cultural and community life.

Subverting the "Cultural Record"

In the winter of 2004, I received a letter in the mail that inspired me to reflect on my projects involving technology and indigenous peoples. The note, from my now friend and colleague Robin Boast of the University of Amsterdam, raised an interesting question: Could my attempts to develop technology to support the ontologies of indigenous communities be applied to the world of museums? Boast was interested in whether we could collaborate with indigenous peoples to create a "digital museum"—a technology that shared museum collections in ways that respected indigenous voices and perspectives.

Since the time of the Enlightenment, museums, archives, and libraries have been responsible for some of the classification schemes that came to "order the world." These have shaped decisions about what counts as knowledge, and how it is to be preserved and made accessible. Boast, who at the time was the deputy director of Cambridge's (U.K.) Museum of Anthropology and Archaeology, was challenging me to consider how we might begin to transform these "cultural institutions" through a collaborative technology project. In so doing, we could transform traditional understandings of "heritage" that were rarely open to the visions of the communities whose objects they held.

I was inspired by Boast's stated vision of applying the fluid community ontology method, as described in the previous chapter, to the domain of the museum. I was also intrigued by his mention of the term *contact zone*, a seductive concept introduced by Spanish and Portuguese language and literature scholar Mary Louise Pratt and advanced by historian and cultural studies scholar James Clifford. I had learned that a contact zone is a space where disparate cultures or communities encounter one another while recognizing past and present asymmetries of power and voice. This concept reminded me of anthropologist Helen Verran's description of the "postcolonial moment" that I discussed in the previous chapter. Both describe a moment where inequality can be recognized and confronted in the hope of changing the future. Both also recognized the power of grassroots community agency and voice. It was fascinating to think that collaboration involving digital technology could shape such a contact zone, and how it might be applied to the world of museums.

Boast and I began to speak by phone, recognizing the possibility of working together with technology to open up indigenous voices that tend otherwise to remain objectified within cultural institutions. We could expand the Tribal Peace project discussed in the previous chapter. Yet instead of merely trying to support indigenous social networks, the goal of this project could be to empower the sharing of *multiple ontologies*. In other words, we could develop a technology that respected a range of knowledge practices and perspectives. We suspected that what we would empower could never be defined by technology design practices, but in what those practices could empower "outside the machine."

First and foremost, we were determined to support the agendas of indigenous peoples, who have long been misrepresented by museums and other cultural institutions. To do so, we had to learn from native communities that had been able to achieve self-determination and autonomy over their lands. One example that has inspired us relates to the Ngarrindjeri aboriginal community of Southern Australia, who were able to take advantage of the national desire for better water resource management to develop and maintain autonomy over initiatives they would lead.[1] This example reveals the power of community agency.

Indigenous peoples are not dead, nor are they entrenched in an exoticized "savage" past. They are not merely victimized subalterns, to be objectified in academic literature and theory. The Ngarrindjeri and other peoples described in this book reveal the power of *tactics*. Grassroots technology users and diverse communities are capable of articulating their expertise in ways that can be comprehensible to institutions of power. Yet they can also fight for the sovereignty of their political goals, values, and ontologies. Many communities practice "code switching," a tactic that frames oneself coherently relative to the perspectives of others without sacrificing one's underlying integrity. While this tactic is less explicitly oppositional, it reveals a mechanism by which power and voice may shift in initiatives that involve cultural institutions and technologies.

Reflecting upon these examples, Boast and I, along with cultural geographer Michael Bravo, wrote a paper outlining our vision of designing technology to support multiple ontologies. We imagined a system that would promote dialogue and conversation to support the differences between the perspectives of different communities rather than collapse all of them into "users." We could avoid top-down precreated classifications imposed by a designer, engineer, or technology corporation.

As we wrote and imagined conceptually, we reflected on an indigenous Inuit object and wrote about how it might be represented in an online system:

> When visitors access a digital image of the [Inuit] kayak from an
> online museum web site . . . they are likely to be captivated by the

carver's memories of the feelings, skills, and textures of kayak travel that inspired the model. The goal of the online system should be to expose the visitors to these deeper sets of knowledge associated with the kayak—the objects, thoughts, and memories. But how likely is the museum collector to have had the time and privilege to have paddled with the carver or to have documented his experiences through a patient oral history? A much stronger likelihood is that the carver's hunting partner or his grandson or granddaughter may want to tell the stories that explain the experiences out of which the model kayak emerged.[2]

I have argued throughout this book that classification and ordering are powerful not simply because categories shape how technologies sort and retrieve information but also because they provide an opportunity to give voice to ontologies that remain invisible or objectified. The fluid ontology method described in chapter 3 empowers communities to assert their control over technology by designing systems according to classifications that are locally meaningful. Applying this approach to a digital museum effort would involve working with the cosmologies and memories of indigenous people while also respecting archaeological and curatorial ontologies whose classifications are based on "scientific" understandings or larger-scale "public" narratives (such as situating an object relative to a region, other tribes, an era, etc.). What are needed are technologies that support these multiple ways of knowing, describing, and classifying objects. Our hope was that this would enrich communication between indigenous peoples, museum curators, and archaeologists, each with potentially valuable perspectives on objects that have entered into the hands of museums.

The challenge at hand goes beyond classification. Ethnic studies scholars such as Kim Christen and Haidy Geismar have pointed out that we must question our assumptions about the circulation of and access to knowledge to consider indigenous and non-Western perspectives.[3] We must question mantras such as "information wants to be free," by respecting that many cultures or communities do not want all knowledge to be made equally available to all. In several indigenous communities, one's age, kinship group, gender, or profession dictates what knowledge one may access. The Western and digitally utopian idea of 'information for all" may be antithetical to the spiritual and moral precepts that support the lives of many indigenous and developing world communities.

Palestinian literature scholar Edward Said famously remarked that Western institutions study societies they have colonized in order to affirm themselves rather than support those they have harmed. Information institutions such as archives or museums can be critiqued on the same grounds. Despite this, it is interesting to note that these institutions have taken on new community-based forms. Community-based archives, local libraries, and tribal museums have expanded greatly in number over the past two decades.[4] Their agendas differ significantly from those of their imperial histories. For example, tribal museums tend to be dedicated to serving their own communities while assigning far lower priority to public visitors. They are less interested than national or regional museums in preserving their artifacts as static objects to be maintained in their current form for posterity, as museum with a Western perspective are likely to do. Tribal museums, in contrast, see living relationships between objects and the peoples, places, and practices that produced and shaped them. Thus, for example, they would relate a piece of pottery to local artistic or religious practices. In this sense, they are focused on community-based activities rather than passive spectatorship.

James Clifford's discussion of *Museums as Contact Zones* discusses a number of ethical, philosophical, and sociopolitical issues at play in the postmodern museum.[5] He argues that at stake is whether the museum will perpetuate a colonial history of inequality or open itself up to acts of appropriation and subversion led by community stakeholders. Contact zones can facilitate the sharing and discovery of new forms of knowledge that emerge through grassroots conversation.

An example of this process can be seen in science and technology studies scholar Ron Eglash's study of the architectural and religious knowledge of West African tribes.[6] His ethnographic and collaborative experiences have brought him back repeatedly to the *fractal*, a recurrent pattern he observed across architectural forms and religious rituals. Eglash points out that the fractal is an emergent example of "vernacular appropriation" whereby communities learn from one another rather than being forced into servitude.[7] It is examples such as these that inspired Boast's and my thinking about how we too could work with new technologies to support the sharing of multiple ontologies.

Kechi:pawa and Tribal Technology

Robin Boast's employer, the Cambridge Museum of Anthropology and Archaeology, owned a notable collection of museum objects that had been recently digitized. These were objects from Kechi:pawa, a village dating back several hundred years and located outside the Zuni Native American Pueblo. The pueblo is in New Mexico (U.S.A.), though the Zuni see their ancestral land as including the neighboring state of Arizona.

Kechi:pawa was excavated in the early 1900s, and as with many collections, objects from this excavation had come into the hands of collecting institutions across the world. Zuni, or A:shiwi, collections may be found in museums as far apart as Cambridge, New York, and even Osaka, Japan. Could Kechi:pawa, which had not been yet been absorbed into and therefore "silenced" by the classificatory ontology of Cambridge's museum, represent a point of departure so Boast and I could pursue our vision? To develop this project, we would need to work closely with the Zuni community from which these objects were taken.

With some funding in hand, we approached Jim Enote, Director of the A:shiwi A:wan Museum and Heritage Center at Zuni. Being on academic and grant-cycle time, I sent an email to Enote while he was traveling, asking whether he would be interested in developing a partnership with us. Reflecting on this now, I recognize the mistake I made in presuming that Enote would respond quickly and affirmatively. My worldview was conditioned by my status as a pretenured faculty member at a top university. I learned a great deal in the years that followed about indigenous sensibilities on matters regarding trust, time, and progress.

Boast and I received a polite response from Enote, asking us to visit him at the Zuni pueblo and explaining that for us to work together we would need to spend time together to build up trust and a collaborative relationship. We would have to confront and overcome many years of misrepresentation by academics, museum curators, and more. Enote explained that although his community had no interest in being studied, observed, or researched, the potential remained for collaboration with outsiders who wished to support Zuni voices and visions. We could wait for the Zuni to seek us out rather than the other way around. If we did so, we could imagine a process whereby we would design and deploy technologies to truly support Zuni voices and ontologies.

Designing a technology to support multiple perspectives and voices is not merely a philosophical goal. Design, like communication, is a process. I would be forced to step away from my existing biases, assumptions, and ambitions.

Zuni Time and Zuni Space

Over a year has passed since our email introductions to the Zuni tribal museum. It is Robin Boast's and my third visit to the Zuni pueblo, and winter has arrived. Blizzards, subzero temperatures, overturned trucks, and zero visibility greet us in December 2006 as we drive across the Continental Divide. We hope to avoid any collisions with elk on the country roads we take as we drive near the border between New Mexico and Arizona.

During our first two visits over the previous year, Boast and I spent several days meeting with the leadership of the A:shiwi Awan Museum and Heritage Center (AAMHC), primarily with director Jim Enote and his staff. On our second trip we were introduced to a number of Zuni elders with whom the museum was collaborating. These elders were leaders of medicine groups in the larger tribe. They were experts in the cosmological, ceremonial, and artistic traditions of the Zuni—from dances to pottery and jewelry making. Although the museum had several collections, some in glass cases, the preservation of these objects was not a priority in the Western sense of ensuring that physical artifacts and objects—the "tangible cultural heritage" of the Zuni—were untouched. Instead, the tribal museum's emphasis was to share its collections to support community activities.

I was struck by how little we had discussed the project that Boast and I had long imagined. In the previous projects I have discussed throughout this book, I had become accustomed to basing my collaborative visits and meetings around various deliverables that I would articulate with my community partners. Thus, the Tribal Peace effort I described in chapter 3 was defined to me as a deliverable by the tribal leadership of San Diego County. While I had learned to put these assumptions at arm's length in my initial meetings at Zuni, the experience ultimately taught me to step away from the entire "research map." In our visits to Zuni, Boast and I were simply putting in "face time" without making

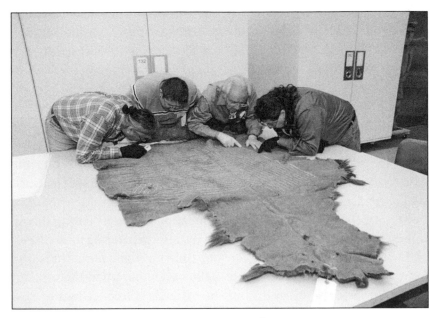

Figure 4.1. Zuni elders and leaders examining an indigenous map.

clear decisions, developing timetables, or articulating deliverables. Our collaboration with Zuni put deliverables and progress reports aside to focus on creating and nurturing relationships.

It is easy to assume that indigenous peoples represent an exaggerated type of "Otherness." Indeed, my discussions throughout this book of community ontologies can be misunderstood as fetishizing diversity to urge academics, professionals, and activists to "save" knowledge that would otherwise be lost. However, our experiences at Zuni could not be further removed from this misguided approach. Indeed, from the start the Zuni community revealed its agency, sovereignty, power, and self-determination. It was clear that the tribal museum staff understood Boast's and my interest in developing technologies to support community voices and ontologies. We were struck by the moments when Enote would summarize our arguments in much clearer language than our own. His story had amazed us—he was a world traveler, spoke fluent Japanese, and made the important choice to come back to his community and assume the leadership of the tribal museum.

Through these initial visits, Boast and I learned that we had to set aside our notions of progress and open ourselves up to the only ethical choice: That of following the Zuni leadership. Developing such a relationship involves embracing humor and the everyday randomness of life, and respecting voices and perspectives that may differ from our own. The Zuni museum staff and I spent time discussing everything from our favorite television programs, the most recent Harold and Kumar movie, life in Los Angeles, Zuni cuisine, and the dogs that would chase us as we walked down the dusty streets of the Pueblo. Our conversations took on a life of their own, and at times included lengthy pauses. I realized that such silence could inspire friendship and collaboration, and our time together need not be spent in verbal communication alone. Listening, being mindful, and present—these were all skills I learned during these visits.

I was fascinated by how rapidly our time together would transition between casual and serious themes. For example, when the topic of "the anthropologist" came up, our Zuni friends voiced feelings of misrepresentation and anger at their objectification. They explained that social scientists would visit their community, exoticize their traditions and customs, and extract what they could to benefit their own agendas rather than those of the community. In some cases, I was told that anthropologists would work with the CIA, the FBI, and the state or national government, claiming to support the Zuni community when in reality they were taking steps "to keep us down."

Despite such a history, Boast and I were cautiously welcomed. When seasonal dances and ceremonies were discussed, I would be told to listen, observe, and be at peace with what was being revealed to me rather than seek out answers to questions I was not entitled to ask. I was being trained to adjust to a Zuni way of life, without full knowledge of what that life was, given my status as an outsider. Curtis Quam, Enote's lead project assistant, was a kind, friendly, and shy collaborator with our team. Politely circumspect, he adopted a "wait and see" approach while gauging our authenticity and level of respect for his tribe. Meanwhile, we built a healthy connection through laughter and joking over many random moments. Yet a respectful distance remained.

Before our third visit, as Boast and I drove through the snowy mountains of New Mexico over the Continental Divide, the Zuni museum team had communicated that the time had come to formally initiate a collaboration between ourselves and the Zuni tribal museum via a conversation with the tribal council. As the museum was independent of tribal governance (as a 501c3 organization), appearing before the council was a matter of respect rather than a legal necessity. At Zuni, respect makes all the difference—and Enote had made it clear that the discussion would be between the museum staff and tribal government. Our role would be to listen and answer questions when asked to do so. As we entered the tribal council room after a long night of driving and on three hours of sleep, Boast and I were asked to sit in the back of the room. Fake plastic plants stood between my chair and the larger table in front where the Zuni museum team was seated. I could barely see the council, given the obstructions to my vision, and wondered whether this was a way of showing us that we were only passive parties to a conversation between Zuni community members.

We greeted the council and were silent while the museum staff and invited elders explained their interest in designing a technology that could allow their community to access digital images of objects sitting in museums across the world. This was the first time I had heard the tribal museum staff articulate their understanding of our collaboration and their vision of a technology we could together create. Enote explained to the council that the system we would design would be the property of the museum, serving the Zuni people *first and foremost*. This was no substitute for repatriating objects that had been stolen, but it could assist in the development of a conversation between community members about images of objects of Zuni patrimony. Most importantly, it could support the community's cultural and educational objectives, empowering youth to take control of different technologies that could help them learn from their elders and one another.

In Zuni, knowledge is *stratified*—different medicine groups have access to different types of knowledge, and one has access to different ways of knowing depending on one's kin, gender, or age. I learned that knowledge emerges through ceremonies and performances between and within medicine groups. In this sense, across the Zuni community lie a range of different knowledge practices, or *multiple ontologies*—which meet and inform one another at particular times and places.

After nearly an hour of conversation, the tribal council gave the museum staff its blessing to develop a technology to support education, learning, and communication within the community. It echoed Enote's perspective that Zuni insights on the objects, when deemed appropriate according to local protocols and classifications, could be shared with museums. This effort would "set the record straight," correcting what the Zuni saw as gross misrepresentations of their culture that had occurred via museum classifications, descriptions, and practices. The tribal council expressed its concern that the Internet and new technologies were complicit in the erasure of indigenous identity and voice, yet also remained open to a new path that we could develop together.

The council asked us to share with it our "human subjects" authorizations from our host universities. Knowing full well that a university's notions of ethics might differ from that of the Zuni, we were nonetheless instructed to submit a project proposal developed with the tribal museum team to the council for approval. As this meeting ended, Enote explained that we were now authorized to develop the specifications of our initiative. The museum team went into a level of detail with us that we had not had before, discussing timelines, budgets, ownership, and local protocols to their satisfaction.

That night we were invited for the first time to attend the winter solstice harvest dances—a multiple, all-night performance in which *Shalako* spirits would dance and bless the community. During these ceremonies, anthropomorphized spirits would come from the sky and earth to dance for the community, and enter and bless particular family homes from different medicine groups. Closed to non-natives in recent years, we were honored by the invitation to witness the dances of these spirits—which are seen as essential to blessing not just the tribe but also the larger world.

For the Zuni, certain types of knowledge are dangerous when they migrate to places outside their lands of origin. The spread of sacred indigenous objects into the hands of art collectors or colonial museums is not only a violation of the Zuni tribe's sovereignty, but also introduces danger into the world by releasing negative spirits outside the tribal lands, where they would be listened to and respected.[8] The tribal museum, like the medicine groups, thus exists to mediate knowledge by respecting such protocols. It is a boundary between Zuni knowledge and spirituality and an external world that tends to ignore and misrepresent the Zuni peoples.

By 11 p.m., the temperature had dropped below zero degrees Fahrenheit. As Boast and I walked to the main plaza of the pueblo, we could hear low, repetitive, and somber rhythms and chants. We walked with Enote and Quam toward the source of these sounds and reached the outside of a house where we saw a number of Shalako dancers. The home belonged to a Zuni family from a medicine clan that was to be blessed by these dancing spirits. We were thus not permitted to enter the home. However, we were allowed to stand outside and listen, watch, and feel, all through a frosted windowpane. In a moment of extreme physical discomfort standing outside in the cold, I was nonetheless grateful for the opportunity to witness the blessings of sacred and timeless spirits on Zuni land. The Shalako beings are believed to come from the sky and the earth, as Zuni cosmologies locate their divine beings above and below Arizona's Grand Canyon.

Our experiences with vision-blocking plastic plants during the tribal council meeting and sub-zero temperatures during the Shalako dances were insightful. They underscored the need to respect and appreciate a radically different way of knowing, performing, and living. We had to open ourselves up to the unknown and unexpected. I saw an opportunity to learn from the Zuni in ways that would not have been possible if we had clung to a pre-existing agenda. This was an opportunity not just to advance my research but my own ethical and cultural awareness. For our research team to respect the fluid ontologies of Zuni life, we would have to listen to "the ontological keys that unlock the doors to diverse, rich, and incommensurable knowledge communities that . . . are diverse 'ways of knowing' about the world that are necessary to organize, find, and use information."[9]

After this, we turned toward the task of designing a digital museum system with Zuni to achieve this objective.

Sharing and Learning from Digital Objects at Zuni

The philosopher John Dewey argued that diverse ways of speaking about, understanding, and reflecting upon a particular issue are fundamental to a thriving democracy.[10] With this in mind, we began to think about how to support a conversation about Zuni objects that placed Zuni voices at the center while including archaeologist and curator partners. We recognized that there was mutual gain in a dialogue that respected the distinctive ontologies of the Zuni and those of archaeologist and museum curator friends and colleagues that already had a positive relationship with the community. Previously, if Zuni had any input in museum technologies it would be absorbed into existing databases and institutional ontologies.

Our goal was to create a space where Zuni voices could be shared without misrepresentation. The only way to do this was to treat Zuni content "as is" and do away with existing classifications and ontologies. As we thought about how to realize this goal through a digital media system, a number of important questions arose. We thought about what digital objects could offer in shaping the communication of knowledge. We also began to reflect on how to maintain ethical appropriateness and respect as we began to more actively collaborate with the community.

To start, we decided that our first effort should be to learn from the accounts and perceptions of digital images of objects by Zuni community members. The museum team had selected a random group of hundred and fifty Zuni members with whom we would share digital images of these objects. The tribal staff asked Zuni community participants to share descriptions and understandings of these objects as well as any other knowledge they wished to present. This process respected the decisions of some not to participate and the anonymity of their responses. The group we worked with was carefully chosen to span a range of social groups at Zuni, considering gender, kinship, and those working in "cultural professions" such as teachers, library staff, the preservation office, and archaeologists. Interviews and surveys were administered by Zuni museum staff rather than by us, outside researchers.

Every aspect of our collaborative research followed the leadership of our colleagues. This helped us ensure that our process would resonate with the priorities and goals of the museum and Zuni community. At their best, participatory methodologies reflect a decentering of the research paradigm away from the "study of" toward "leadership by."[11] Yet we were also mindful that protocols, rules, and underlying systems of political economy are often perpetuated in the name of participation. Our intention was to engage our community partners at every level, including imagining what the project could become—such as its name, goals, and schedule.

The Zuni museum staff selected two hundred professionally photographed objects from the Cambridge Museum's collection. This was chosen based on categories that the team deemed would be of interest to community members. We attempted to avoid objects that would be considered religiously sensitive. Jewelry from different kinship groups, pottery, fetishes, and deities were circulated to the hundred and fifty members surveyed and interviewed.

The research team asked each participant about their knowledge, feelings, and experiences of the images of the selected objects, presenting one to three images per object to each community member. They also asked each community member about their thoughts on heritage, the role of the tribal museum, and their experiences and interests in new technology. Fully mindful that the image of an object is not a good proxy for its physical materiality, even when viewed within a glass case or "white cube,"[12] we were still interested in whether digital images could inspire and cultivate the sharing of local ontologies at Zuni. The researchers provided very little information during the interview if participants were unable to identify what they were looking at immediately or what connections they felt they or their kinship group had to the object. Often, toward the end of the interview and especially if the participant had trouble identifying an object, the interviewer would tell the participant the name of the object and offer some basic Zuni-specific information about it.

These conversations were conducted almost completely in Zuni not only because Zuni is a first language for many elder tribal members, but also because it is the only language actively used in cultural and religious discussions. Boast, I, and our university research teams were not involved in the direct interviews. As language is a window into the ontologies of culture and community, it made sense that indigenous knowledge was best expressed through the semantics and syntax of the Zuni language. This issue further forced our research team to make what are sometimes painful adjustments for those of us within Western academies. We learned to be comfortable with translations that are necessarily imperfect and interpretive.

As the Zuni museum team conducted interviews with their fellow community members over the next six months, we learned that the knowledge shared by the tribe about these objects differed significantly from that contained in existing archaeological and curatorial records. What was striking was not the fact that these differences existed, but their nature—the difference between personal, embodied connections to objects versus "rational" and detached understandings.

Figure 4.2 reveals significant distinctions between the descriptions found in the museum catalog on the right side of the Venn diagram, and Zuni responses on the left side. The diagram shows responses from five selected basketry, pottery, and jewelry pieces. These results were

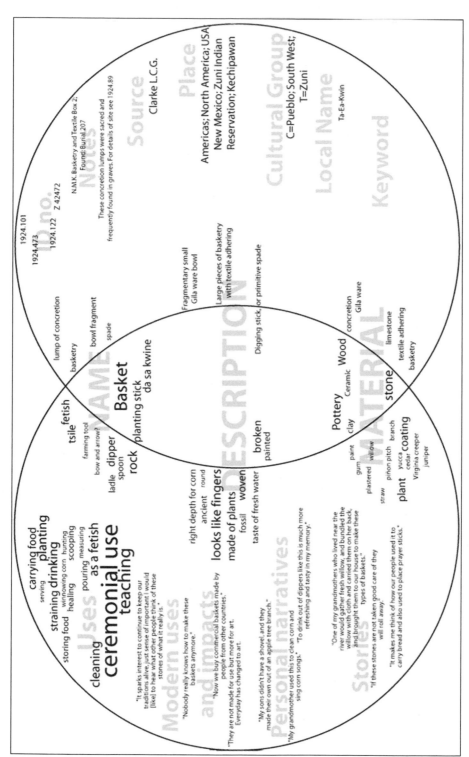

Figure 4.2. Distinctions between Zuni community and museum ontologies.

broadly applicable to the majority of digital objects shared with community members.

While there are some overlaps in naming and titles between entries on the two sides of this diagram, the differences are revealing. The Zuni responses focus on culturally specific *practices* and *narratives* through which these objects are experienced. Objects, even those that no longer exist in the community, are still active through memories or everyday experiences. Zuni do not understand a piece of pottery in a neutral vacuum. Instead, its meaning is *relational*—expressed through the object's connections to economic, religious, or political practices and memories. Thus, although the fetish of a bear may not be part of everyday life at Zuni, it still lives on through its associations with stories, myths, and memories.

In contrast to Zuni responses, we observed how the feedback shared by the archaeologists and curators reflected epistemologies of heritage, persistence, and preservation. Thus, in terms such as "lump of concretion," the archaeological records associated with the objects contain abstract terms like *concretion*, or geometric terms like *lump*. These are part of a specialized scientific vernacular and like the Zuni responses, are examples of ontologies that deserve to be treated as they stand. The key distinction between these ontologies relates to *abstraction* versus *embodiment*. The connection between a given object and the emotional, spiritual, economic, or political elements of Zuni life were mostly absent in the curatorial and archaeological databases that we consulted. Yet they are integral to the Zuni way of knowing.

The stories shared by the Zuni speak to the context in which an object was produced, circulated, and at times returned to the earth. While these contexts are subject to change, as are all stories, their connections to place and community are notable. One cannot read an object independently from the values, practices, and knowledges of the community. To cite an example, a fifty-five-year-old male tribal elder, exposed to the digital image of a mortar object, shared the story below:

> [This mortar reminds me of] grandfather making black paint. This same grandfather also survived the smallpox epidemic in the early 1900s, and [he] was passed for being dead but came back to life after three days of being comatose, [which] proved how strong he was but [he] was forever scarred by the smallpox. (viewing MAA Z42477)

One can see an infusion of life and energy in this elder's engagement with the mortar and imagine how an exposure to such images can unlock personal, emotional, spiritual, and other material associations and memories.

Sociologists of science John Law and Annamarie Mol explain that objects, whether from cultural, scientific, or other backgrounds, are carriers of different types of knowledge, emerging from local cultures, peoples, and places.[13] However, when an object is made to travel to distant museums where it is asked to "speak" about its place of origin, that local object becomes a public spectacle, interpreted by diverse publics, each maintaining their own cultural imaginations as they react to it.[14]

Of course, curators and archaeologists are open to stories. They tell stories of their own and sometimes design exhibitions based on the stories they gather from the communities with which they collaborate. Indeed, we all tell stories regardless of our professional or cultural identities. Yet such fluidity is rarely encoded into the underlying systems that classify these objects—the catalog record and associated museum databases. These *command* how knowledge is remembered and valued.

In addition to memories and storytelling, community members also related the images they viewed to their *practices*, or their activities with and uses of those objects. Nearly two-thirds of the interviewees referred to the actual uses of objects (99 of 150 object interviews). Zuni participants expressed an interest in how these objects compared to others in contemporary use. They asked us repeatedly why there was no mention in the archaeological and curatorial catalog entries of activities and practices associated with the images we shared. The stories told by Zuni tribal members were replete with references to particular places, peoples, and families. While these may not always make sense to a museum curator or archaeologist, it was critical to our project design to empower these narratives and design the technology accordingly.

Cultural anthropologist Arjun Appadurai has argued that Western common sense, given its scientific and philosophical traditions, treats traditional cultural objects as "inert and mute," and it is only the agency of diverse communities and cultures that gives these objects knowable meaning.[15] The perceived opposition between words and objects implies that only through the activity of verbal expression can the meaning of objects circulate and be understood as part of human thought and agency.[16] The mistaken principle at play is that "things by themselves" are inherently enigmatic, and only when words are applied to these "things" can we understand and impart significance to them.[17] Yet left invisible in such catalogs and records are the processes behind the interpretation of museum objects. Knowledge, in contrast, can be seen as process-based, embodied, and performed, relating to anthropologist Tim Ingold's expression that we "know as we go." If we treat knowledge as static, formal, logical, and easily classified, we lose sight of the performances, memories, and practices associated with objects.

By sharing these objects at Zuni, we learned the value of questioning categories and systems that classify knowledge rather than simply accepting them as universal truth. We also were reminded of the importance of being critical of the invisible so-called "mind of God" by which search algorithms have been identified. If we trust algorithms from major search engines as "blind truth," the ontologies of the powerful will continue to dominate all others.[18] This is particularly troubling as indigenous knowledge can be miscast according to the logics of the market or state, as my search for "Zuni pottery" revealed (see Figure 4.3). The top result here is an eBay link that treats what may be a sacred tribal object as a commodity to be bought and sold.

Figure 4.3 reveals that when it comes to search results, neither bits nor users are equal.[19] My Zuni colleagues expressed disgust at this search re-

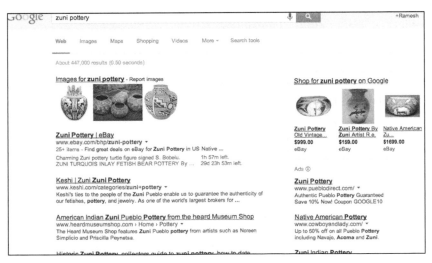

Figure 4.3. Google search results for "Zuni Pottery" (April 5, 2015).

sult, while clearly also recognizing that intervening in such spaces was not their priority compared to their need to focus on supporting their own community. Yet the absence of Zuni voices in these results adds to the false impression that these peoples are no longer living. It is thus far easier to buy and sell their objects as if they were any other commodity. We can only imagine an alternate search experience that would both consider and prioritize actual Zuni voices in the results, insofar as this community is interested in correcting various wrongs and misrepresentations.

Digital Repatriation

Zuni community members never saw the photos we shared from museum collections around the world as substitutes for the physical objects of their patrimony. The digital image, although maintaining a materiality of its own right, could never appropriately represent the physicality and originality of actual excavated materials. Nonetheless, there was meaning and value in engaging with digital objects, particularly when images of higher resolution were provided. Community members would commonly ask for further images from multiple angles of various objects, so they could zoom in on various parts of the image. They would also ask us to describe an object's tactility. Tribal members would explain to us that specific details such as a color blending, etching, or small symbol, were important in their identification of the object's social or cultural meaning.

A large number of Zuni participants expressed the conviction that *repatriating*, or recovering physical objects taken from their tribe, is paramount, even if digital images have value. This insight speaks to the thorny character of repatriation discussions since the passage of the Native American Graves Protection and Repatriation Act (NAGPRA). Repatriation can be politically challenging when tribally run institutions stand for values and beliefs which differ from those who possess the objects they wish repatriated.[20] Such a clash of epistemologies was notable in 1990 during the well-known controversy surrounding the Zuni war gods.[21] Zuni leaders argued that these objects must be returned to the land from which they came by being placed on the tops of sacred Mesa mountains. A return to the land would mean that the gods would be able to bless the people and be blessed by the home from which they came.

Yet from the perspective of the collecting institutions, the ensuing bio-degradation of the items would mean a loss of these objects for preservation purposes. This example, like so many others discussed throughout this book, reveals a clash between ontologies that fail to neatly fit together. Situations such as these are an opportunity for us to give up power and embrace and respect the perspectives of an indigenous community rather than misrepresent or ignore it. We can think about collaborative technology projects within the framework of this ethos. The tribal museum thus rejects the emerging discourse of "virtual repatriation." Jim Enote has made it clear that despite the previously explained value of digital objects, "It may be virtual, but it's not repatriation."[22]

The digital image may inspire reflection in ways that are similar to my descriptions of the village of Ardhavaram in chapter 2. Community members noted that digital objects were valuable because of how easily they could be shared and copied for use in schools, institutions, and homes. We found their comments particularly interesting as the participants who came up with this rationale for favoring the idea of digital objects did so without any prompting from the researchers.

Digital objects were also seen as a useful way to extend the accounts of Zuni tribal members, when appropriate, for effective use by other communities with which the Zuni might choose to share their knowledge. Yet such sharing is carefully mediated by tribal protocols. One community member noted that "when [a description] comes from a Zuni person, they know exactly how much information can be presented without disclosing everything the public wishes to know." She also pointed out that Zuni insights could correct historical and ongoing misrepresentations in nontribal museums, archives, and libraries.

Autonomous Networks

From this book's first chapter onward, I have argued that mere access to technology is not sufficient to reverse political or economic inequality, and indeed may even promote stratification. What is needed is a rethinking of technology from the perspectives of culturally diverse communities traditionally marginalized as users. Collaboration with diverse communities and users is a game changer in a world where notions such as innovation or creativity are limited to elite first-world laboratories. We can rid ourselves of the myth of infinite resources that is blind to the "dark side" of technology innovation—from e-waste to drone strikes and surveillance.

Boast and I were inspired by cultural geographer David Turnbull's argument that knowledge is processual—it travels and is dynamically shaped over time by diverse communities and cultures.[23] Turnbull served as an adviser to our effort from the beginning, visiting the Zuni pueblo in a leadership workshop our team held several years ago. As he sees it, knowledge is not something separate from what we do. It is embodied and performed. We observed this in action as we shared digital images at Zuni, and were reminded that knowledge and communication are intertwined, they are both practices. Community members narrated, remembered, and communicated their reactions to the images they observed.

We have focused on developing a digital network that supports the voices and perspectives across and between three partners (a set of archaeologists, museum curators, and Zuni participants) whose conversations would respect whatever each of them chose to share. We wished to create a decentralized network that respected the autonomy and sovereignty of not only the Zuni but also the archaeologists and curators with whom they were interested in communicating.

Paul Baran's (1964) sketch of a decentralized network in part (b) of Figure 4.4 inspired our project design. Baran is the inventor of the packet-switching technology, a digital network communications model that dominates the technical workings of the Internet. A decentralized network, however, need not solely be a technical diagram but can also be interpreted as an architecture by which power and voice are decentralized. In theory, this network would allow each node within it to interact with others as the people in that node saw fit.

Our collaboration with the Zuni is not merely focused on the structure of decentralized communication, but also on the *semantics* of what flows within a network of nodes and what the links between them mean over time. In other words, it is not enough to create a system that links the Zuni, the archaeologists, and the curators together—the system must also reject any preexisting classifications or categories. By privileging this supposed "rawness" of communication, we have seen fascinating examples whereby each partner has been able to learn from the others in ways that could not have been predicted from the start.

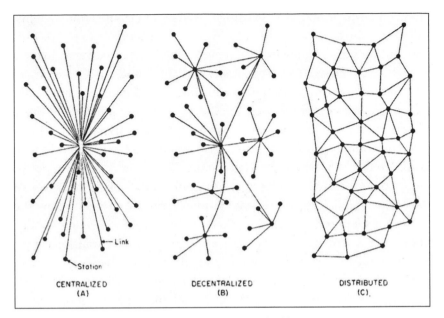

Figure 4.4. Three types of networks. Source: http://4.bp.blogspot.com.

The system we first designed was built using the "Pub Sub" open source protocol which allows communications to be shared via a "hub" that manages what is shared between "publishers" and "subscribers."[24] While most hubs index the information shared by each partner, gathering metadata and sorting information within existing classifications, our design simply gathers whatever is shared by each partner (the Zuni, the archaeologists, and museums) without treating or analyzing the data. Each partner can engage with the digital objects shared by the hub using whatever local system they wish to use. The system we have designed now serves our archaeologist, curator, and Zuni partners. Each user group can log in to our network to share what they wish about the 800+ digital objects of Zuni patrimony today. Our hope remains that through projects such as ours diverse communities can work with technology to speak on their own terms.

Most networked communication systems and databases tend to be optimized for what is called *interoperability*—the technical challenge of designing systems to "work" with one another across institutional and organizational boundaries. To do so, data are "cleaned" and analyzed so they can be associated with existing metadata or classification systems. What is lost when one sacrifices autonomy in this way are the incommensurable ways of knowing that make us different and diverse. In their recent book, *Interop*, legal scholars John Palfrey and Urs Gasser argue that bureaucratic, organizational, and commercial choices made about interoperability shape the social, political, and economic lives of those absent from these boardrooms.[25] When systems work with classifications that simply "sort things out," they command how the world is to be ordered.[26] What are supported are the discourses of those in power rather than the diverse voices or communities they claim to serve. To serve the "public" appropriately, standards cannot merely follow the logic of a supposedly neutral market, but also what technology policy researcher Adam Thierer describes as "experimental, evolutionary interoperability."[27] They must, in other words, respect diverse knowledge systems, not just those more popular according to market metrics.

The drive to achieve interoperability at all times is all the more prevalent, given the present obsession with "Big Data."[28] Anthropologist Tom Boellstorff argues for the power of shifting our understanding of data away from the precreated and socially constructed algorithms and toward "parahuman, complexly material, and temporally emergent ways that do not always follow a preordained, algorithmic recipe."[29] We must open ourselves up to multiple ways of creating, sharing, and classifying data and technology rather than simply buying into the hype of big data (like the technological instruments designed to work with it) as autonomous and universal.

The system Boast and I designed in collaboration with the Zuni is built upon the premise that interoperability can be achieved through conversation and communication rather than via precoded algorithms or database classifications. Networks and ontologies must be treated as autonomous.

The Story of Amidollane

To move between philosophical and ethnographic perspectives, I wish to provide a glimpse into the Zuni experience of our networked system, recognizing that this is but one story of many from our experiences over nearly a decade of fieldwork and collaboration. By "thickly describing"[30] one site at one period of time within the larger networked conversation our technology supports, I hope to reveal some of the complex social and cultural factors that shape technology design and deployment.

This story focuses on how our Zuni partners have begun to work with the technologies we have collaboratively designed. At the core of this story is *Amidollane*, the Zuni word for rainbow. This metaphor was chosen by our tribal community partners to describe their approach toward our partnership. It is the name of the local system used at Zuni and the decentralized networked web-based system described in the previous section. On a metaphorical level, Amidollane relates to the Zuni experience of being interconnected with the world, engaging with a spectrum of objects, people, ideas, and effort. Amidollane has no end, while reaching far and wide in every direction to foster cultural, spiritual, and religious energy.

Enote's team has worked diligently to clarify the meaning of Amidollane, metaphorically and as a technology, so as to appropriately communicate with the larger Zuni community. The system is described with the subtitle: "Supporting authentic Zuni narratives from the source." In a promotional document circulated to the entire pueblo and other stakeholders outside of Zuni, Amidollane has been described by the tribal museum as strengthening "Zuni-led and controlled knowledge sharing in order to sustain Zuni philosophy, language, and arts for generations to come" (December 14, 2012). Enote's team has also clarified that the audiences for this system are primarily local (museum staff, schools, artists, the historic preservation office, and religious leaders) and secondarily subscribing museums, collections institutions, archaeologists, anthropologists, and ethnographers. Table 4.1 clarifies the core principles that justify and inspire the Zuni effort, making clear who our effort truly serves.

Developed by Jim Enote and his team, this table describes a set of protocols developed by the museum staff, intended to carefully mediate the relationship between this new technology and the complexity of Zuni life. It is also intended to signal to the community that this technology will support the authenticity of Zuni storytelling and knowledge. It explains how Amidollane counters a long-standing asymmetry of power and voice around objects of Zuni heritage. At the same time, the above document reveals a strong interest in intervening in institutions that

TABLE 4.1. Zuni Knowledge Protocols, Developed by the Tribal Museum

ZUNI ITEMS IN PUBLIC AND PRIVATE COLLECTIONS ARE FREQUENTLY MISREPRESENTED BY NON-ZUNI NARRATIVES	ZUNI EXPERTS HAVE INTUITIVE AND LEARNED KNOWLEDGE ABOUT ZUNI ITEMS IN COLLECTIONS	AMIDOLLANE IS A CATALOG SYSTEM THAT STRENGTHENS ZUNI NARRATIVES	AMIDOLLANE IS A DIFFERENT KIND OF COLLECTION MANAGEMENT SYSTEM
Zuni items in museum collections are cataloged and described by Non-Zuni museum professionals; Non-Zuni descriptions are inadequate and often incorrect in their representation of Zuni items; Museums use a particular form to describe Zuni items that is very different from the way Zuni describes items; Museums use conventional terms and qualifications to describe items; Digitized collections are generally more accessible to the public including Zuni tribal members; Access to digitized collections means more people are accessing inadequate or incorrect representations of Zuni items	We have thousands of years of accumulated knowledge pertaining to Zuni and Zuni items; We are familiar with the making and purpose of Zuni items; We engage Zuni collections as if they are still in Zuni; We describe items using Zuni language when appropriate or relevant; Our knowledge can enhance museum strategies and create more powerful learning solutions; Zuni experts and museum professionals have complementary motives that can strengthen an understanding of the Zuni world	Amidollane is a collaborative catalog system; Zuni knowledge about items in museum collections can be registered in a variety of ways; Items can be described using text, photos, or audio recordings	Amidollane builds on the work and experience of previous sharing systems; We are concerned about the asymmetry of authority and the control over sharing systems and catalogs in general; Amidollane is located at the A:shiwi A:wan Museum in the Zuni community; Zuni controls the input and sharing of knowledge on Zuni terms

may have imperialistic histories. It represents what Enote has described as a "middle way," respecting the values, ontologies, and memories at Zuni while being realistic about the issues the community must navigate in relation to the wider world.

Zuni community members demonstrate the middle way in many ways. They have adopted tropes of Westernized archaeology and curatorship within a richly indigenous framework that sees peoples and their places as inseparable. What we see here is strategic and flexible "code-switching" in action.[31] Zuni museum staff practice aspects of museology while at other times they engage with indigenous ontologies that can never be appropriately translated into the canons of museum practice. Code switching is a practice by which the Zuni can move between existing ontologies, holding them in productive tension. Just as when one learns a different language and thus a different ontology or way of describing and knowing the world, the opportunity to move between different ever-evolving knowledge practices can be cultivated through technologies we collaboratively design.

A Sacred Anahoho

We came upon Amidollane metaphorically, ethically, and conceptually. But how could it support and be supported by the lives of the indigenous community? To underscore the insight of this chapter that technologies can support the ontologies of community not merely by the way they are coded and designed, but also by the way they relate to powerful performances of knowledge, this section shares a story of the collective viewing of an ancient spirit, the *Anahoho*.

In May 2013, I was invited to join a group of Zuni tribal members at the pueblo's museum. The Amidollane system had been phased into community life by being introduced to spiritual leaders, teachers, and high school and college aged youth. Both the museum staff and our research team were interested in understanding how the system may interact with these different publics. We could then refine its design and deployment to support the larger community. Amidollane was built on the Filemaker Pro platform. I anticipated that the twelve individuals visiting the museum would each open up their own laptop to access the system. Instead I was very surprised to see them sitting next to one

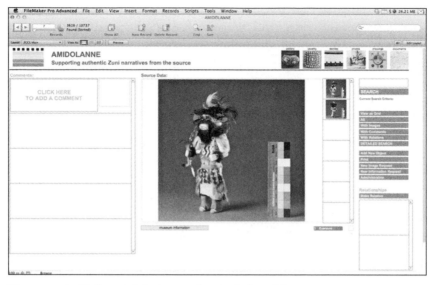

Figure 4.5. *Amidollane* and the image of an Anahoho spirit.

another with only one tribal member, Curtis Quam, directly interacting with a single laptop computer. A large screen was used to display the laptop to the group of visitors. Collectively viewing images shared by the system, the visitors launched into conversations related to each object they viewed.

As Quam scrolled through the objects in the system, a colorful figurine image came onto the screen, featuring a headdress, shoes, and ornate clothes. The audience asked him to zoom in on the image of the object and wanted to find any other images of it they could. Quam was also told that there was no need to click on the system's "museum information" tab that reveals metadata and classifications from the collecting institution and curator.

The image we were looking at was of an ancient spirit, the Anahoho. As the Zuni viewed this image together, a lively discussion ensued. It took place in the Zuni language, while every several minutes Quam wrote notes down in English. I was fascinated to observe several Zuni youth looking down and putting their fingers in their ears, thereby excluding themselves from the conversation at particular moments. An hour later, after the discussion about the figurine came to an end, another image appeared on the screen. This one was sadly of human re-

Figure 4.6. Collective knowledge in the making at Zuni.

mains. Collective silence filled the room. Then the group proceeded to view an image of a piece of pottery. One of the elders noted that this image looked nearly identical to the pottery his great grandfather would make.

Why did some people put their fingers in their ears while we viewed the images of the Anahoho? Why did a dozen people watch a single computer screen? Why were the several laptops in the room left unused, given that everyone could use the Amidollane system on their own? Why was the discussion so lively between the Zuni elders who already knew one another? Why was the Zuni language spoken so often with only small parts of this discussion written into the system, and that too in English? And what determined the difference between the speaking and writing of English versus Zuni?

Clearly, the experience raised more questions than answers. Nonetheless, having had the privilege of being invited to observe these conversations and reflect upon these moments, I believe that this vignette revealed the ways in which knowledge for the Zuni emerges through conversation and communication, and the possibility of thinking about how technologies may support the cultivation and sharing of these ontologies. Zuni knowledge is embodied, brought to life through collective performance and conversation. It became clear to me that Zuni knowledge could never be truly represented from afar via classification systems or databases designed by museum professionals.

In these ethnographic moments, I was also able to learn how this community delineates its boundaries between what knowledge is "open versus closed." As I later learned, the action youth took to put their fingers in their ears respects the indigenous practice of "silo-ing knowledge." Zuni are born into kinship groups based on a maternal ancestral line and a variety of factors determine whether they are permitted or excluded from access to various types of social and cultural knowledge. Out of respect for the different elders in the room, some youth were permitted to listen to comments from their own kin yet prohibited from hearing the comments of others. Hence, they put their fingers in their ears at certain times.

The Anahoho image we had looked at was of a spirit that was no longer part of contemporary religious practice, but was still known to some of the elders in the room. The ability to see this image and engage with the digital object stimulated a rich discussion between elders from different kin groups. From my observation, it was also captivating to the youth who were eager to learn about it while remaining attentive to religious protocols.

As some elders later explained, it is only the Zuni language that contains the concepts and categories that could adequately speak to this powerful figurine. Yet they were uncomfortable writing this language down, as it was rarely transcribed. The oral conversation that I witnessed was revealing of the collective, yet situated, production of knowledge at Zuni. Tribal members together were responsible for articulating and communicating these ontologies in ways that carefully negotiated traditions and values with the realities of the "here and now." Zuni knowledge in its true form resists representation. It cannot be fully "coded" into a system or made to fit into an existing metadata or classification system. The system in this sense was not the container of knowledge, but just one actor in a room with several others that shaped an important conversation. The insight this chapter aims to share is that we think of technology similarly.

What was the knowledge being shared and produced in this conversation? The elders were telling stories, locating the meaning of this image relative to various cultural folk tales. Much like what we learned as we shared digital images with community members, it was clear that the communication and representation of knowledge at Zuni was all about stories. Stories connect the objects shared by the system to contemporary practices within the community. At this particular point, the knowledge from the museum catalog was not what was most important to these elders. Instead, the important task was to empower the oral and conversational practices of Zuni life.

As the meeting ended that day, George Ishak, an elder, master craftsman, and artist in the room told me a story of the Anahoho. He explained that the spirit would come to life during initiations to bless and purify people's houses and would use pottery and willow stick baskets in the process. He explained that it was important that individuals not touch these figurines, or they would become "clumsy."

Clumsy? Clearly the concept does not lend itself well to translation into the English language, yet it was widely understood by the Zuni speakers in the room. This reveals how local knowledge practices often defy simple translation, and that we should do away with the myth that that we can simply "translate" cultures, languages, or ontologies into one another. Yet I believe that the confounding experience of trying to grapple with the Zuni concept of what is "clumsy" is a unique opportunity to respect Zuni knowledge practices as they stand. Our effort with Amidollane indeed made possible such valuable encounters with the incommensurable.

Scholarship and activity in the field of human-computer interaction (HCI) tends to look at technology use as *teleological*—focused on achieving an optimal outcome. Processes are often ignored unless they are critical to understanding how to reach a desirable end point. Much of HCI is thus geared to resolve what information scientist Nick Belkin calls an "anomalous state of knowledge."[32]

No standard model of technology use could predict what I observed and learned on this day. In the one hour that the Anahoho koko was on the screen, I was exposed to multiple languages, emotional states, and physical performances (such as fingers being placed in ears). There is value in developing this technology collaboratively with community members and to consider how to design it accordingly. Yet I also recognized that the technology we had developed could best support the ontologies at Zuni not merely through its design method, but also by the responses it provoked and inspired. The technologies we develop must be devoted to supporting performances, cosmologies, emotions, and ethics, and other such timeless practices. Amidollane is a digital system indeed, though technology is but a small part of the larger story. A far richer understanding would see the system as an actor within a network of peoples and other entities that support Zuni ontological life—the rituals, performances, and interactions between different participants. As one tribal teacher told me in an anonymous interview:

> For us, support is not clicking a button on a technology, or calling up someone far away in New York—it is knocking a door of our neighbor, or talking to our aunt in the pueblo. . . . A computer that replaces human interaction or attempts to sum up who we are would make us lose ourselves. . . . Amidollane is different because it is a technology that is all about us, human beings, the museum, the elders, the youth and those personal connections that may have changed recently but in a sense have always been part of who we are. . . . [W]e just use the technology to remind us of who we are and provide us with new pathways forward.

Technology both shapes and is shaped by cultural and social life at Zuni. While this insight emerges from the experiences I share in this chapter, it can be extended more widely as we think about the two-way relationships between technologies and cultures. Our process of designing the *Amidollane* system respected the ontologies articulated by community members and went on to consider how to create various components of technology (interfaces, databases, and design affordances) based on these perspectives. In so doing, the technology was able in turn to shape and empower the ontologies on which its design was based.

Zuni elder George Ishak explained to me that many years ago he had worked with computers while consulting for scientists from outside the community who were interested in his folk knowledge of the sawmill. Based on this experience, he was inclined to see the computer as "computational," which he defined as mathematically optimized as distinct from his indigenous values and practices. Yet his perspective had opened up as he collaborated with our team, and particularly as he saw the potential of a technology to reintroduce the image of the Anahoho to his community.

My Zuni colleagues have pointed out that despite the continued presence of indigenous festivals and ceremonies on their land, their tribe has in part gone the way of many others in today's world. The experience of life is increasingly individualized, stratified by the brick and mortar of single-family households. I was particularly taken by the words of one young Zuni man who wished to remain anonymous for our interview. He talked about being torn between his desire to be "of the world" while remaining "one with his people." How he and other Zuni negotiate these boundaries remains a major issue for the community. As a medicine leader explained:

> Our culture used to be more intimate, where we learned between families, kin, and our common forms of identity. But we no longer live together, we no longer connect with our elders in the same ways. In the 1970s we still lived together, allowing us to share and learn from one another through conversations and our initiation status—but no more. We are the same every year, but we're different. The right type of technology would allow us to be the same yet different in a way that supports not just who we were but who we aspire to be.

My hope is that Amidollane can support forms of agency that have existed at Zuni long before we began our collaboration with this community. Internet and technology access have been slow to come to the Zuni, but are now far more ubiquitous than when Robin Boast and I first visited the community in 2007. Tribal members are concerned that these infrastructures have worked to support individuality rather than collectivity and are in tension with the traditions and practices that many are determined to keep alive. This destiny for technology need not be written in stone, as I have argued throughout this book. Instead, we can rethink how we design and deploy technology to consider the voices and perspectives that come from engaged collaboration.

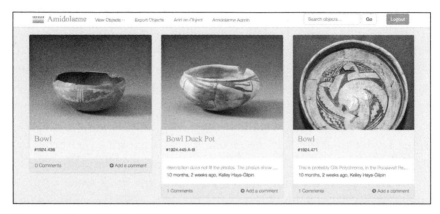

Figure 4.7. The online Amidollane system.

My story reveals the ethical challenges and opportunities involved in thinking about technologies in the service of multiple ontologies. As Octavius Seowtewa, a widely respected elder, religious leader, and master jeweler, pointed out to me, "It is important for the world, not just for us, what objects and knowledge flow to which places. Otherwise people will lose their money, get ill, or even die. We elders at Zuni are here to guard knowledge not just for our own good but also for the protection of the world. When our knowledge goes to the wrong people and places, it is bad for everyone."

Figure 4.7, our online system that supports "raw" conversations around selected Zuni objects continues to engage archaeologists, curators, and the Zuni in a dialogue that respects the ways each chooses to share what they know. The A:shiwi A:wan tribal museum at Zuni has assumed the mantle of leadership over both the local Amidollane system that lives at Zuni (Figure 4.6) and this online system to cultivate such dialogues around digital images of museum objects while sharing what it wishes to with its curator and archaeologist partners. The museum at Zuni is a legitimate central node in our reimagined digital network—one that maintains full autonomy over what it shares and how it chooses to speak about the objects it shares. This community museum is now at the center of a new network that supports and respects the ontologies of its community. Museum leadership has now shared *Amidollane* with other centers of culture within the Zuni Pueblo, working with different schools and historic preservation offices run and managed by fellow tribal members.

Knowledge as Process and as Performance

As the Zuni elders, teachers, and students together viewed the Ana-hoho, they too produced knowledge *collectively*, partly in relation to one another but also in relation to other objects and tools in their environment, such as the Amidollane system. The Zuni would collectively arrange themselves in front of the computer, defying the model of one person per computer or one user per session. That practice of technology use differed significantly from what we have seen with our archaeologist and museum curator partners (not to mention my own uses of technology). In these moments the community deferred to Curtis Quam as the "user" of the technology, despite our attempts to recruit others to do the scrolling, typing, and clicking, or to expand system use by asking each Zuni individual in the room to use their own laptop to help us evaluate the system we had designed. While I first saw this as a project roadblock, I eventually recognized that it spoke to the ways roles are usually decentralized at Zuni. This setting confirmed Enote's words that "here at Zuni everyone has a role." To assume that the only role in relation to a technology is that of the user behind the laptop is evidence of the limiting and objectifying ways in which we often see how new technology *should* be used, rather than how it *can* serve local cultural or community-based agendas.

The stories I have shared here reveal that we cannot think of ontology as being reducible to the affordances of tools, whether by this we mean database architectures, algorithms, or interfaces. Knowledge cannot be reduced to design specifications, even if the process of design is conducted with full respect for the classifications, value systems, and protocols of a community. My experiences reveal that ontologies are produced through processes, conversations, and practices that are larger than technology, although technologies can be recoded to consider the ways in which databases, algorithms, or interfaces are designed. Sociologists of science and technology have long reminded us that knowledge is produced through *practices* rather than simply through *representations*. Practices are process-based, embodied, and bridge verbal and nonverbal interaction. Practices can incorporate language, infrastructure, identities, emotions, performances, and many other aspects of what can be described as "material arrangements."[33] When we design and deploy technologies with the aim of empowering the processes and performances of community life, we take an important step toward arriving at a world where multiple ways of knowing can flourish.

Ontology is an ambiguous term, described representationally both in the computer sciences and in some of my own work, for example through a system of categories and classifications. Yet we can open this term up when we respect the fact that knowledge is enacted, performed, processed, and situated. Ontology can thus also be seen as being in line with performance studies scholar Diana Taylor's description of *repertoire*, where bodies, peoples, and places are integrated in particular times and places to communicate, perform, and collectively know.[34] Repertoire neither can nor should be frozen into static, solid, and historically continuous categories. It is a system of transmission, performing history via mediums of immediacy and dissipation. Repertoire transmits knowledge in ways that representational technologies cannot. Indeed, if we live in a world where ontology is limited to the types of storage technologies discussed in chapter 1 and to archives and museum databases as discussed in this chapter, "only the literate and powerful could claim social memory and identity."[35]

Our work with Amidollane and the Zuni reveals that technologies do not "contain knowledge" but can act to inspire reflection, communication, and sharing. The sociologist of science and technology Andrew Pickering has argued that we must understand the production of knowledge in relation to the "dialectic of resistance and accommodation." Describing his ethnographic studies of quark scientists, Pickering points out that he had initially oversimplified modeling as a technical predetermined process without looking at the other social modalities at play in the process of producing scientific knowledge. Pickering elaborates:

> To understand why people believed what they did, it seemed one had to understand how specific items of knowledge fitted in with the practice of their producers and users. . . . Practice as modeling, I thus realized, has an important real-time structure, with the contours of cultural expression being determined by the emergence in time of resistances.[36]

We must not make the same mistake when we develop technologies to support diverse communities and users. Technologies are neither "solutions" to problems people face nor can they ever appropriately "capture" the knowledge that people practice and perform. In this sense, the potential of technology to work with and support local, fluid, and community ontologies requires two steps. First, while communities can appropriate technologies from afar, such as we see with mobile phones and other examples I provide in chapter 2, there is great power in designing systems in ongoing active and ethical collaboration with local communities, using the types of fluid ontology techniques I have discussed regarding both the Tribal Peace and Amidollane systems in this and the previous chapter. Second, collaborative design can empower knowledge in ways that neither could nor should be predicted or modeled from afar. If a technology were simply "exported" to the Zuni rather than considered within the embodied process of listening, learning, and being of service, then the variety of material metaphors (fingers in ears, performances, switching of languages, oral storytelling) I shared in this chapter would remain absent. Sadly, my contribution would perpetuate misunderstanding and indigenous objectification.

As our project is ongoing, our team does not yet know whether our emphasis on supporting multiple local ontologies in conversation with one another will affect or inspire our archaeologist and curator partners. Yet I feel confident that through our collaboration a new space has opened up which counters a long history of hopelessness relative to those who have long held power over knowledge. Every Zuni member our team interviewed referred to the feeling that his or her voice has never mattered when it came to the long-standing asymmetries of power they have faced in relation to governments, cultural institutions, universities, and more. This may explain the strategic use of language switching (between Zuni and English) that concurrently shares and conceals knowledge from outsiders like myself.

Zuni community members now speak about the changed possibility of sharing knowledge on their terms, setting the record of misrepresentation straight, and engaging with a world that has attempted to oversimplify and thereby silence their sovereignty and at times their very existence. The Zuni wish to tell the world that they are indeed present and very active in shaping their destiny, but most importantly in doing so on their own terms. *Amidollane*, the technology we collaboratively developed, is but one factor among many supporting this agenda.

5

Taking Back Our Media

Long interested in the indigenous-led uprisings of the early 1990s in the rural southwestern Mexican state of Chiapas, in 2012 my wife and I traveled to the remote regions of the Lacandon jungle to understand the Zapatista struggle for autonomy against the privatization of their lands. Invited by artist friends who had built a rapport with these communities by painting murals on Zapatista land, we had the opportunity to visit the community centers, or "caracoles," of Morelia and Roberto Barrios. These two caracoles were two of the five Zapatista district centers, each of which housed decentralized governments that supported nearby farms and villages. I knew about the tactics employed by the Zapatistas in 1994 to publicize their struggle internationally through their strategic uses of early Internet forums such as Usenet newsgroups.[1] The appropriation of these forums allowed the community to frame its local political struggle to attract international attention and sympathy. The Zapatistas cleverly spun their story by utilizing the technologies of the day to manage and articulate a range of narratives to their own communities, others in Mexico, and publics across the world.

We see similar practices at work today in terms of the media spectacles produced by the Islamic State (ISIS) movement in Syria and Iraq. This jihadist movement's prowess in appropriating social media environments such as Twitter, SoundCloud, or YouTube had led to great concern and surprise. It is entirely possible that this creative use of technology has influenced the Islamic State's global visibility and its ability to recruit disaffected youth from across the world.

Both the Zapatista and ISIS cases, despite their diametrically different political orientations, remind us that political, social, and "terrorist" movements cannot be understood without looking at their modes of mediation. Indeed, contemporary activism today, whether we speak of violent and brutal acts of terror or nonviolent grassroots struggle, must be partially viewed through the prism of their engagements with media

Figure 5.1. A Zapatista workshop for appropriate technology in the jungles of Chiapas, Mexico.

and technology. Drone strikes on targets in Afghanistan where the perpetrator sits behind a computer thousands of miles away from the target, well-produced ISIS videos showing the beheadings of hostages, the hijacking of Twitter hashtags, or the collection of suspicious individual phone data—these are all contemporary examples of how technology is appropriated for geopolitical ends.

I remember feeling connected with the Zapatista cause as a high school student some twenty years ago without knowing any of the details. These sentiments were inspired by the occasional messages I read on Unix-powered machines that hosted Usenet discussion groups. I note now as a scholar that the creative use of technology at the grassroots is critical to shaping both local and global strategies. Different "publics" can be influenced and coordinated through an organized campaign that bridges a range of media strategies and tactics.

The Zapatista use of technology in the mid-1990s inspired identification with their cause despite the fact that very few in Mexico or the outside world had specific knowledge of the conditions the people were experiencing. The protesters forced the mainstream media to discuss the story, for example via the widely viewed American CBS program *60 Minutes*, which covered the story for an audience of millions in 1994.[2] Subcomandante Marcos, a public spokesperson for the movement who was neither indigenous nor from Chiapas, was seen as an inspirational figure by people across the world. Mexican audiences increasingly sympathized with a rural movement taking place within their own borders, thanks partially to the ways in which the international media networks influenced the domestic sphere. The Zapatista case thus illustrated how a "new" media technology of the time could be appropriated to influence a range of audiences and was one factor amongst several helped this movement reach a wide domestic and global audience.

Zapatista technology use speaks to the importance of communications within the battlefield. The negative international press attention given to this rural and regional movement pressured the Mexican regime to capitulate to the protesters' demands. Yet in contrast to their use of new technology with global publics, Zapatista activists communicated with one another and their stakeholder communities orally, through familial or political networks, or via the powerful technology of community radio, which I have recently begun to study in Bolivia. Short-wave radio, in particular, was used as a communication platform by Zapatistas in their responses to the encroachments by the Mexican military.

I was grateful for the opportunity to visit two of these caracoles in 2012, given my interest in thinking past universalist metaphors such as "global village." After several hours' travel, we arrived at the Morelia caracol and sat outside the local office waiting to meet the junta, a rotating group of community members who formed the local government. The junta included different Zapatista subgroups, including teenagers and women. Masks covered everything but the eyes of junta members. I introduced myself as a scholar of media studies and explained my interest in learning how the technologies of the day could be appropriated to support the Zapatista cause, much as the community had done nearly twenty years before in its use of online news and discussion groups.

I noticed many beautiful murals throughout the community, including one of a skeleton figure by the graffiti artist Banksy. This mural was

Figure 5.2. Banksy mural on Zapatista land. Source: http://stirtoaction.com.

displayed next to a shack painted with the words "Taller Appropriada Technologia" or "workshop for appropriate technology." The appropriate technology movement dates back to writings from the 1960s questioning the meaning of technology for local communities.[3] The writings of Fritz Schumacher, in particular, were concerned with how technology could support sustainability. They criticized the "technology transfer" model that was popular at the time. In contrast, this movement was interested in imagining efforts with technology that could be less capital and energy intensive.

A young member of the Morelia junta told me I could learn more about his people if I spent time establishing rapport with them through the creation of mutual trust and respect. This resembled my experience with the Zuni discussed in the previous chapter. We were thus encouraged to visit this community and other Zapatista caracoles across Chiapas. A week later, my wife and I visited the caracol of Roberto Barrios elsewhere in the province, located about sixty kilometers from the famous Mayan archaeological site of Palenque. We waited for over an hour before the junta opened its doors to us. When I asked community leaders how I could be of service, the response I received was "Quien sabe?" or "Who knows?" I pressed on, asking what the goals of the Zapatista movement were, and received the same two-word response. Finally, when I asked what the best route was to return to Palenque, their response was the same: "Quien sabe?"

Reflecting on these experiences, I sensed that "Quien sabe," like the stories I shared of plastic plants and frosted windowpanes at Zuni in chapter 4, speaks to how the Zapatista communities could be persuaded to collaborate with a scholar like myself but only on their own terms and for their own purposes. It is a set of local, community-specific understandings that frame how the caracoles choose to engage with the external world. Following the argument of this book, we must think about the design and meaning of technology in the same spirit of supporting community voices.

"Quien sabe" may not speak directly to the ethical questions surrounding collaboration, but it may offer a glimpse into the knowledges and cosmologies of these communities. "Caracol" in Spanish means "snail" in English, and perhaps like "Quien sabe" reflects a slow, internally reflective process by which nature and temporality are processed. The ancestors of the Zapatistas lived during an era when memory and movement were primarily defined by the ecology and environment of the places in which they lived. Their descendants, of primarily Mayan indigenous ethnicity, were interested in maintaining these practices. In that sense the Zapatista cause is an epistemological rebellion against how we know and think. As Thomas Urban, a graduate student in archaeology in Oxford University, points out:

> The potential of the Zapatista ideals, if fully realized through the agency of the sign, manifests in the larger world outside. . . . [T]he Zapatistas connect with their past and communicate this to the world with signs that reference that past as an agent for a better future through specific actions in the present. Ideas about the past, whether real or perceived, are relayed by the symbol of the snail, a small conduit in a very large symbolic action, the connection between past and future, local and global, the diminutive *caracol de Resistencia* (snail of resistance), is indeed a vast repository of meaning.[4]

The characteristics described here are in contrast with the instantaneity, speed, and violence of neoliberal information markets that pride themselves on their use of predictive analytics, "big data," and just-in-time decisions.[5] Unlike the metaphysics of the *caracol*, the French philosopher Paul Virilio has argued that notions of speed encoded into globalizing technologies *virtualize* our experiences of the here and now, detaching us from the present. By controlling the infrastructures of technology those in authority have a great deal of power over the shaping of experience. Coining the term "dromology," or the science of speed, Virilio states, "Whoever controls the [technology] possesses it . . . not [because of] laws and contracts, but first and foremost [due to] a matter of movement and circulation."[6] From Virilio's perspective, contemporary technologies remove us from the local—the here and now. Yet to assume that technologies inherently and immutably serve the purposes of technocrats overlooks the possibility that they could be rethought through collaborations with communities across the world.

The Zapatista movement is neither an illustration of utopic, Western-centric narratives of the "digital revolution," nor does it validate the dystopic belief that new technologies inherently serve neoliberalism. Rather, it is a community strategically appropriating a number of technologies, old and new, to support its practices and values.

Webs and Spiders

In March 2013, my wife and I traveled briefly across New Mexico and Arizona in the American Southwest from a meeting at the Zuni Native American reservation. We journeyed to Spider Rock in Canyon De Chelly on the Navajo reservation in rural Arizona. As we approached the canyon overlook, we were amazed to see a giant spiraled pillar rising hundreds of feet above the earth. We peered over the canyon walls at the spire and pondered the meaning of this sacred site to the Navajo people and their ancestors. Inscribed on a plaque next to the overlook was the passage:

> As the myth goes, Spider Woman began her many creations by spinning and chanting (or singing), first developing the universe in four Chapters—- east, west, north, and south. Within the space sprung the birth

of the sun, moon, and stars, which immediately banished darkness from the world. Next, she took shells of turquoise, red rock, yellow stone, and clear crystal [with which] she next created the mountains, oceans, and desserts. Then the earth goddess herself became the womb from which mankind sprung over time; gradually, as is the case with childbirth. To create various races, it is believed that [she] used many different kinds and colors of clay. Using her remaining thread, the goddess bound each of her human creations directly to her. . . . The Navajo culture also credits Spider Woman for their unusually talented weaving abilities. As the story goes, a young Indian girl wandered into the desert where she viewed a wisp of smoke coming from a hole in the ground. Peering into the hole, the girl saw Spider Woman spinning a blanket.[7]

The myth of the Spider Woman, described in the above quotation, explains how the world is a web of interconnectedness, woven by ancestral beings. This web connects the peoples and beings under the earth and above the sky.[8]

Our experience at Spider Rock is a reminder that the "web" has long been a metaphor among diverse communities and cultures. The word "web" existed long before its incorporation into today's digital vocabulary. From the Navajo perspective, a web, produced through the act of weaving, is a living architecture that integrates spirituality, history, and aspiration. Sociologist of science David Turnbull offers the following example of weaving from the Incan people of South America:

Textiles were the primary visual medium for the expression of ideas, the fundamental art form of the Andean peoples. Their "weaving insists that messages be embodied in and expressed by structure." Stories join ideas, string joins things together, and both are dependent on tension. String and cordage derive their connective capacity from tension in knots, binding, or twining. Weaving depends on the tension between the warp and the weft.[9]

I share my experience with the Zapatistas and my journey to Spider Rock as a reminder that the digital tools of today are neither neutral nor universal, but rather socially constructed by the imaginaries of their creators. Technologies, just like metaphors such as the "web," can be rei-

Figure 5.3. Spider Rock—Canyon De Chelly, Navajo Reservation, Arizona, U.S.A.

magined in relation to a range of epistemologies and ontologies. Yet we seem to have reached a moment in time when we ascribe metaphors to new technology in ways that are far removed from actual human experiences and histories.

The Last Billion

The vast majority of people in our world have been left out of the discussion of how networked digital technologies are developed, for what purposes, and with what meaning. While we evangelize terms such as "global village" in our discussions of technology, we fail to consider the economies, voices, and agendas behind its infrastructural, social, political, or economic deployment. The elites of the world have power over not only the metaphors by which we think about technology, but over its actual design and deployment. Users and communities across the world are supposed to passively accept a narrative of technological immateriality, inevitability, and evolution defined primarily by the rich and powerful. Terms such as the "last billion" are increasingly circulated to define those who remain digitally disconnected. With such homogenizing language, 15 percent of the world's population is reduced to a single category and presumed to be technologically "needy." Not only does this terminology ignore the many different facets of and reasons for being disconnected; it more perniciously presumes that "our" tools can edify the "other."

During the TED 2014 conference in Vancouver, Larry Page, cofounder of Google, was interviewed by journalist Charlie Rose about his hopes and dreams for the company.[10] Page spoke with great pride about the Google Loon project,[11] which deploys a set of high-altitude balloons to remote regions of the world in order to connect people in these remote areas to the Internet. Stating that "[our project] can provide hope to two-thirds of the world population that does not have strong Internet," Page's assumptions became transparent. Listening live to the conversation as an invitee to the TED Active meeting, I wondered whether Page believed that billions of people were hopeless without Internet access. Did he assume that access to digital tools was more important than access to water or food? It seemed like Page presumed that that the Internet access these communities would want would be based on his company's terms of service. As I have argued, initiatives like Google Loon and Facebook's drone connectivity make possible certain forms of access while precluding others, limiting what the Internet can be for these new users. Sadly, it seems impossible to block these objectives from moving forward. How, for example, can rural users protest against an automated system thousands of meters above their heads in the sky?[12]

It is far more meaningful to re-envision technology from the perspective of these communities cast as "users." We can turn our gaze away from the stratospheres where Google balloons or Facebook drones fly and remember that at the end of the day technologies exist to serve human beings and the richly diverse communities within which they live.

Disciplining Knowledge

This book has pointed to the ambivalences associated with "participation" in new media technology. It has praised the creative practices through which users have approached digital platforms and recognized the opportunities these uses have presented so they can support themselves in an increasingly networked world. Yet we must continue to ask, When is a creative use of technology still a reenactment of the agendas of those with power and privilege? Whether one speaks of participating in technology efforts led by the government, or open data projects supported by a company or nongovernment organization, French philosopher Michel Foucault's lectures on "governmentality" speak to how passive engagement with technology can threaten freedom and autonomy.[13]

I discuss this Foucauldian critique not to dismiss the world of social media as it stands but to provoke us to think about the conditions which enable technologies to limit users' discursive control and manipulation. Governmentality describes the ways in which citizens can be *disciplined* via seemingly innocuous policies adopted by states, corporations, or organizations. One can imagine a similar outcome emerging from the way technologies are designed and deployed. If we simply accept the world as it stands, we fail to question the underlying voices and agendas that drive the initiatives that appear on the surface to be neutral. We can imagine other possibilities by first critiquing that which exists.

This book has discussed governing institutions from Indian policy makers to colonial museums, both of which are obvious candidates for the Foucauldian critique. However, theories of governmentality encourage us to consider more public institutions, such as hospitals or schools. Foucault argues that disciplined subjects enact discourse as they "freely participate" in such systems—for example, by choosing which schools to attend. Similarly, citizens would seem to hold agency in their choice to participate in public technology efforts such as the project I describe in this chapter. I believe that we must think critically about Foucault's idea of governmentality in relation not only to the types of projects I have discussed throughout this book, but also more broadly in environments today where "open" projects in government, science, culture, and the arts are lauded far and wide. We must think long and hard about what types of open projects truly speak to the democratic labeling with which they are associated. We can ask a number of important questions. For example, do projects that make data open for grassroots use mask agendas associated with data collection, monetization, surveillance, or the feeding of algorithms?

Social theorist Nikolas Rose has argued that a Foucauldian critique of technology can best be undertaken in terms of two categories, *technologies of self* and *technologies of market*.[14] "Technologies of the self" relate to the construction of identity while "technologies of the market" relate to the social world. Rose explains that "expertise" is a key component of the disciplining of self. The protocols in systems of neoliberalism discipline subjects by suggesting and popularizing various categories as reference points by which users define themselves. To live a quality life, you must conform to the protocols through which rewards are given and avoid actions that generate punishment. As this is often framed in relation to the language of empowerment, it demonstrates how discourses of governmentality provide a user with an illusory sense of freedom and autonomy. For example, people receive rewards and badges through their online participation on sites such as Foursquare or Yelp, the number of followers they may have on Twitter, and so on.

"Technologies of the market," Rose's second category, extend the notion of "self" into the social and economic world. Confirmations of identity and acts of aspiration are coded to affirm the privileged position of those who profit from "open" market patterns. These technologies brand commodities to affirm "free choice." One can think of the predictive analytics suggested by various technology companies, ranging from Amazon to Netflix, as examples of "free choice" underlying ontological prescriptions and protocols. Discourses of power and inequality are reenacted through initiatives framed as democratic and participatory.

Applying the critique of governmentality to new technology is insightful. It reveals how much of today's contemporary experience of the Internet across the world is rooted in the flexible framework of neoliberalism whereby a technology user is presented with a series of "free" choices, including access to open data, that may lead to outcomes that support the agenda of the organization designing the information or technology system. At stake in the numerous examples I share in this book is the tension between the top down and the bottom up, the global and the local, and the preclassified and the emergent. Foucault's writings are a useful compass to keep in mind as we navigate the multiple ambivalences associated with digital technology and its global spread.

Provincializing New Media

This book has argued that mere access to new technology neither creates "open societies" nor resolves existing forms of economic and social stratification. The "global village" has not come to pass. We know that multiple linguistic Internets exist in parallel and that one's use of social media technology often promotes demographic homogeneity. We also know that Twitter is a heavily African American space of conversation, but very few of these conversations cross ethnically demographic boundaries. We know that a massive Chinese Internet exists that rarely intersects with pages written in other languages or published via social media networks.

While it is important to learn about other people, cultures, and communities on their terms, we must respect the power and importance of local, cultural, indigenous, and community-based creative uses of technology. Conversations that surpass the bounds of community can and should emerge but only when the voices of their participants are truly respected. From this perspective, the "global village" is the problem rather than the solution. We must reject assumptions about technology and culture that are dictated by Western concepts of cosmopolitanism.

To embrace diverse voices and rethink technologies, we can attempt to "provincialize" digital media by locating the collaborations we create within the situated realities of time, place, and community. Anthropologist Gabriella Coleman draws on theorist Dipesh Chakrabarty[15] to discuss what provincializing may make possible:

> To provincialize digital media is not to deny their scale and global reach, particularly in the circulation of finance capital and in the aspirations of transnational corporations; rather, it allows us to consider the way these media have become central to the articulation of cherished beliefs, ritual practices, and modes of being in the world; the fact that digital media culturally matters is undeniable but showing how, where and why it matters is necessary to push against peculiarly narrow presumptions about the universality of digital experience.[16]

Technologies can support diverse communities when they are not thought of autonomously but as part of a process of ethical, respectful collaboration. What they produce and how they are designed can be powerfully opened up, considering the examples I have provided throughout this book. Instead of perpetuating the false metacategory of "technology" as some sort of given, the task of provincializing should consider the materialities and design practices associated with specific devices and tools within the context of community life. We should recognize the importance of designing technologies with the cultures and communities they are supposed to serve. In so doing, they can support not only the local ontologies and voices of these peoples but empower performances and practices that bind and sustain community.

Chapter 2 has described how the process of telling stories through the use of video cameras can support greater collective reflection and mobilization in rural India. Chapters 3 and 4 have extended this analysis to demonstrate how the codes of digital technology—its databases, algorithms, and interfaces—can be rewritten to support the knowledge practices, or ontologies, of indigenous Native Americans. When we remember the people and places which give shape to technology, we stop thinking of people and communities as objectified 'users.' We can engage with technology without being 'captured' by it.

Cosmopolitan Solutions

Jan Chipchase, corporate ethnographer of technology, explains in his 2007 TED talk that rural Africans and inner-city Chinese use mobile phones because they want to be part of "the conversation."[17] His perspective is that as new technologies are developed, it is only a matter of time before everyone on the planet comes within their embrace. Yet who is "everyone" and who defines what this "conversation" is? If we ask this question and reflect on it honestly, we must recognize that terms such as "everyone" mask the reality that very few voices are included in the conversation. To illustrate my argument that contemporary thinking around technology fails to focus on the lived realities and visions of developing world communities, I would like to discuss two recent texts that have made an impression on scholars, activists, and a public interested in where the Internet is headed.

Civic media scholar Ethan Zuckerman's *Rewire: Digital Cosmopolitans in the Age of Connection*,[18] and technology critic Evgeny Morozov's *To Save Everything Click Here*,[19] poignantly critique the oversimplifications of technospeak. Yet neither of them sufficiently emphasizes the power of grassroots community agency. Morozov, building on his previous book *The Net Delusion*,[20] takes aim at the dreams of "solutionists" or those who believe in introducing technologies that solve problems that may not even exist. He explains that this denies society the opportunity to reflect, discuss, and collectively imagine alternative futures outside the ideologies and practices of Silicon Valley. Zuckerman in contrast discusses how the digital world may isolate rather than connect peoples from different cultures and nations. He thus argues that we need to rewire the Internet so that people across the world can interact with one another easily, explaining that the big problems in the world are global in scale. Zuckerman is particularly focused on how the Internet tends to support trivial and local experiences at the cost of cross-cultural awareness. While scholars have long been concerned with increased civic disinvestment in the United States since the 1950s, Zuckerman's concerns are almost the opposite. He argues that the world faces global challenges and if the technologies of our time fail to empower global conversations, we need to rewire the Internet.

I appreciate both these texts because neither writer accepts the world of technology as it stands. "Solution"-providing technologies should not replace the public imagination nor should they be limited to cultural, national, or demographic bubbles. Yet the focus of both authors on elite technologists or journalists is limited, as in so doing they fail to sufficiently consider the experiences and voices of the marginalized themselves, specifically in the global South. Zuckerman's work certainly is sympathetic to this critique, as his advocacy for the Global Voices effort represents an attempt to bring together activist bloggers who support stakeholder communities.

Morozov's critique of a culture of gadgets and apps is advanced through a critique of "technological exceptionalism," or the overstated prophecies that accompany new technologies. He notes that the term "Internet" (with a capital "I") has become hallowed ground that can never be questioned. Such deification blocks the possibility of productive reimagining. No one dares critique terms like "openness," "generativity,"[21] or the "Internet" in such a world. Yet how these terms are interpreted depend on who holds the power to define and apply them: "Before the idea of 'the internet' hijacked our imaginations, we made such trade-offs all the time. No serious philosopher would ever proclaim that either transparency or openness is an unquestionable good or absolute value to which human societies should aspire."[22]

Sociologists and historians of science have long made the types of arguments that Morozov popularizes. Historian Peter Galison has written about a technology-obsessed world in which "progress" marches onward at the cost of experimentation, reflection, and improvisation.[23] Similarly, sociologist Bruno Latour asks us to question the methods by which facts are made public, describing the distinction between "matters of fact" and "matters of concern."[24] "Matters of fact" often produce a narrowing of vision, blocking a far more complex reality. Latour argues that just as we need transparency in the social construction of truth, we also need a social tool called "reversibility" which makes visible the concerns, actors, and chains of events that shape an agenda to which science or technology is deployed.[25] From this perspective, we can view our public as "ever in the making,"[26] open to improvisation and new possibilities rather than coded by the invisible algorithm of some "app."

Unlike Morozov, whose writing is primarily critical, Zuckerman's piece is a call to arms. We must rewire digital infrastructures and networks so they will support value systems consistent with cosmopolitan connectivity. The Global Voices project, initiated by Zuckerman and Internet freedom advocate Rebecca Mackinnon, connects bloggers and citizen journalists across the world. The effort is dedicated to presenting news that has not been editorialized by the mainstream media or filtered by social media technologies. Global Voices stories can shape mainstream media coverage and reach users worldwide, thanks to the project's emphasis on translation. While language represents powerful "glue" that creates and supports community, to Zuckerman's thinking it is also a barrier that can separate people. Zuckerman's point that multiple linguistic Internets exist in parallel, most notably on the Chinese and English language networks, underscores his belief in the importance of bridging such divisions. Zuckerman thus celebrates the xenophile, the one person who loves the other, arguing that this individual can become a "bridge figure" who links communities that are currently linguistically, culturally, and technologically disconnected.[27]

I had the privilege of attending the most recent Global Voices summit in Nairobi, Kenya, over several days in the summer of 2012. I fondly recall interacting with a youthful, open-minded group of volunteers who shared a belief in the undelivered promise of digital technology networks to bring peoples and cultures together. Indeed, Zuckerman's argument is seductive—many scholars who attended the summit openly wondered what the world, let alone the Internet, would look like if it were more like the Global Voices community.

Zuckerman is correct to say that many of today's challenges, such as climate change, require global conversation and cross-cultural awareness. Yet not all challenges are global and that indeed thinking globally about people's traditions, knowledges, struggles and identities may unintentionally exclude them from positions of control and power. We should not be forced to think globally at the cost of our own communities, particularly when globalization has contributed to their disenfranchisement. For example, one "problem" that is not global is the crisis the world faces around disappearing linguistic and cultural diversity. Engaging with this challenge must require respecting the voices and knowledges of local communities who represent such diversity. It cannot be modeled from afar or above. Indeed, imposing a rewired Internet upon these cultures could threaten rather than support diversity.

I have paid special attention here to presenting major arguments drawn from Morozov and Zuckerman's recent books, as I believe both authors' views represent provocative and mainstream perspectives toward the question of how new technologies can better support diverse communities and cultures worldwide.

A local community should not be an implementation site for a development project or a venue to gather more technology users. As chapter 2 has argued, we should not make assumptions about information, communication, or technology before thinking about what development means from a community's perspective, recognizing that it is something all of us can strive toward, independent of place and culture. By supporting the decentralized networks that the Internet was supposed to be founded upon, we can respect the diverse ways in which people may choose to live their lives, and consider how technologies may be designed or used to achieve such an aim. Supporting diversity does not have to be at the cost of cross-cultural communication. Yet perhaps the best way to confront global problems is to recognize and respect our differences. We can think about new technologies similarly.

A Third Space for Technology

Perhaps it is time to move past the pro- versus anti-technology conversation to consider a third space, one that focuses on the actions we take and sees technologies as part of processes and relationships. Cultural studies scholar Homi Bhabha describes his notion of a "third space" as an alternative to the false binaries which, he believes, were produced through centuries of colonialism:

> The theoretical recognition of the split-space of enunciation may open the way to conceptualizing an international culture, based not on the exoticism of multiculturalism or the diversity of cultures, but on the inscription and articulation of culture's hybridity. It is the in-between space that carries the burden of the meaning of culture, and by exploring this Third Space, we may elude the politics of polarity and emerge as the others of our selves.[28]

Bhabha is asking us to recognize that the stories we present are partly about ourselves as well. To serve as a force of mobilization, the third space cannot be promised or dismissed from afar. It could, however, direct our attention toward local communities—their ontologies, practices, and ethics.

We should remember that living experiences are far more diverse than the ways in which technologies may code them. Anthropologist Clifford Geertz cleverly describes the humanistic experience of living as an *ethnographic algorithm*.[29] In contrast to this, many popular terms today such as "big data," "search," or "personalization" are blindly embraced as neutral, progressive, and innovative. Each reflects particular regimes of interpretation that "take place within horizons of culture that are embedded in contexts of power."[30] This is why it is all the more important to move past the blank acceptance of such language to consider more deeply our actions and intentions around technology. With this in mind, I think of sociologist of technology Phil Agre's concerns that globalization and its interactions with networked technology would bring about a world of "shallow diversity."[31] Agre's discussion of "deep diversity," in contrast, considers the importance of respecting local knowledge.

How can we think about technologies similarly? We need to develop projects that respect rather than ignore the multiple ways of knowing, or ontologies, that are part of a diverse community life. They may have to consider that no knowledge can ever be fully represented by a database, algorithm, or interface, no matter how it was designed. Shallow diversity, in contrast, is perpetuated when the framework of knowing is predetermined, when architectures for managing knowledge are developed independently of the experiential and interactive possibilities of that knowledge. Agre argues that there is a great deal at stake in such a decision:

A world without deep diversity would leave us poorer as human beings. Perhaps we will maintain always-on connections to everyone we know, but that will do us little good if none of those people knows or feels anything that is deeply different from what we know or feel in our own lives. It is only through the encounter with difference that we are able to question our own assumptions, and it is only through the encounter with difference that we can distinguish between our own heads and the radical strangeness and challenge of the real world. In a world of shallow diversity, we will prosper and we will die. We must learn to value and conserve deep diversity, and we must learn what it would even mean to replenish what has been lost.[32]

Our deeper differences are at stake if we push forward with technology efforts that export shallow diversity. A world of deep diversity would respect the sovereignty and autonomy of cultural difference and consider technology accordingly.

Taking the Digital Up

Eric Schmidt, former CEO of Google, and Jared Cohen, head of Google Ideas and a former U.S. State Department employee, argue in their latest book, *The New Digital Age: Transforming Nations, Businesses, and Our Lives*, that the global spread of technology will naturally support liberal, democratic values.[33] They suggest that there is something "natural" in networked digital technologies that spreads these values. Cohen and Schmidt, together with a number of other writers, presume that the Internet is a naturally open space. They apply this thinking to their discussion of politics and governance, arguing that nations such as China that reject "transparency" will find themselves increasingly excluded and isolated.

In a *New Republic* piece, Evgeny Morozov lambasts Schmidt and Cohen's views as hype, citing the Singer brochure of the nineteenth century that was full of similarly overstated rhetoric about the sewing machine: "Schmidt and Cohen are full of the same aspirations—globalism, humanitarianism, cosmopolitanism—that informed the Singer brochure. . . . The goal of books such as this one is not to predict but to reassure—to show the commoners, who are unable on their own to develop any deep understanding of what awaits them, that the tech-savvy elites are sagaciously in control."[34]

Morozov's point is that all new technologies are accompanied by a great amount of overstated hype. Far from being simple bluster, such hype can reinforce the power and privilege of those who create these machines. By being blindly celebrated rather than critically scrutinized, technocrats are supposedly able to impose their political and economic wills on a silent public. Yet this perspective, according to cultural anthropologist Faye Ginsburg, fails to recognize that many communities across the world cannot be defined by these false utopias.

> The discourse of the digital age smuggles in a set of assumptions that paper over cultural differences in the way things digital *may be taken up* ... (invoking) neo-developmentalism that assumes that less privileged cultural enclaves with little or no access to digital resources—from the South Bronx to the global South—are simply waiting, endlessly, to catch up to the privileged West.[35]

Morozov's focus on overstated rhetoric ignores a reality, namely, that while the sewing machine never fulfilled its utopic prophecies, it was still deeply meaningful to particular communities and their livelihoods. This is because many communities carve their own destinies around technology in ways that cannot be predicted. They *take the digital up.*

For example, if we only consider the hype associated with the sewing machine, we tend to ignore groups such as the International Ladies' Garment Workers' Union, one of the largest grassroots organizations that fought for social justice related to women's rights and labor practices.[36] The workers' union was not trapped by a "liberation versus doomsday" conversation about how they should organize around this technology. We can recognize the strategic means by which technologies are being appropriated by communities throughout the world in similar fashion.

Ginsburg illuminates the importance of paying attention to how the "digital is taken up." Such an understanding reveals how labor movements, geographies, and identities shape and modify their practice around technology to support their agendas. These social and cultural actions cannot be captured only by the "magic" of technology, and are better described by how it was "taken up." Feminist scholar of science and technology, Sandra Harding, has argued that all knowledge attempts are socially situated, grounded by peoples and places. Yet in stratified societies, "the activities of those at the top both organize and set limits on what [the] persons [who] perform such activities can understand about themselves and the world around them."[37]

Jared Cohen, Eric Schmidt, and even critic Evgeny Morozov's perspectives reflect "standpoints" of power, restricting the social and cultural meanings of digital technology. Yet from Harding's perspective, these views are nothing but standpoints, stories like any others that claim the mantle of truth. This false dualism erases another story that recognizes the agency of local communities and reimagines digital technology accordingly. This standpoint imagines a new path forward toward collaborating and supporting community-driven technology efforts.

Revolution and Repair

To offer a contemporary example of my argument that we can best understand the meaning of technology by how it is "taken up," I turn to the misguided discussion of "social media revolutions" with which I began this book's first chapter. I revisit this theme in the hope that the preceding chapters can inform a deeper reading of the actions people around the world are taking to fight for justice and change. I speak here of the wave of revolutionary movements that have occurred in several regions of the world since late 2010, spanning student protests in Europe and South America, regime-changing Arab Spring revolutions in Tunisia and Egypt, and the struggle for economic and social justice in the Western world. Given the insights from this book, it is clear that the notion of these revolutions being "technologically powered" falsely emphasizes the exceptionalism of new technologies and their creators.

We see yet again here the fallacies of technocentric thinking that ignores local context. While there has been important empirical work that has examined media and technology use contextually in these movements,[38] most popular punditry remains fixated on blindly praising the democratizing potential of social media tools or categorically dismissing them. Neither seems particularly interested in "culture" or "people-first" stories that examine the meaning of these tools in relation to the tactics, knowledges, and practices of activists on the ground.

Clay Shirky's "Political Power of Social Media" argues that "when we change the way we communicate, we change society."[39] Shirky's position implies that any contemporary political discussion must place social media and the Internet at its center. In contrast, writers like Malcolm Gladwell, in his *New Yorker* piece from October 2010 entitled "Small Change—Why the Revolution Will Not Be Tweeted" argue that while social media may promote "shallow" information sharing, it could also support the agendas of despotic regimes. Shirky's writing lauds exceptional cases in which decentralized groups of activists come together via a Facebook group, while also extrapolating from Internet memes, such as "cute cats," to make the claim that social media brings people together. Gladwell's article, in contrast, discusses examples of "slacktivism," such as clickable petitions that fail to translate into a sustained political movement.

These examples of technology use are interesting yet problematic because they simplify our understanding of what technology can mean by failing to discuss the deeper contexts of place, community, or culture. The fact that an activist blogs or creates a Facebook page is not as important as who he or she is attempting to reach by using this media or how this social media activity coordinates with other nondigital actions undertaken by that same person. Indeed, activists may use such tools to spread misinformation rather than supporting Shirky's overstated notion of "building community." By focusing on the hybrid manners (online, offline, both, or neither) that activists use to shape the world around them, powerful stories emerge that cannot be limited to a conversation about the "nature" of technology. Instead, they are all about how the digital is "taken up." What is missing on both sides of this debate is the recognition of local community voices and knowledge, which if considered would open up a multiplicity of explanations for how technologies may or may not assist a political movement. Looking at places and peoples provides valuable insights that consider how people struggling for social change shape newer and older technologies.

With the goal of respecting and humanizing the peoples and places in the political landscape of the Arab Spring, I have collaborated with activists in Egypt since 2011. My ethnographies have revealed that activists have increasingly learned how to exploit different technologies to achieve their own aims, not by using them simply as prescribed but by creatively appropriating them to support grassroots goals and priorities.[40] From this perspective nothing in these tools "naturally" generates revolution. They may, however, be wielded to support the visions of activists on the ground.

As of January 2011, Cairo—the most infrastructurally advanced Egyptian city—had less than 10 percent Facebook and 5 percent Twitter connectivity. Some scholars have assumed that the revolutionaries had no means of communicating with one another without such technology, described as the "collective action problem."[41] Yet this assumption is confounded by the reality that very few of those who protested actually had access to the technology. I learned how activists strategically used technologies to influence the far more pervasive mainstream media, shaping a larger "media ecology" whereby television networks and social media platforms inform one another. This influenced the coverage on networks like Al Jazeera and Al Arabiya, which are broadcast into millions of homes throughout Egypt, where satellite television access has been nearly ubiquitous since its deregulation in the early 1990s. I was stunned in the midst of my fieldwork in 2011 to discover a shack on a rooftop in the old Islamic neighborhood of Cairo that only had one electricity outlet connected to a makeshift satellite dish that could access these channels.

Journalists are increasingly subject to a twenty-four-hour, "always on" news cycle, and thus turn to social media platforms as a useful way to help source their stories. This gives activists who use social media the opportunity to amplify what they wish to share. While this is hardly sufficient to make a revolution possible, it is an example of how activists may manipulate and influence journalists and their audiences through the creative use of social media. My research in Egypt reveals the creativity, bravery, and intuition that drove this revolutionary movement's goals of achieving "bread, freedom, and social justice."[42] Within the overall research there is space for writing about the appropriation of technology. What we cannot do, however, is continue to believe the hype that revolutions are somehow made possible by social media and the Internet.

When we continue to debate the "native" capacities and potential of particular tools and technologies without considering the far more interesting question of how diverse communities shape such tools in accordance with their own visions, aspirations, and ontologies, we insulate ourselves in an elite, technocratic narrative that defies the reality on the ground. This manner of speaking places the elite technologies of the developed world at the start and the end of each such story. The heroic youth we see in the mainstream media are portrayed as willing and eager "users" of technology, rather than creative and dedicated activists devoted to transforming their nation through whatever means possible.

Figure 5.4. A shack on a rooftop in Islamic Cairo, where I observed the indirect effects of social media.

Egyptian blogger and activist Gigi Ibrahim, featured on the cover of *Time* magazine's February 28, 2011 issue, explained to me that the West "needs to believe that we could not have [made revolution possible] without their digital toys." The *Time* magazine story filters out many facets of her identity, including her political values, connection to a fifteen-year-old labor movement, her history of protest, and knowledge of the street. She is fetishized as a young Arab technology user, part of the "social media generation changing the world."[43]

The longer we speak about digital technologies as disembodied, the longer we perpetuate myths that disrespect the power and potential of communities and cultures worldwide. Not only do we misunderstand revolutions but we also fail to recognize how technologies are shaped and often "repaired" to support grassroots agendas and economies. Sociologist and cofounder of New Delhi's Sarai collective, Ravi Sundaram, has written vivid ethnographies of the "grey markets" of South Asia, where technologies are hacked on the street and recontextualized within informal local economies. He points out that we should understand the diffusion of digital technologies as a type of "recycled modernity" in a dynamic world of instability.[44]

Consistent with Sundaram's narratives, information scientist Steven Jackson discusses decay, erosion, and "repair cultures" in the developing

Figure 5.5. Social media revolutionaries?

world.[45] His work contrasts dramatically with squeaky-clean innovation discussions that are increasingly part of technospeak. Jackson tells another story about technology that considers the risk, uncertainty, and improvisation in parts of the world where certain digital tools may have spread. In this world dialectics and dichotomies abound—we marvel at the creative ways in which the iPhone is soldered on the street in inner cities worldwide, while recognizing how exposure to e-waste is shaping a cancer epidemic in West Africa. Jackson asks us to pay attention to the flows by which such devices travel and recognize how their spread shapes power and privilege. We can humanize peoples, places, histories and stories.

Indeed, while we embrace a narrative of growth and progress from the perspective of the "heroic innovators" who first developed digital technologies telling stories of Bill Gates or Steve Jobs, when we trace the uncanny movement of industrial ships to the shores of Bangladesh or landfills of Central Africa, different realities become visible. It all depends on our frame of articulation—how we choose to[46] understand and process a range of different realities. Jackson's research is a reminder of the need to respect and learn from the creativity, resilience, and reinvention exhibited by communities on the margins. Yet it is also a reminder that such practices are interconnected with environmental devastation and e-waste as part of an unjust world.

Innovation and repair are thus two sides of the same coin, demonstrating that we cannot understand technology simply as it is developed. Instead, as these tools spread to different places and communities over time other realities reveal themselves.

In this spirit, Jenna Burrell's research in West Africa looks at how technologies shape the aspirations and tactics of Ghanaian and Nigerian scammers. She shows how the obsolete technological junk of the elite world is appropriated by these communities to shape "rumors."[47] Instead of seeing the scammers as desperate criminals or as antithetical to the Internet's "ideals" from a privileged perch, Burrell humanizes their communities, revealing their agency to act as they can in an unequal world.

Western mantras such as "global village" or "social media revolution" hardly apply to the examples that abound in Jackson or Burrell's fieldwork. Instead, what we see are examples of improvisation and intuition. They defy farcical narratives of innovation, described by philosopher

Shiv Viswanathan as the "tyrannies of official science." As Portuguese sociologist Boaventura Santos and colleagues argue:

> Over the last decades there has been a growing recognition of the cultural diversity of the world, with current controversies focusing on the terms of such recognition. . . . The epistemological privilege granted to modern science from the seventeenth century onwards, which made possible the technological revolutions that consolidated Western supremacy, was also instrumental in suppressing other non-scientific forms and knowledges. . . . [It is now time] to build a more democratic and just society and . . . decoloniz[e] knowledge and power.[48]

These scholars argue that a democratic and just society does not mandate what counts as knowledge but instead learns from its communities and constituencies. At the same time Nobel laureate and Harvard economist Amartya Sen, in his keynote address at the recent World Culture Forum, warns us to not valorize diversity at the cost of remembering the rights and values that bind us all.[49]

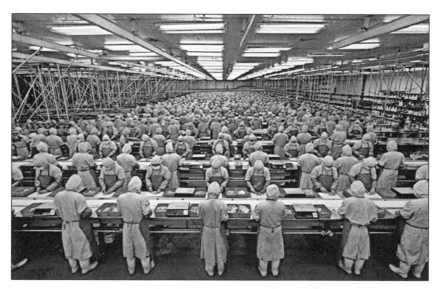

Figure 5.6. Laborers assembling the iPhone in the FoxConn corporation (Shenzen, China). Source: http://armored-column.com.

Figure 5.7. A Congolese laborer extracting Coltan, panning for minerals for more than twelve hours per day. Source: http://www.dailymail.co.uk.

Sen's book, *Identity and Violence*,[50] explains that cultural categories, when blindly embraced, may work to sow enmity rather than support dialogue and mutual understanding. For example, overstating science or technology as simply Western is problematic, given that many who "produce" these tools, perhaps in subservient positions of technology support or call centers, live in different parts of the world.[51]

As Figures 5.6 and 5.7 illustrate vividly, we too cannot fully grasp the meaning of an iPhone or any technology or infrastructure without recognizing the spaces in which it is produced, such as the factories of Fox-Conn in Shenzen, China, or the places from which its Coltan mineral is harvested, such as the mines in remote regions of the Democratic Republic of Congo. Just as we must peer into the repair practices by which technologies may be re-constructed long after their moments of planned obsolescence, we have the opportunity to become familiar with the environmental and labor practices that go into making the technologies we hold in our hands. We can think ethically and politically about these practices as we make decisions about how we choose to consume and interact with technologies and the corporations that produce them.

Ontologies and Seeing Like a State

Many of the community-based projects described throughout this book may be criticized for their specificity. Technology efforts are launched with *scale* in mind, considering policy making and developmental funding realities tied to initiatives that claim to achieve broader impacts. With larger numbers in mind, researchers, professionals, and funders can make more general arguments about the meaning of technology, at times extrapolating too broadly from specific examples.

The tension between community-centered and scale-based thinking is worth thinking about. I believe our work with community ontologies need not always come at the expense of macro-level thinking. Perhaps striving for scale is naturally not a priority for most such community-based efforts, which are notable for the value they attach to specific personal and place-based relationships. That said, in some cases communities are understandably interested in turning outward to build up relationships with external institutions and publics.

Political scientist and anthropologist James C. Scott makes an important contribution to this discussion in his book *Seeing Like a State*, a historical and political analysis of the relationships between information, stakeholder communities, and policy making.[52] The book is about how well-intended schemes administered by governments to improve the lives of citizens often fail. Scott argues that the problem is not simply poor infrastructure, inadequate services, or corruption, but also how citizens are framed, measured, and quantified. One challenge is thus to know how knowledge is articulated, represented, and exploited, in this case specifically how the state chooses to identify its constituent citizens. Scott explains that states must "make a society legible to arrange the population in ways that [simplify functions] of taxation, conscription, and the prevention of rebellion."[53] These practices are part of the legacy of high modernism and indebted to theories of scientific and rational planning.

Not only is the government approach that Scott describes far messier than meets the eye, but its method of quantifying citizens and resources is also limited. The problem is that scientific planning approaches often assume that abstract categories can describe development issues for a vast range of communities. It is troubling to apply master models from the state that fail to adapt to the voices of its citizens or learn from their local ontologies. Yet in other cases it is understandable—it would seem that the responsibility of governing a state requires seeing the world in ways that differ significantly from bottom-up grassroots experiences. Categories can force conformity by making certain types of knowledge public and acceptable, and others invisible and silent. In the process, these forms of misrepresentation can discredit local ontologies. While communities may engage in "metis" or tactical actions, the ontologies by which they are governed will by definition fail to consider their priorities.

What then can be done to reconcile the ways of policy and scale with the importance of respecting community ontologies? One approach may be to work *with* rather than to ignore incommensurability. With my colleague Jessica Seddon, a developmental economist based in South India, I have explored two interventions in the context of citizen grievances in the South Indian state of Karnataka. Our first approach has been to open up data gathered by the state for local reuse and appropriation, consistent with the move an increased interest today in big data and "open government." Our second approach has been to design systems whereby communities can articulate their grievances according to their own locally crafted fluid ontologies. Both allow data to be shared "as is" and open up a space for a group, whether a policy maker or local community, to reinterpret the data as they choose.

To illustrate our argument, Seddon and I have explored the ways in which slum dwellers in inner-city Bangalore, India, articulate concerns that they wish to report to the government and how this differs from the Karnataka provincial government's means of recording the very same experiences. These grievances are gathered by the government using a variety of information technologies deployed at kiosks and mobile applications throughout the city. One example we have explored relates to "waterlogging," a category used by policy makers to describe the many ways in which flooding and intense rain impacts regions in South Asian cities. Seddon and I found that this term made little sense to the inner-city communities who were supposed to report on this via the public grievance technology. The communities had specific, richly contextual ways of describing the flooding that would affect them, none of which lent themselves to the bureaucratic terms used by the government. Inner-city dwellers in the city of Bangalore, for example, would describe the effects of waterlogging using dozens of distinct terms, none of which were based on the abstraction of this meta-ontological term.

Our work on mismatched ontologies speaks to the danger of ignoring, filtering, or dismissing local knowledge. Yet it also considers what can be gained by uncovering bridges when community voices and ontologies are given the power to shape the practices of policy making.

Stepping away from Theories

I have shared stories of my collaborations with communities across the world to argue for a rethinking of how we design and understand the meaning of new technologies. Awareness of cultural diversity is essential as we think about the global yet asymmetric diffusion of new digital tools and systems. We must remember that "culture" or "community" are far too easily objectified when our discussions of new technology confine themselves to innovation-speak. We can embrace the process of learning from one another rather than clinging to narratives developed from afar. This should apply not only to how we analyze what technologies mean, but to the theories we, as activists, researchers, or publics, use as we attempt to understand the significance of technology across the world.

I have gained a great deal from this lesson of detaching myself from early-stage hypotheses and to learn instead from the communities with which I collaborate. This reveals itself in the stories I have shared throughout this book's chapters. My effort to explore the potential of video storytelling in India in chapter 2 was driven by the hypothesis that such a process could inspire new reflections and conversations. Yet my hypothesis was hardly relevant to what I learned about how such tools could be appropriated by villagers to support their literacy practices and political and social struggles. Similarly, the Tribal Peace effort described in chapter 3 can be evaluated in relation to a hypothesis that theorized learning or usability outcomes in Native community-created interfaces or databases. It turns out that this aim was only a small part of a story that taught me to respect the power of disagreement, human networks, and community-based knowledge. My work with the Zuni and our Amidollane effort, described in chapter 4, could be articulated in terms of the hypothesis of increasing Zuni participation in conversations where they had too often been silenced. While this goal remained part of our collaboration, the stories I share in chapter 4 showed that knowledge cannot simply be captured in the realm of abstraction but must include the things we do, namely, our daily practices. This collaboration reveals the power of indigenous voices to subvert a museum-centric view of the world in favor of one that respects community diversity.

Each of these efforts taught me that the confirmation or rejection of a hypothesis means little when the original questions we ask come from a misguided place. We cannot presume to know what "technology questions" must be studied from afar—whether we live in an ivory tower or a state-of- the-art research laboratory. Viewing the projects I have shared through a technology-first lens miscasts the larger realizations of this book, that is, the unanticipated and emergent experiences that come from collaboration. Trained as a designer and engineer, I recognize my innate tendency to valorize my power to come up with a set of solutions for any challenge at hand. Yet every project I have described illustrates the valuable insights gained when I put aside my own agenda and bias as much as possible to open myself up to experiences that could not have been predicted from afar. From this perspective, design is not simply about aesthetics and usability but also a process of supporting conversation and communication.

There is a significant body of research that discusses how designers can support the diverse social and cultural values articulated by the communities with whom they collaborate.[54] Within the different cultures, communities and environments I describe throughout this book, it has been important not to see design as providing solutions, or even worse as a form of social engineering. My time in Egypt, for example, taught me that I should only put on my "design hat" when requested. There is important work to be done in gathering and sharing stories that recognize the power and sovereignty of the activists and their struggles.

As we think cross-culturally about the Internet and new technology, I believe it is time to tip the scales away from *world-making* and instead to embrace *world-listening*. We should consider whether there is a new path forward for scholars, policy makers, and activists to put their agendas aside, even for a few minutes, to consider "Whose Global Village" we choose to support. As scholars, activists, or professionals we have been inculcated with a range of worldviews. We must recognize these while opening ourselves up to collaborations that reveal perspectives and ontologies that differ from our own.

This argument is not to declare that we are meaningless in such collaborations but rather that we should place ourselves first and foremost at the service of our friends and partners. As my colleagues at Zuni pointed out repeatedly, "If you are here to support our goals and visions, then you are welcome." Complementing this point of view, an activist in Egypt explained to me, "We do not need another NGO or a new dialog.com to solve our problems—we just need you to listen, support our voices, and pay attention to what we do."

My research and public practice have been transformed thanks to the experiences narrated in this book. Today I ask my partners how I can be of service to them in furthering their aims and visions and navigate the ambiguity of this process together with the demands of academic publishing and research. My role in Egypt, for example, has been to observe, listen, and attempt to be of service. The greatest honor has come via the invitations I have received to discuss with activists what I have learned over the past few years spent in their nation and by sharing my professional and personal knowledge of media and social movements in other regions of the world. Having been invited to share stories of Egyptian activism with Zapatistas, Tibetans, indigenous peoples in Bolivia, and other communities across the world has been a reminder to me of how I can learn from diverse peoples and communities, and the stories they choose to share.

Splintered Networks

With 6 billion mobile phones now in the hands of people worldwide, no longer can we think of our study of technology through simple prognostications from afar or a top-down analysis. The arguments I have made across this book have raised a provocative question: What would it mean to step away from top-down understandings of the Internet and instead 'splinter' the way we think about technologies and the communities they may support?

Many technologists continue to push forward with their desire to "unify," "open," and "reform," with only their assumptions in mind. This may originate from the best of intentions, but it lacks faith that global dialogues can indeed emerge from the bottom up by respecting local communities. We have an opportunity to listen to and support diverse communities without ignoring the global conversations and challenges collectively faced by peoples across the world.

It is notable that activists—whether through bit coins, proxy servers, block chains, mesh networks, or encryption software—have embraced the "splinternet," or an Internet that is split along technical, commercial, political, ethnic, religious, or other social lines. Technology journalist Doc Searls describes the splinternet as the "growing distance between the ideals of the Internet and the realities of dysfunctional national-isms . . . which contribute to the various and sometimes incompatible standards which often make it hard for search engines to use the data."[55] Searls's solution is to "standardize information and technology to make the world better, to make the Net work."[56]

There is great peril in following such a path. It is notable that Searls assumes that a networked technology (the Internet) has an "ideal," with-out revealing whose values power this vision. In contrast, activists, not just in the developing world of the global South, but in the postindus-trial West, have begun to recognize that an open Internet increasingly means greater surveillance and policing. They have thus begun to fight for autonomy. The following activist brief indicates as much:

> Using "mesh network" technology, activists recognize that "when you run your own network . . . nobody can shut it down. . . . It harkens back to the early days of the digital universe when the network consisted mostly of university scientists and researchers communicating among themselves without corporations sitting in the middle or government (that we know of) monitoring their chats. The goal then, as now, was both connection and control: an internet of one's own."[57]

I have pointed out the perils of an increasingly homogeneous Internet, a network that claims to democratize while also functioning to support top-down political and economic agendas. I also have briefly pointed to the challenges of working with digital technology in a moment where our data can be increasingly captured and controlled by surveillance institutions and corporations. The splinternet may not be the answer to the dilemma we face, yet it is increasingly the direction taken by activists and grassroots communities concerned with where their data goes and how it is used. That said, a fragmented Internet runs the risk of isolating cultures and societies from one another, making it impossible to work together on global issues such as climate change, conflict resolution, or human rights. Purely local "intranets' face the challenge of being unable to scale, cutting short. While this book's chapters primarily emphasized the potential of collaboration, they revealed what can be gained when we *balance* the local and global in ways that respect the sovereignty of grassroots voices in informing global communication.

It is incredible to think about what may be possible when we think about technology locally and culturally rather than globally. The question is one of values, control, and voice. We are at a point in time where we can either embrace diversity or ignore it. We can embrace incommensurability without getting trapped by identity politics. We can accept that the promise of digital equality is unfulfilled. To accept these challenges, we need to stop, look, listen, and collaborate.

If we take the current Internet, as articulated by Facebook, Google, Microsoft and their ilk for granted, we are supposed to simply trust our gateways to the digital world rather than scrutinize them to imagine alternatives that are noncommercial, public, or considerate of cultural diversity. When we uncritically evangelize language such as the "cloud," or even "Internet freedom," we homogenize the experiences of diverse peoples. We even sell ourselves short in the Western world by failing to reconsider how networked technology can support our families, communities, and cultures. We are supposed to blindly accept the technologies we use today as "innovative," and dismiss those who raise alternatives. But there is another path. We can instead think *culturally*—of values, knowledges, aspirations, and practices—to reimagine what technology can mean.

From the Lacandon jungle in the mountains of Chiapas, Mexico, Subcomandante Marcos argued in 1997 that our world had entered an era of neoliberalism which had objectified the invisible majority of the world's population. He explained that media industries only exist for elites, presenting seductive spectacles of movie stars and politicians, designed for consumption rather than autonomy or empowerment. Yet we still do have a choice:

> We have a choice: we can have a cynical attitude in the face of the media, to say nothing can be done about the dollar power that creates itself in images, digital communication, and computer systems that invade not just with an invasion of power, but with a way of seeing that world, or how they think the world should look. . . . But there is a third option that is neither conformity, nor skepticism, nor distrust: that is to construct a different way—to show the world what is really happening—to have a critical world view and become interested in the truth of what happens to the people who inhabit every corner of this world.[58]

Many years after this interview, Marcos's point still rings true. Neoliberalism's excesses have prompted social movements and revolutions across the world. The utopias associated with a global Internet have been tempered by a world in which robotic drones are sent far and wide to "manhunt."[59] The spectacular revelations brought to light by whistleblower Edward Snowden have raised concerns across the world about technologized surveillance and manipulation. Now more than ever it is time to consider Marcos's third way. That path cannot be master wired from above, but like all historical examples of powerful democratic change, must emerge from the people. By asking the question "Whose Global Village?" we can start to think about technology futures that truly respect cultural and community diversity across the world.

NOTES

INTRODUCTION

1 Page, 2014.

2 Negroponte, 2006.

3 Haraway, 1991.

4 NBC News, 2015.

5 McLuhan, 1962, 1994.

6 Turnbull, 2009, par. 4.

7 Agre, 2000b.

8 Hammersley and Atkinson, 1983.

9 Ellingson and Ellis, 2008.

10 Adelman, 1993; Lewin, 1946; Whitehead and McNiff, 2006.

11 O'Brien, 2001.

12 Gilmore, Krantz, and Ramirez, 1986.

13 Richard Winter (1996) identifies six key principles as the core of action research:
   1. A critique of one's reflexivity and bias;
   2. Understanding shared language, including the language of conflict and divergence;
   3. An understanding that both researcher and community are equals; no longer is the community an object of study but the leader of an initiative;
   4. Understanding that risk to ego is necessary and healthy;
   5. Taking multiple paths, actions, and interpretations so that research is neither over-instrumentalized nor viewed from a distance; and
   6. Balancing actions and theory to reinforce and transform each other, with neither being stable or seen as having greater importance.

14 I have discussed this philosophical position from a level of abstraction, but how does one actually develop such initiatives using these ethical and methodological precepts? Information scholars Rudy Hirschheim and Heinz Klein (1994) suggest a few basic techniques:
   1. Provide an equal opportunity to all participants to raise issues, points, and counterpoints to other views through discussion;
   2. Place every participant on an equal footing with respect to their power positions;
   3. Encourage a participant's questioning of the clarity, veracity, sincerity, and social responsibility of the proposed actions proposed; and

4. Encourage all participants to take an equal opportunity to articulate their feelings or doubts or concerns.

15 Freire, 2000.

16 Freire, 2000, 72.

17 Various cultural critics (Cheah and Robbins, 1998; Joseph, 2002; Robbins, 1999) have argued that it is important to embrace existing inequalities and work to enact agendas from the grassroots up rather than simply apply a donor or a bureaucratic "poverty alleviation agenda" (Gujit and Shah, 1998). Nongovernmental organizations (NGOs), often seen as important enactors of development programs, are frequently complicit, as they have to balance downward versus upward accountability (Lewis and Madon, 2004). The further a researcher can step away from standardization and embrace multiple practices on the ground, the higher the possibility of achieving a more democratized vision of a project.

18 Gujit and Shah, 1998.

19 Cooke and Kothari, 2001.

20 Chambers, 1997, 196.

CHAPTER 1. TECHNOLOGY MYTHS AND HISTORIES

1 Gustin, 2011, www.wired.com

2 Dubai School of Government, 2011.

3 Hier and Greenberg, 2007; Lyon, 2013; Marx and Muschert, 2007.

4 Aneesh, 2001; Suchman, 2007.

5 C. Anderson, 2006; Brownstone, 2014; Galloway, 2004.

6 Jenkins, 2006.

7 McChesney, 2013.

8 Galloway, 2004.

9 Gillespie, 2013.

10 Terranova, 2004.

11 Noble, 2011.

12 C. Anderson, 2006.

13 Shirky, 2010.

14 Lovink and Rossiter, 2007; Rossiter, 2003; Terranova, 2000.

15 Fromm, 1941.

16 Feenberg, 1995, 87.

17 Bowker, Baker, Millerand, and Ribes, 2010; Graham, 2010.

18 Bowen, 2015.

19 Wells and Mayne, 1938.

20 Bush, 1945.

21 Shirky, 2008, 2010.

22 Shirky, 2008, 2010, 2011.

23 Brown and Duguid, 2002.

24 Knobel and Bowker, 2011.

25 Gitelman, 2006; Wardrip-Fruin and Montfort, 2003.

26 Fish, 2013.
27 Kay, 2000.
28 Ingalls, Kaehler, Maloney, Wallace, and Kay, 1997.
29 Bardini and Friedewald, 2003, 204.
30 Bardini and Friedewald, 2003; Bardini, 2000.
31 Engelbart, 2001; Goldberg and Kay, 1977; Kay, 1990.
32 Rousseau, 2002.
33 De Bellaigue, 2007.
34 Buck and Hull, 1966.
35 Diderot and d'Alembert, 1751.
36 Shapiro, 1996.
37 Meinong, 1904.
38 Husserl, 1913.
39 Corrazon, 2010.
40 Woolgar and Lezaun, 2013.
41 Law, 2002; Mol, 1999, 2002.
42 Law and Mol, 1995, 277.
43 Balsamo, 2011.
44 Heidegger, 1954.
45 Boast, forthcoming.
46 T. Mitchell, 1992.
47 Manovich, 2001.
48 Chun, 2008b, 159.
49 Vítězslav, 1996.
50 Chun, 2008b, 160.
51 Chun, 2008b, 160.
52 Latour, 1986.
53 E. G. Coleman, 2013; Nissen, 1998.
54 Dourish and Mazmanian, 2012.
55 Parks, 2013.
56 Bowker and Star, 2000.
57 Bogost and Montfort, 2009.
58 Montfort, 2012.
59 A Timeline of Database History," n.d.
60 Anderson and Zalta, 2004.
61 Dourish, 2014.
62 Dourish and Bell, 2007.
63 Geismar and Mohns, 2011, 152.
64 Bijker and Law, 1992.
65 Bodker, Kensing and Simonsen, 2004.
66 Bidwell and Winschiers-Theophilus, 2014.

CHAPTER 2. DIGITAL STORIES FROM THE DEVELOPING WORLD

1 Couldry, 2008; Lambert, 2013; Nelson and Hull, 2008.
2 Ito, 2003, 2006.
3 Tulloch and Jenkins, 1995.
4 Michaels, Hebdige, and Langton, 1994.
5 Hardt and Negri, 2009.
6 Friedman, 2000, 2006.
7 Appiah, 2010; Kant, 1784; Poster, 2008.
8 Castells, 1996, 2000.
9 DiMaggio, Hargittai, Celeste, and Shafer, 2004; Hargittai, 2008; Zillien and Hargittai, 2009.
10 Parikh and Lazowska, 2006.
11 Internet and Mobile Association of India, 2007.
12 Hargittai, 2008; Howard, Busch, and Sheets, 2010; Warschauer, 2006.
13 Rogers, 2010.
14 Zillien and Hargittai, 2009, 288.
15 Warschauer, 2003, 13.
16 Lanier, 2014, 9.
17 Lanier, 2014.
18 Chun, 2011.
19 Chun, 2008a.
20 Hardt and Negri, 2009.
21 Orlikowski, 2008, 411.
22 Ginsburg, 2008; Srinivasan, 2013b.
23 Castells, 2000, 2011.
24 Koolhaas, 2007.
25 Aneesh, 2006; Shome, 2006.
26 Sassen, 1998, 2000, 2003.
27 Srinivasan, 2013a.
28 Appadurai, 2000, 5.
29 Tongia and Wilson III, 2011.
30 Samarijava and Shields, 1990.
31 Prahalad, 2004.
32 Rajagopal, 2013.
33 Keniston and Kumar, 2003; Van Dijk and Hacker, 2003; Warschauer, 2003.
34 Srinivasan, 2012a.
35 Mitra, 2003, 2005.
36 Negroponte, Bender, Battro, and Cavallo, 2006.
37 Arora, 2007; Warschauer, 2001, 2004.
38 Warschauer, 2001, 2003.
39 Warschauer, 2006.
40 Philip, Irani, and Dourish, 2010.

41 Philip, Irani, and Dourish, 2010, 3.

42 Philip, Irani, and Dourish, 2010, 3.

43 W. Anderson, 2002.

44 Negroponte, 2006, 3:54.

45 These include: *Economic barriers*: The lack of access to information, markets, and opportunities; *Physical barriers*: The problems with distances and infrastructures that disadvantage primary rural and occasionally inner-city communities; *Political barriers*: The lack of transparency to governmental, legal and human rights services; *Social and health barriers*: The divisions that end up marginalizing who fail to speak, write, or read particular languages, and those who lack access to educational or health resources.

46 Appadurai, 2000, 3.

47 Kothari, 1999.

48 Gandhi, Verraraghavan, Toyama, and Wang, 2007.

49 Wallack and Srinivasan, 2009.

50 F. Cleaver, 1999.

51 Puri and Sahay, 2003.

52 Banerjee, Duflo, Chattopadhyay, and Shapiro, 2007; Scott, 1998; Wallack and Srinivasan, 2009.

53 Barzilai-Nahon, 2006.

54 Keniston and Kumar, 2003.

55 Burrell and Toyama, 2009.

56 These authors argue that all ICTD research must consider:

1. Accuracy through a justification of one's methods.

2. Transparency by making explicit the methods and approaches taken to study an issue.

3. Empiricism by considering evidence "of the world" as opposed to speculation alone.

4. Novelty by advancing the field and building on rather than repeating established insights or biases.

5. Disciplinary relevance: Build on an emerging field and show its relationship to other studies, theories, and/or research.

6. Generalizability: Maintain a mindfulness of how case studies and statistics may be generalizable, and recognize the limits of the generalizability of what one studies.

57 Suchman, 2002.

58 Gitelman, 2006.

59 Fast Company Staff, 2011.

60 Aker and Mbiti, 2010.

61 Porteous, 2006.

62 Chipchase, 2007.

63 Ndiwalana, Morawczynski, and Popov, 2010.

64 Geertz, 1978.

65 Michaels, Hebdige, and Langton, 1994.
66 Graham and Marvin, 2001; Horst and Miller, 2006; Larkin, 2008.
67 Parks, 2014a, 243.
68 Parks, 2014a, 244.
69 Zielinski, 2006.
70 D. Miller and Slater, 2000.
71 Horst and Miller, 2006.
72 Caron and Caronia, 2007.
73 Lechner, 1985.
74 Lievrouw, 2001, 12.
75 Bowker and Star, 2000.
76 Heeks, 2008.
77 Appadurai, 2004; Sen, 1995; Srinivasan, 2006b.
78 Bowker and Star, 2000, 379.
79 Spivak, 1988.
80 Sawhney and Suri, 2008.
81 Parks, 2014b.
82 Jenkins, 2003, 2006, 2013.
83 Barber, 2003; Shalom, 2008.
84 Berker, Hartmann, Punie, and Ward, 2005; Silverstone and Haddon, 1996; Silverstone and Hirsch, 1992.
85 Putnam, 2000.
86 Jenkins, 1992.
87 Fiske and Hartley, 1978; Poster, 2008.
88 Baym, 2000.
89 Watkins, 2005.
90 Hall, 1977.
91 Hebdige, 1984.
92 Williams, 1985.
93 Lipsitz, 1994, 2007.
94 Lipsitz, 2007.
95 Ginsburg, 2008.
96 Ginsburg, 2008, 139.
97 Ginsburg, 2008, 139.
98 T. Turner, 1992.
99 Ginsburg, Abu-Lughod, and Larkin, 2002.
100 Boast, Bravo, and Srinivasan, 2007; Srinivasan, 2006a.
101 Michaels, Hebdige, and Langton, 1994.
102 T. Turner, 1992.
103 Michaels, Hebdige, and Langton, 1994, 65.
104 Cleaver, 1998, par. 4.
105 Cleaver, 1998.
106 Ginsburg, 1991.

107 Arora, 2008.
108 Brookfield, 1998; Dewey, 1933; Ulrich, 2000.
109 Boud, Keogh, and Walker, 1985.
110 Heeks, 2008.
111 Appadurai, 2000, 6.
112 Appadurai, 2004, 66.
113 Srinivasan, M., 2016.
114 de Certeau, 1984; Goffman, 1959.
115 Appadurai, 2004.
116 Appadurai, 2000, 65.
117 Kundu, 2000.
118 Freire, 2000.
119 Lofland, Lofland, Delamont, and Coffey, 2001; Spradley, 1980.
120 Aronson, 1994.
121 Lievrouw et al, 1987.
122 Sen, 2007.
123 Rogers, 2010.
124 Girvin, 1947.
125 Kretzmann and McKnight, 1993.
126 Frankel, Miller, and Jeffrey, 2000; O'Donnell, 2011.
127 Fukuyama, 2002; Sen, 1993.
128 Searle, 1990.
129 McAdam, 2006.
130 Hirschman, 1970.
131 Heeks, 2008.
132 www.digitalgreen.org

CHAPTER 3. NATIVE AMERICANS, NETWORKS, AND TECHNOLOGY

1 Srinivasan, 2013b.
2 Suchman, 2002.
3 Néret-Minet Tessier and Sarrou, 2013.
4 Clifford and Marcus, 1986.
5 Derrida, 1996.
6 Crawford and Lipschutz, 1998; Galtung, 1990.
7 Galtung, 1969; Gilligan, 1996.
8 Foucault and Sheridan-Smith, 1972; Foucault, 1975.
9 Foucault, 1981.
10 Isaac, 2005.
11 Enote, 2013, par. 1.
12 "Paris auction house sells Hopi masks despite tribe's objection," 2013.
13 Appadurai, 1990.
14 Turnbull, 2009, par. 4.
15 Davis, n.d.

16 Turnbull, 2009, par. 5.
17 Philip, Irani, and Dourish, 2010, 6.
18 Verran, 2002.
19 Verran, 2002, 730.
20 Verran, 2002, 743.
21 Haraway and Teubner, 1991, 21.
22 Agrawal, 1995.
23 Bowker, 2005.
24 Bowker and Star, 2000.
25 Star and Griesemer, 1989.
26 Furner, 2007, 158.
27 Star and Griesemer, 1989.
28 Star, 1983, 1999, 2002.
29 Star, 2002.
30 Star, 1983, 2002.
31 Bowker and Star, 2000, 605.
32 Kwasnik, 1992.
33 Kwasnik, 2000, 24.
34 Buckland, 1991; Houser, 1986; Lund, 2009; Riles, 2006.
35 Olson, 2000, 2007.
36 Plumwood, 1993, 437.
37 www.cidoc-crm.org
38 Allen, Karanasios, and Norman, 2013; Slater, 2012.
39 Ihde, 2005; Winsberg, 2010.
40 Berggren, 1985.
41 Pariser, 2011.
42 A. Aneesh describes the hybridity of algorithm and human labor as "algocracy" (Aneesh, 2001, 2006), explaining that we must look carefully at the hidden patterns and practices of labor and power as they influence algorithms, technologies, corporations, and eventually, users. This question becomes even more challenging when we consider digital social enterprises, which wield labor and algorithms for an ostensibly socially conscious outcome (Fish and Srinivasan, 2012). Algorithms are not just implicated in conversations centered on labor and ethics, but also discussions around surveillance and privacy. Citing the work of scholars like Robert McChesney (2013) and Dan Schiller (2000), Lucas Introna and Helen Nissenbaum (2000) argue that the work of corporate algorithms continues a larger assault on public spheres by regimes that have economic and social power (Agre, 2000a).
43 Minsky, 1988.
44 One such system with which I became familiar is CyC (www.cyc.com), which at the time was one of the largest knowledge representation databases found in Artificial Intelligence. Thematically similar to CyC, the ABC ontology (Lagoze and Hunter, 2006) that I also learned about at this time was developed with the purpose of supporting interoperability between different types of metadata while

providing users with a framework they could use to develop their own descriptions within the ABC structure. Other ontology models within the computer and information sciences include the OWL Web Ontology Language (www.w3.org) used for publishing and sharing ontologies across the World Wide Web and XML Topic Maps (www.topicmaps.org), which provide a model and the grammar to represent the structure of the information resources used to describe topics and their associations.

45 Boast, Bravo, and Srivasan, 2007; Srinivasan and Huang, 2005; Srinivasan, 2006a.
46 de Certeau, 1984.
47 DiSalvo, 2009, 52.
48 Joseph, 2002; Robbins, 1999.
49 Srinivasan and Huang, 2005, 193.
50 Gilliland, Lau, and McKennish, 2013.
51 Flores, Graves, Hartfield, and Winograd, 1988, 152.
52 http://sctdv.net
53 Sandvig, 2013, 172.
54 Shipek, 1988.
55 Ackleson, 2005; M. Coleman, 2005; Dunn, 1996; U.S. Government Accountability Office, 2006.
56 Shipek, 1988.
57 Durkheim, 1915/2012.
58 Sandvig, 2013.
59 Sandvig, 2013, 176.
60 Genachowski, 2010.
61 Brescia and Daily, 2007; Minority Rights Group International, 2009, U.S. Census Bureau, 2008.
62 Sandvig, 2013, 170.
63 Howe, 1998, 27.
64 Sandvig, 2013, 188.
65 Sandvig, 2013, 174.
66 James, 2006; Srinivasan, 2006a; Terranova, Thomas, and Wyatt, 2002.
67 Akrich, 1992.
68 Von Hippel, 2005; Zittrain, 2008.
69 Sandvig, 2013, 190.
70 Frank, in preparation.
71 B. Anderson, 2006.
72 Srinivasan, 2006a.
73 Said, 1978.
74 Couldry, 2008; Lambert, 2013; Lundby, 2008; Nelson and Hull, 2008.
75 Brown and Duguid, 2002.
76 Foucault, 1970.
77 Carey, 2008.
78 Sawhney and Suri, 2008.

79 Sawhney and Suri, 2008, 364.

80 Chan, 2014.

81 Medina, 2011.

82 Aki, 2014.

83 Bowker, 2005.

CHAPTER 4. MULTIPLE VOICES

 1 Hemming and Rigney, 2010.

 2 Boast, Bravo, and Srinivasan, 2007, 396.

 3 Christen, 2012; 2006.

 4 Lau, Gilliland, and Anderson, 2012; Stevens, Flinn, and Shepherd, 2010.

 5 Clifford, 1997.

 6 Eglash, 2004.

 7 Eglash, 2004.

 8 Colwell-Chanthaphonh and Ferguson, 2006.

 9 Srinivasan, Becvar, Boast, and Enote, 2010, 738.

10 Dewey, J, 1927; 2002.

11 Smith, 1999.

12 O'Doherty, 1999.

13 Law and Mol, 1995.

14 Appadurai, 1996.

15 Appadurai, 1986.

16 Appadurai, 1986; Ingold, 2007.

17 Pearce, 1994.

18 Rule, 2013.

19 Dourish, 2004, 2013.

20 Fuller, 1992; Simpson, 2012.

21 Suro, 1990.

22 Boast and Enote, 2013.

23 Turnbull, 2000.

24 http://redis.io/topics/pubsub.

25 Palfrey and Gasser, 2012.

26 Bowker and Star, 2000.

27 Thierer, 2012.

28 Boyd and Crawford, 2012; Snijders, Matzat, and Reips, 2012; Borgman 2015.

29 Boellstorff, 2013, sec. 5, par. 6.

30 Geertz, 1973.

31 Auer, 1995, 2013.

32 Belkin, 1980.

33 Pickering, 2010.

34 D. Taylor, 2003.

35 D. Taylor, 2003, xvii.

36 Pickering, 2010, ix.

CHAPTER 5. TAKING BACK OUR MEDIA

1 Cleaver, 1998; Martinez-Torres, 2001; Russell, 2001.
2 Subcomandante Marcos/TKO/The Getaway Drivers, 1994.
3 Ghosh and Morrison, 1984; Hazeltine and Bull, 1998; Schumacker, 1973.
4 Urban, 2007, par. 9.
5 Castells, 1999; Virilio, 1986.
6 Virilio, 1986, 47.
7 Spider Rock Plaque, Canyon de Chelly National Monument, Arizona.
8 Bird, 2002.
9 Turnbull, 2011.
10 Ha, 2014.
11 www.google.com/loon
12 Fish, 2015.
13 Foucault, 1978.
14 Rose, 1999.
15 Chakrabarty, 2009.
16 Coleman, 2010, 489.
17 Chipchase, 2007.
18 Zuckerman, 2013.
19 Morozov, 2013a.
20 Morozov, 2011.
21 Zittrain, 2008.
22 Morozov, 2013a, 68.
23 Galison and Hevly, 1992.
24 Latour, 2004.
25 Latour and Woolgar, 1979; Latour, 2004.
26 Lippmann, 1946.
27 Zuckerman, 2008, 2013.
28 Bhabha, 1994, 38.
29 Geertz, 1973.
30 Boellstorff, 2013.
31 Agre, 2000b.
32 Agre, 2000b, 76.
33 Schmidt and Cohen, 2013.
34 Morozov, 2013b.
35 Ginsburg, 2008, 130.
36 Tyler, 1995.
37 Harding, 2013, 54.
38 Howard and Parks, 2012; Iskandar, 2007; Srinivasan, 2013a.
39 Shirky, 2011.
40 Srinivasan and Fish, 2011; Srinivasan, 2012b, 2013a, 2013c.
41 Tufekci, 2011.

42 Srinivasan and Fish, 2011.
43 *Time Magazine*, cover, June 13, 2011.
44 Sundaram, 1999.
45 Jackson, Ahmed, and Rifat, 2014; Jackson and Kang, 2014; Jackson, 2014.
46 Star and Strauss, 1999.
47 Burrell, 2012.
48 Santos, Nunes, and Meneses, 2007, xix.
49 Amartya Sen Keynote, *World Culture Forum*: The Power of Culture in Sustainable Development, November 24–27, 2013, Bali, Indonesia.
50 Sen, 2007.
51 Sassen, 2000, 2003.
52 Scott, 1998.
53 Scott, 1998, 2.
54 Binder, Ehn, De Michelis, Jacucci, Linde, and Wagner, 2011; Bruckman, 2004; Schultz 2015; Fry, 2009; Escobar, 2012; Latour 2008; and much more.
55 Searls, 2008, par. 1.
56 Searls, 2008.
57 Thompson, 2013.
58 Statement of Subcomandante Marcos to the Freeing the Media Teach-In," 1997.
59 Chamayou, 2011.

REFERENCES

A timeline of database history. (n.d.). Retrieved August 13, 2014 from http://quickbase. intuit.com

Ackleson, J. (2005). Constructing security on the U.S.–Mexico border. *Political Geography, 24*(2), 165–184.

Adelman, C. (1993). Kurt Lewin and the origins of action research. *Educational Action Research, 1*(1), 7–24.

Agrawal, A. (1995). Dismantling the divide between indigenous and scientific knowledge. *Development and Change, 26*(3), 413–439.

Agre, P. E. (1994). Surveillance and capture: Two models of privacy. *Information Society, 10*(2), 101–127.

———. (2000a). Infrastructure and institutional change in the networked university. *Information, Communication and Society, 3*(4), 494–507.

———. (2000b). The market logic of information. *Knowledge, Technology and Policy, 13*(3), 67–77.

Aker, J. C., and I. M. Mbiti (2010). Mobile phones and economic development in Africa. *Journal of Economic Perspectives,* 207–232.

Aki, A. (2014, August 22). QandA: Never alone brings Alaska native culture to life. Retrieved from http://blogs.voanews.com

Akrich, M. (1992). The de-scription of technical objects. In W. E. Bijker and J. Law (eds.), *Shaping Technology/Building Society* (205–224). Cambridge, Mass.: MIT Press.

Allen, D. K., S. Karanasios, and A. Norman (2013). Information sharing and interoperability: The case of major incident management. *European Journal of Information Systems, 23*(4), 418–432.

Anderson, B. (2006). *Imagined Communities: Reflections on the Origin and Spread of Nationalism.* London: Verso.

Anderson, C. (2006). *The Long Tail: Why the Future of Business Is Selling Less of More.* New York: Hyperion.

Anderson, D. J., and E. N. Zalta (2004). Frege, Boolos, and logical objects. *Journal of Philosophical Logic, 33*(1), 1–26.

Anderson, W. (2002). Introduction: Postcolonial technoscience. *Social Studies of Science, 32*(5/6), 643–658.

Aneesh, A. (2001). Rethinking migration: On-line labor flows from India to the United States. In W. A. Cornelius, T. J. Espenshade, and I. Salehyan (eds.), *The Interna-*

tional Migration of the Highly Skilled (351–370). University of California, San Diego: Center for Comparative Immigration.

———. (2006). *Virtual Migration: The Programming of Globalization.* Durham, N.C.: Duke University Press.

Appadurai, A. (ed.). (1986). *The Social Life of Things: Commodities in Cultural Perspective.* Cambridge, U.K.: Cambridge University Press.

———. (1990). Difference and disjuncture in the global cultural economy. *Theory, Culture and Society, 7*(2), 295–310.

———. (1996). *Modernity at Large: Cultural Dimensions of Globalization* (vol. 1). Minneapolis: University of Minnesota Press.

———. (2000). Grassroots globalization and the research imagination. *Public Culture, 12*(1), 1–19.

———. (2004). The capacity to aspire: Culture and the terms of recognition. *Culture and Public Action,* 59–84.

Appiah, K. A. (2010). *Cosmopolitanism: Ethics in a World of Strangers (Issues of Our Time).* New York: W. W. Norton.

Aronson, J. (1994). A pragmatic view of thematic analysis. *The Qualitative Report, 2*(1).

Arora, P. (2007). The ICT Laboratory: An analysis of computers in schools in rural India. *Association for the Advancement of Computing in Education Journal, 15*(1), 57–72.

———. (2008). Instant-messaging Shiva, flying taxis, Bil Klinton and more: Children's narratives from rural India. *International Journal of Cultural Studies, 11*(1), 69–86.

Auer, P. (1995). The pragmatics of code-switching: A sequential approach. In L. Milroy and P. Muysken (eds.), *One Speaker, Two Languages: Cross-Disciplinary Perspectives on Code-Switching* (115–135). Cambridge, U.K.: Cambridge University Press.

———. (2013). *Code-Switching in Conversation: Language, Interaction and Identity.* London: Routledge.

Autonomic, P. (2004, October 24). DJ/Rupture's Diasporic Breakbeats. Retrieved from http://autonomicforthepeople.blogspot.com

Badone, E. (2004). Crossing boundaries: Exploring the borderlands of ethnography, tourism, and pilgrimage. In E. Badone and S. R. Roseman (eds.), *Intersecting Journeys: The Anthropology of Pilgrimage and Tourism* (180–189). Urbana: University of Illinois Press.

Balsamo, A. (2011). *Designing Culture: The Technological Imagination at Work.* Durham, N.C.: Duke University Press.

Banerjee, A., E. Duflo, R. Chattopadhyay, and J. Shapiro (2007). Targeting efficiency: How well can we identify the poor? *Serie de Documentos de Trabajo* (21).

Baran, P. (1964). On distributed communications networks. *Communications Systems, IEEE Transactions on, 12*(1), 1–9.

Barber, B. R. (2003). *Strong Democracy: Participatory Politics for a New Age.* Berkeley: University of California Press.

Bardini, T. (2000). *Bootstrapping: Douglas Engelbart, Coevolution, and the Origins of Personal Computing.* Stanford: Stanford University Press.

Bardini, T., and M. Friedewald (2003). Chronicle of the death of a laboratory: Douglas Engelbart and the failure of the Knowledge Workshop. *History of Technology, 23,* 191–212.

Barzilai-Nahon, K. (2006). Gaps and bits: Conceptualizing measurements for digital divide/s. *Information Society, 22*(5), 269–278.

Baym, N. (2000). *Tune In, Log On: Soaps, Fandom, and Online Community.* Thousand Oaks, Calif.: Sage.

Belkin, N. J. (1980). Anomalous states of knowledge as a basis for information retrieval. *Canadian Journal of Information Science, 5,* 133–143.

Berggren, J. L. (1985). History of mathematics in the Islamic world: The present state of the art. *Middle East Studies Association Bulletin, 19*(1), 9–33.

Berker, T., M. Hartmann, Y. Punie, and K. Ward (eds.) (2005). *Domestication of Media and Technology.* Berkshire, U.K.: McGraw-Hill International.

Bhabha, H. K. (1994). *The Location of Culture.* London: Psychology Press.

Bidwell, N., and H. Winschies-Theophilius (eds.) (2014). *At the Intersection of Traditional and Indigenous Knowledge and Technology Design.* Santa Rosa, Calif.: Informing Science Press.

Bijker, W. E., and J. Law (eds.) (1992). *Shaping Technology/Building Society: Studies in Sociotechnical Change.* Cambridge, Mass.: MIT Press.

Binder, T., P. Ehn, G. De Michelis, G. Jacucci, G. Linde, and I. Wagner (2011). *Design Things.* Cambridge, Mass.: MIT Press.

Bird, L. (2002, December 26). 0024-Our Voices-Ehep Legend.

Boast, R. (forthcoming). *The Machine in the Ghost: A Media Archaeology of the Digital.*

Boast, R., M. Bravo, and R. Srinivasan (2007). Return to Babel: Emergent diversity, digital resources, and local knowledge. *Information Society, 23*(5), 395–403.

Boast, R., and J. Enote (2013). Virtual repatriation: It's virtual, but it's not repatriation. In P. Biehl and C. Prescott (eds.), *Heritage in Context of Globalization: Europe and the Americas.* New York: Springer Press.

Bodker, K., F. Kensing, and J. Simonson (2004). *Participatory IT design: Designing for Business and Workplace Realities.* Cambridge, Mass.: MIT Press.

Boellstorff, T. (2013). Making big data, in theory. *First Monday, 18*(10). Retrieved from http://firstmonday.org

Bogost, I., and N. Montfort (2009). *Racing the Beam: The Atari Video Computer System.* Cambridge, Mass.: MIT Press.

Booth, R. (2009, September 7). Lost world of fanged frogs and giant rats discovered in Papua New Guinea. *Guardian.* Retrieved from www.theguardian.com

Borgman, Christine. (2015). *Big Data, Little Data, No Data: Scholarship in the Networked World.* Cambridge, Mass.: MIT Press.

Boud, D., R. Keogh, and D. Walker (eds.) (1985). *Reflection: Turning Experience into Learning.* Abingdon, U.K.: Routledge.

Bowen, W. (2015). Posthumous interview with Democracy Now! www.democracynow.org

Bowker, G. C. (2005). *Memory Practices in the Sciences.* Cambridge, Mass.: MIT Press.

Bowker, G. C., K. Baker, F. Millerand, and D. Ribes (2010). Toward information infrastructure studies: Ways of knowing in a networked environment. In J. Hunsinger, L. Klastrup, and M. Allen (eds.) *International Handbook of Internet Research* (97–117). London: Springer.

Bowker, G. C., and S. L. Star (1996). How things (actor-net) work: Classification, magic and the ubiquity of standards. *Philosophia*, 25(3–4), 195–220.

———. (2000). *Sorting Things Out: Classification and Its Consequences*. Cambridge, Mass.: MIT Press.

Boyd, D., and K. Crawford (2012). Critical questions for big data: Provocations for a cultural, technological, and scholarly phenomenon. *Information, Communication and Society*, 15(5), 662–679.

Brescia, W., and T. Daily (2007). Economic development and technology-skill needs. *American Indian Quarterly*, 31(1), 23–43.

Brookfield, S. (1998). Critically reflective practice. *Journal of Continuing Education in the Health Professions*, 18(4), 197–205.

Brown, J. S., and P. Duguid (2002). *The Social Life of Information*. Cambridge, Mass.: Harvard Business School Press.

Brownstone, S. (2014, July 31). Should you be paid for your social media posts? Retrieved from www.fastcoexist.com

Bruckman, A. (2004). Co-evolution of technological design and pedagogy in an online learning community. In S. Barab, R. Kling, and J. Gray (eds.), *Designing for Virtual Communities in the Service of Learning* (239–255). Cambridge, U.K.: Cambridge University Press.

Buck, R. C., and D. L. Hull (1966). The logical structure of the Linnaean hierarchy. *Systematic Biology*, 15(2), 97–111.

Buckland, M. K. (1991). *Information and Information Systems*. ABC-CLIO.

Burrell, J. (2012). *Invisible Users: Youth in the Internet Cafés of Urban Ghana*. Cambridge, Mass.: MIT Press.

Burrell, J., and K. Toyama (2009). What constitutes good ICTD research? *Information Technologies and International Development*, 5(3), 82–94.

Bush, V. (1945). As we may think. *Atlantic Monthly*, 101–108.

Carey, J. W. (2008). *Communication as Culture: Essays on Media and Society*. Rev. ed. New York: Routledge.

Caron, A. H., and L. Caronia (2007). *Moving cultures: Mobile communication in everyday life*. Montreal: McGill-Queen's University Press.

Castells, M. (1996). *The Rise of the Networked Society*. Cambridge, Mass.: Blackwell.

———. (1999). The social implications of information and communication technologies. *The World Social Science Report*. Retrieved from www.chet.org.za—no longer available.

———. (2000). The rise of the fourth world. In D. Held and A. McGrew (eds.), *The Global Transformations Reader: An Introduction to the Globalization Debate*. London: Blackwell.

———. (2011). *The Rise of the Network Society: The Information Age: Economy, Society, and Culture* (vol. 1). Chichester, U.K.: John Wiley and Sons.

Chakrabarty, D. (2009). *Provincializing Europe: Postcolonial Thought and Historical Difference*. Princeton: Princeton University Press.

Chamayou, G. (2011, October). The manhunt doctrine. *Radical Philosophy*. Retrieved from www.radicalphilosophy.com

Chambers, R. (1997). *Whose Reality Counts? Putting the First Last*. London: Intermediate Technology Publications Ltd (ITP).

Chan, A. S. (2014). *Networking Peripheries: Technological Futures and the Myth of Digital Universalism*. Cambridge, Mass.: MIT Press.

Cheah, P., and B. Robbins (1998). *Cosmopolitics: Thinking and Feeling beyond the Nation* (vol. 14). Minneapolis: University of Minnesota Press.

Chipchase, J. (2007). *The Anthropology of Mobile*. Retrieved from www.ted.com/talks

Christen, K. (2006). Tracking properness: Repackaging culture in a remote Australian town. *Cultural Anthropology*, 21(3), 416–446.

———. (2009). Access and accountability: The ecology of information sharing in the digital age. *Anthropology News*, 50(4), 4–5.

———. (2012). Does information really want to be free? Indigenous knowledge systems and the question of openness. *International Journal of Communication*, 6, 24.

Chun, W. H. K. (2008a). *Control and Freedom: Power and Paranoia in the Age of Fiber Optics*. Cambridge, Mass.: MIT Press.

———. (2008b). The enduring ephemeral, or the future is a memory. *Critical Inquiry*, 35(1), 148–171.

———. (2011, August 1). *Imagined Networks, Affective Connections*. UCHRI's SECT VII from the University of Hawaii at Manoa. Retrieved from www.youtube.com

Cilliers, P. (1998). *Complexity and Postmodernism: Understanding Complex Systems*. London: Psychology Press.

Cleaver, F. (1999). Paradoxes of participation: Questioning participatory approaches to development. *Journal of International Development*, 11(4), 597–612.

Cleaver, H. (1998). *The Zapatistas and the Electronic Fabric of Struggle*. Retrieved from http://la.utexas.edu

Clifford, J. (1989). The others: Beyond the "salvage" paradigm. *Third Text*, 3(6), 73–78.

———. (1997). Museums as contact zones. In *Routes: Travel and Translation in the Late Twentieth Century* (188–219). Cambridge, Mass.: Harvard University Press.

Clifford, J., and G. E. Marcus (1986). *Writing Culture: The Poetics and Politics of Ethnography*. Berkeley: University of California Press.

Cohen, I. B. (2005). *The Triumph of Numbers: How Counting Shaped Modern Life*. New York: W. W. Norton.

Coleman, E. G. (2010). Ethnographic approaches to digital media. *Annual Review of Anthropology*, 39, 487–505.

———. (2013). *Coding Freedom: The Ethics and Aesthetics of Hacking*. Princeton: Princeton University Press.

Coleman, M. (2005). U.S. statecraft and the U.S.-Mexico border as security/economy nexus. *Political Geography*, 24(2), 185–209.

Colwell-Chanthaphonh, C., and T. J. Ferguson (2006). Memory pieces and footprints: Multivocality and the meanings of ancient times and ancestral places among the Zuni and Hopi. *American Anthropologist*, 108(1), 148–162.

Cooke, B., and U. Kothari (2001). *Participation: The New Tyranny?* New York: Zed Books.

Corning, P. A. (2002). The re-emergence of "emergence": A venerable concept in search of a theory. *Complexity*, 7(6), 18–30.

Corrazon, R. (2010). Birth of a new science: The history of ontology from Suárez to Kant. Retrieved from www.ontology.com

Couldry, N. (2008). Mediatization or mediation? Alternative understandings of the emergent space of digital storytelling. *New Media and Society*, 10(3), 373–391.

Crawford, B., and R. D. Lipschutz (1998). The myth of "ethnic conflict": Politics, economics, and "cultural" violence. *Research Series 98*, University of California, Berkeley.

Crovitz, G. (2012). Who really invented the Internet? *Wall Street Journal*, A11.

Dammbeck, L. (2003). *The Net* (original title: *Das Netz*). Documentary.

Davis, W. (n.d.) Dreams from endangered cultures, TED talk, retrieved from www.ted. com

De Bellaigue, C. (2007). *Educating Women: Schooling and Identity in England and France, 1800–1867*. New York: Oxford University Press.

de Certeau, M. (1984). *The Practice of Everyday Life*. (S. Rendall, trans.) Berkeley: University of California Press.

Dean, M. (2010). *Governmentality: Power and Rule in Modern Society*. London: Sage.

Derrida, J. (1996). *Archive Fever: A Freudian Impression*. Chicago: University of Chicago Press.

Dewey, J. (1927, 2002). *The Public and Its Problems: An Essay in Political Inquiry*. (M. L. Rogers, ed.) University Park: Penn State University Press.

———. (1933). *How We Think: A Restatement of the Relation of Reflective Thinking to the Educational Process*. Lexington, Mass.: Heath.

Diderot, D., and J. L. R. d'Alembert (1751). *Encyclopédie ou Dictionnaire Raisonné des Sciences, des Arts et des Métiers* (vol. 2). Paris: Chez Briasson.

DiMaggio, P., E. Hargittai, C. Celeste, and S. Shafer (2004). Digital inequality: From unequal access to differentiated use. In K. Neckerman (ed.), *Social Inequality* (355–400). New York: Russell Sage Foundation.

DiSalvo, C. (2009). Design and the Construction of Publics. *Design Issues*, 25(1), 48–63.

Dourish, P. (2004). *Where the Action Is: The Foundations of Embodied Interaction*. Cambridge, Mass.: MIT Press.

———. (2013). *Designing for Zombies*. Retrieved from www.dourish.com

———. (2014). No SQL: The Shifting Materialities of Database Technology. *Computational Culture*, 1(4).

Dourish, P., and G. Bell (2007). The infrastructure of experience and the experience of infrastructure: Meaning and structure in everyday encounters with space. *Environment and Planning B: Planning and Design, 34*(3), 414.

Dourish, P., and M. Mazmanian (2012). Media as material: Information representations as material foundations for organizational practice. In P. Carlile, D. Nicolini, A. Langley, and H. Tsoukas (eds.), *How Matter Matters: Objects, Artifacts and Materiality in Organization Studies* (92–118). Oxford, U.K.: Oxford University Press.

Dubai School of Government (2011). Arab Social Media Report, May (2011), http://unpan1.un.org

Dunn, T. J. (1996). *The Militarization of the U.S.-Mexico Border, 1978–1992: Low-Intensity Conflict Doctrine Comes Home.* Austin: University of Texas Press.

Durkheim, E. (1915). *The Elementary Forms of the Religious Life.* London: Courier Dover Publications.

Eglash, R. (2004). *Appropriating Technology: Vernacular Science and Social Power.* Minneapolis: University of Minnesota Press.

Ellingson, L. L., and C. Ellis (2008). Autoethnography as constructionist project. In J. A. Holstein and J. F. Gubrium (eds.), *Handbook of Constructionist Research* (445–466). New York: Guilford Press.

Engelbart, D. C. (2001). Augmenting human intellect: A conceptual framework. In R. Packer and K. Jordan (eds.), *Multimedia. From Wagner to Virtual Reality* (64–90). New York: W. W. Norton.

Enote, J. (2013, March 13). Zuni museum director responds to the auctioning of Hopi and Zuni masks in Paris. *Indian Country Today.* Retrieved from http://indiancountrytodaymedianetwork.com

Escobar, Arturo. 2012. Notes on the Ontology of Design (draft). University of North Carolina, Chapel Hill.

Fast Company Staff. (2011, May 18). Most Creative People 2011: Jan Chipchase. *Fast Company.* Retrieved from www.fastcompany.com

Feenberg, A. (1995). *Alternative Modernity: The Technical Turn in Philosophy and Social Theory.* Berkeley: University of California Press.

Fish, A. (2013, January 18). Who built the Internet? Studly genius individuals! (Part 4). Retrieved from http://savageminds.org

———. (2015). Who really benefits from the Internet space race? https://theconversation.com

Fish, A., and R. Srinivasan (2012). Digital labor is the new killer app. *New Media and Society, 14*(1), 137–152.

Fiske, J., and J. Hartley (1978). Bardic television. In *Reading Television* (56–80). New York: Routledge.

Flores, F., M. Graves, B. Hartfield, and T. Winograd (1988). Computer systems and the design of organizational interaction. *ACM Transactions on Information Systems (TOIS), 6*(2), 153–172.

Foucault, M. (1970). *The Order of Things: An Archaeology of the Human Sciences.* New York: Vintage.

———. (1972). *The Archaeology of Knowledge.* (A. M. Sheridan Smith, trans.) New York: Pantheon Books.

———. (1975). *The Birth of the Clinic: An Archeology of Medical Perception.* (A. M. Sheridan-Smith, trans.) New York: Vintage.

———. (1978). *Discipline and Punish: The Birth of the Prison.* New York: Pantheon Books.

———. (1981). *The Order of Discourse.* In R. Young (ed.), *Untying the Text: A Post-Structuralist Reader.* London: Routledge.

Frankel, E., F. D. Miller, and P. Jeffrey (eds.). (2000). *Natural Law and Modern Moral Philosophy.* New York: Cambridge University Press.

Freire, P. (1968). *Pedagogy of the Oppressed.* New York: Seabury Place.

———. (2000). *Pedagogy of the Oppressed* (30th anniversary edition. Translated by Myra Bergman Ramos, with an Introduction by Donaldo Macedo). New York: Continuum International Publishing.

Friedman, T. L. (2000). *The Lexus and the Olive Tree: Understanding Globalization.* New York: Macmillan.

———. (2006). *The World Is Flat: A Brief History of the Twenty-First Century.* Updated and expanded ed. New York: Macmillan.

Fromm, Eric. 1941. *Escape from Freedom.* New York: Holt, Rinehart and Winston.

Fry, Tony. 2009. *Design Futuring.* Oxford: Berg; Sydney: UNSW Press.

Fukuyama, F. (2002). Social capital and development: The coming agenda. *SAIS Review, 22*(1), 23–37.

Fuller, N. J. (1992). The museum as a vehicle for community empowerment: The Ak-Chin Indian Community Ecomuseum project. In S. D. Lavine, I. Karp, and C. M. Kreamer (eds.), *Museums and Communities: The Politics of Public Culture* (327–365). Washington, D.C.: Smithsonian Institution Press.

Furner, J. (2007). Dewey deracialized: A critical race-theoretic perspective. *Knowledge Organization, 34*(3), 144–168.

Galison, P., and B. W. Hevly (1992). *Big Science: The Growth of Large-Scale Research.* Stanford: Stanford University Press.

Galloway, A. R. (2004). *Protocol: How Control Exists after Decentralization.* Cambridge, Mass.: MIT Press.

———. (2007, September 12). We are the gold farmers. Retrieved from http://cultureandcommunication.org

———. (2012). *The Interface Effect.* Cambridge, U.K.: Polity Press.

Galtung, J. (1969). Violence, peace, and peace research. *Journal of Peace Research, 6*(3), 167–191.

———. (1990). Cultural violence. *Journal of Peace Research, 27*(3), 291–305.

Gandhi, R., R. Verraraghavan, K. Toyama, and R. Wang (2007). *Digital Green Preliminary Report.* Retrieved from www.digitalgreen.org

Geertz, C. (1973). Thick description: Toward an interpretive theory of culture. In *The Interpretation of Cultures* (311–323). New York: Basic Books.

———. (1978). The bazaar economy: Information and search in peasant marketing. *American Economic Review*, 68(2), 28–32.

Geismar, H., and W. Mohns (2011). Social relationships and digital relationships: Rethinking the database at the Vanuatu Cultural Centre. *Journal of the Royal Anthropological Institute*, 17(s1), S133–S155.

Genachowski, J. (2010, March 2). Prepared remarks of FCC Chairman Julius Genachowski. Presented at the 2010 Executive Council Winter Session, Washington, D.C. Retrieved from http://hraunfoss.fcc.gov

Ghosh, P. K., and D. E. Morrison (1984). *Appropriate Technology in Third World Development*. Westport, Conn.: Greenwood Press.

Gillespie, T. (2013). The relevance of algorithms. In T. Gillespie, P. Boczkowski, and K. Foot (eds.). *Media Technologies: Paths Forward in Social Research*. Cambridge, Mass.: MIT Press.

Gilligan, J. (1996). *Violence: Reflections on a National Epidemic*. New York: Vintage.

Gilliland, A., A. J. Lau, and S. McKemmish (2013). Pluralizing the archive. In K. Fujiyoshi (ed.), *Archives for Maintaining Community and Society in the Digital Age* (65–74). Koyasan University, Japan.

Gilmore, T., J. Krantz, J., and R. Ramirez (1986). Action-based modes of inquiry and the host-researcher relationship. *Consultation: An International Journal*, 5(3): 160–176.

Ginsburg, F. (1991). Indigenous media: Faustian contract or global village? *Cultural Anthropology*, 6(1), 92–112.

———. (2008). Rethinking the digital age. In D. Hesmondhalgh and J. Toynbee (eds.), *The Media and Social Theory* (127–144). New York: Routledge.

Ginsburg, F., L. Abu-Lughod, and B. Larkin (eds.). (2002). *Media Worlds: Anthropology on New Terrain*. Berkeley: University of California Press.

Girvin, R. E. (1947). Photography as social documentation. *Journalism Quarterly*, 24(3), 207–220.

Gitelman, L. (2006). *Always Already New: Media, History and the Data of Culture*. Cambridge, Mass.: MIT Press.

Gladwell, M. (2010, October 4). Small change: Why the revolution will not be tweeted. *New Yorker*. Retrieved from www.newyorker.com

Goffman, E. (1959). *The Presentation of Self in Everyday Life*. New York: Doubleday.

Goldberg, A., and A. Kay (1977). Personal dynamic media. *IEEE Computer*, 10(3), 31–41.

Graham, S. (2010). When infrastructures fail. In S. Graham (ed.), *Disrupted Cities: When Infrastructure Fails* (1–26). New York: Routledge.

Graham, S., and S. Marvin (2001). *Splintering Urbanism: Networked Infrastructures, Technological Mobilities and the Urban Condition*. London: Psychology Press.

Greg's Cable Map. (n.d.). Retrieved from www.cablemap.info

Guijt, I., and M. K. Shah (1998). Waking up to power, conflict and process. In I. Guijt and M. K. Shah (eds.), *The Myth of Community: Gender Issues in Participatory Development* (1–23). London: IT Publications.

Gustin, S. (2011) Social media, sparred, accelerated, Egypt's revolutionary fire. *Wired Magazine*, February 11, 2011, www.wired.com

Ha, T.-H. (2014, March 19). Computing is still too clunky: Charlie Rose and Larry Page in conversation. Retrieved from http://blog.ted.com

Hall, S. (1977). Culture, the media and the "ideological effect." In J. Curran, M. Gurevitch, and J. Woollacott (eds.), *Mass Communication and Society*. London: Arnold.

Hammersley, M., and P. Atkinson (1983). *Ethnography: Principles and Practices*. London: Tavistock Press.

Haraway, D. (1991). A cyborg manifesto: Science, technology, and socialist-feminism in the late 20th century. In D. Haraway and U. Teubner, *Simians, Cyborgs and Women* (149–181). New York: Routledge.

Haraway, D., and U. Teubner (1991). *Simians, Cyborgs, and Women*. New York: Routledge.

Harding, S. (2013). Rethinking standpoint epistemology: What is strong objectivity? In L. Alcoff, L. M. Alcoff, and E. Potter (eds.), *Feminist Epistemologies* (49–82). New York: Routledge.

Hardt, M., and A. Negri (2009). *Empire*. Cambridge, Mass.: Harvard University Press.

Hargittai, E. (2008). The digital reproduction of inequality. In D. Grusky (ed.), *Social Stratification* (936–944). Boulder, Colo.: Westview Press.

Hayes, E. N., and T. Hayes (1970). *Claude Lévi-Strauss: The Anthropologist as Hero*. Cambridge, Mass.: MIT Press.

Hayles, N. K. (2002). *Writing Machines*. Cambridge, Mass.: MIT Press.

Hazeltine, B., and C. Bull (1998). *Appropriate Technology; Tools, Choices, and Implications*. San Diego, Calif.: Academic Press.

Hebdige, D. (1984). *Subculture: The Meaning of Style*. New York: Methuen.

Heeks, R. (2008). ICT4D 2.0: The next phase of applying ICT for international development. *Computer*, *41*(6), 26–33.

Heidegger, M. (1954). The question concerning technology. In C. Hanks (ed.), *Technology and Values: Essential Readings* (99–113). Chichester: Wiley-Blackwell.

Hemming, S., and D. Rigney (2010). Decentring the new protectors: Transforming Aboriginal heritage in South Australia. *International Journal of Heritage Studies* *16*(1): 90–106.

Hickman, L. A. (1990). *John Dewey's Pragmatic Technology*. Bloomington: Indiana University Press.

Hier, S., and J. Greenberg (2007). *The Surveillance Studies Reader*. Maidenhead, U.K.: McGraw-Hill International.

Hirschheim, R., and H. K. Klein (1994). Realizing emancipatory principles in information systems development: The case for ethics. *MIS Quarterly*, *18*(1), 83–109.

Hirschman, A. O. (1970). *Exit, Voice, and Loyalty: Responses to Decline in Firms, Organizations, and States* (vol. 25). Cambridge, Mass.: Harvard University Press.

Horst, H., and D. Miller (2006). *The Cell Phone: An Anthropology of Communication*. Oxford, U.K.: Berg.

Houser, L. (1986). Documents: The domain of library and information science. *Library and Information Science Research*, 8(2), 163–188.

Howard, P. N., L. Busch, and P. Sheets (2010). Comparing digital divides: Internet access and social inequality in Canada and the United States. *Canadian Journal of Communication*, 35(1), 109–128.

Howard, P. N., and M. R. Parks (2012). Social media and political change: Capacity, constraint, and consequence. *Journal of Communication*, 62(2), 359–362.

Howe, C. (1998). Cyberspace is no place for tribalism. *WICAZO-SA Review*, 13(2), 19–28.

Hull, M. S. (2003). The file: Agency, authority, and autography in an Islamabad bureaucracy. *Language and Communication*, 23(3), 287–314.

Husserl, E. (1913). *Ideas: General Introduction to Pure Phenomenology*. Abingdon, U.K.: Routledge.

Ihde, D. (2005). Philosophy of technology. In P. Kemp (ed.), *Philosophical Problems Today* (91–108). Dordrecht: Springer.

Ingalls, D., T. Kaehler, J. Maloney, S. Wallace, and A. Kay (1997). Back to the future: The story of Squeak, a practical Smalltalk written in itself (318–326). In *ACM SIGPLAN Notices* (vol. 32). ACM.

Ingold, T. (2000). *The Perception of the Environment: Essays on Livelihood, Dwelling and Skill*. London: Psychology Press.

———. (2007). Materials against materiality. *Archaeological Dialogues*, 14(01), 1–16.

International Telecommunication Union. (2012). *Measuring the Information Society 2012*. Geneva, Switzerland. Retrieved from www.itu.int

Internet and Mobile Association of India. (2007). *Internet in India*. Retrieved from www.iamai.in

Introna, L. D., and H. Nissenbaum (2000). Shaping the Web: Why the politics of search engines matters. *Information Society*, 16(3), 169–185.

Isaac, G. (2005). Mediating knowledges: Zuni negotiations for a culturally relevant museum. *Museum Anthropology*, 28(1), 3–18.

Iskandar, A. (2007). Lines in the sand: Problematizing Arab media in the posttaxonomic era. *Arab Media and Society*, 1–47.

Ito, M. (2003). Technologies of the childhood imagination: Media mixes, hypersociality, and recombinant cultural form. *Items and Issues*, 4(4), 2003–2004.

———. (2006). Japanese media mixes and amateur cultural exchange. In D. Buckingham and R. Willett (eds.), *Digital Generations: Children, Young People, and New Media*. New York: Routledge.

Jackson, S. J. (2014). Rethinking repair. In T. Gillespie, P. Boczkowski, and K. Foot (eds.), *Media Technologies: Essays on Communication, Materiality and Society*. Cambridge, Mass.: MIT Press.

Jackson, S. J., S. I. Ahmed, and M. R. Rifat (2014). Learning, innovation, and sustainability among mobile phone repairers in Dhaka, Bangladesh. In *Proceedings of the 2014 conference on Designing Interactive Systems* (905–914). ACM.

Jackson, S. J., and L. Kang (2014). Breakdown, obsolescence and reuse: HCI and the art of repair. In *Proceedings of the 32nd annual ACM Conference on Human Factors in Computing Systems* (449–458). ACM.

James, K. (2006). Identity, cultural values, and American Indians' perceptions of science and technology. *American Indian Culture and Research Journal, 30*(3), 45–58.

Jenkins, H. (1992). *Textual Poachers: Television Fans and Participatory Culture.* New York: Routledge.

———. (2003). Quentin Tarantino's Star Wars? Digital cinema, media convergence, and participatory culture. In D. Thorburn and H. Jenkins (eds.), *Rethinking Media Change: The Aesthetics of Transition* (281–312). Cambridge, Mass.: MIT Press.

———. (2006). *Convergence Culture: Where Old and New Media Collide.* New York: NYU Press.

———. (2013). *Textual Poachers: Television Fans and Participatory Culture.* New York: Routledge.

Joseph, M. (2002). *Against the Romance of Community.* Minneapolis: University of Minnesota Press.

Kant, I. ([1784] 2010). Idea of a universal history with a cosmopolitan purpose. In G. W. Brown and D. Held, *The Cosmopolitanism Reader* (17–26). Cambridge, U.K.: Polity Press.

———. (1934). *Critique of Pure Reason. Translated by Norman Kemp Smith.* (N. K. Smith, ed.). London: Macmillan.

Kay, A. (1990). User interface: A personal view. In B. Laurel (ed.), *The Art of Human-Computer Interface Design* (191–207). Boston: Addison-Wesley.

———. (2000). Dynabooks: Past, present, and future. *Library Quarterly,* 385–395.

Kelly, Kevin. *The Next 5,000 Days of the Web.* (2007). Retrieved from www.ted.com

Keniston, K., and D. Kumar (2003). The four digital divides. *Online Erişim, 21,* 2010.

Kirschenbaum, M. G. (2008). *Mechanisms: New Media and the Forensic Imagination.* Cambridge, Mass.: MIT Press.

Kitching, G. N. (1988). *Karl Marx and the Philosophy of Praxis.* New York: Routledge.

Knobel, C., and G. C. Bowker (2011). Values in design. *Communications of the ACM, 54*(7), 26–28.

Koolhaas, R. (2007). *Lagos: How It Works.* Zurich, Switzerland: Lars Müller.

Kothari, B. (1999). Same language subtitling: Integrating post literacy development and popular culture on television. *Media and Technology for Human Resource Development, 11*(3), 111–117.

Kretzmann, J., and J. McKnight (1993). *Building Community from the Inside Out.* Chicago: ACTA Publications.

Kundu, A. (2000). Globalising Gujarat: Urbanisation, employment and poverty. *Economic and Political Weekly,* 3172–3182.

Kwasnik, B. H. (1992). The role of classification structures in reflecting and building theory. *Advances in Classification Research Online, 3*(1), 63–82.

———. (2000). The role of classification in knowledge representation and discovery. *Library Trends, 48*(1), 22–47.

Lagoze, C., and J. Hunter (2006). The ABC ontology and model. *Journal of Digital Information*, 2(2).

Lakoff, G. (1987). *Women, Fire, and Dangerous Things: What Categories Reveal about the Mind*. Chicago: University of Chicago Press.

Lambert, J. (2013). *Digital Storytelling: Capturing Lives, Creating Community*. New York: Routledge.

Lanier, J. (2013). *Who Owns the Future?* Retrieved from www.youtube.com

———. (2014). *Who Owns the Future?* New York: Simon & Schuster.

Larkin, B. (2008). *Signal and Noise: Media, Infrastructure, and Urban Culture in Nigeria*. Durham, N.C.: Duke University Press.

Latour, B. (1986). Visualization and cognition: Drawing things together. *Knowledge and Society*, 6, 1–40.

———. (2004). Why has critique run out of steam? From matters of fact to matters of concern. *Critical Inquiry*, 30(2), 225–248.

———. (2008). A cautious Prometheus? A few steps toward a philosophy of design (with special attention to Peter Sloterdijk). Networks of Design Conference, Cornwall.

Latour, B., and Woolgar, S. (1979). *Laboratory Life: The Social Construction of Scientific Facts*. Beverly Hills: Sage.

Lau, A. J., A. J. Gilliland, and K. Anderson (2012). Naturalizing community engagement in information studies: Pedagogical approaches and persisting partnerships. *Information, Communication and Society*, 15(7), 991–1015.

Law, J. (2002). On hidden heterogeneities: Complexity, formalism and aircraft design. In J. Law and A. Mol (eds.), *Complexities: Social Studies of Knowledge Practices* (116–141). Durham, N.C.: Duke University Press.

Law, J., and A. Mol (1995). Notes on materiality and sociality. *Sociological Review*, 43(2), 274–294.

Lechner, F. J. (1985). Modernity and its discontents. *Neofunctionalism*, 1, 157.

Lewin, K. (1946). Action research and minority problems. *Journal of Social Issues*, 2(4), 34–46.

Lewis, D., and S. Madon (2004). Information systems and nongovernmental development organizations: Advocacy, organizational learning, and accountability. *Information Society*, 20(2), 117–126.

Lewontin, R. C. (1983). Gene, organism, and environment. In D. S. Bendall (ed.), *Evolution from Molecules to Men* (273–285). Cambridge, Mass.: Cambridge University Press.

———. (2001). *The Triple Helix: Gene, Organism, and Environment*. Cambridge, Mass.: Harvard University Press.

Lievrouw, L. A. (2001). New media and the pluralization of life-worlds: A role for information in social differentiation. *New Media and Society*, 3(1), 7–28.

Lievrouw, L. A., E. Rogers, C. Lowe, and E. Nadel. (1987). Triangulation as a research strategy for identifying invisible colleges among biomedical scientists. Social Networks, 9 (winter), 217–248.

Lim, H., B. Fan, D. G. Andersen, and M. Kaminsky (2011). SILT: A memory-efficient, high-performance key-value store. In *Proceedings of the Twenty-Third ACM Symposium on Operating Systems Principles* (1–13). ACM.

Lippmann, W. (1946). *Public Opinion*. New Brunswick, N. J.: Transaction Publishers.

Lipsitz, G. (1994). *Dangerous Crossroads: Popular Music, Postmodernism and the Poetics of Place*. London: Verso.

———. (2007). *Footsteps in the Dark: The Hidden Histories of Popular Music*. Minneapolis: University of Minnesota Press.

Liu, A. (2004). *The Laws of Cool: Knowledge Work and the Culture of Information*. Chicago: University of Chicago Press.

Lofland, L., J. Lofland, S. Delamont, and A. Coffey (2001). Participant observation and field notes. In P. Atkinson, A. Coffey, S. Delamont, J. Lofland, and L. Lofland (eds.), *Handbook of Ethnography* (356–357). Thousand Oaks, Calif.: Sage.

Lovink, G., and N. Rossiter (2007). *My Creativity Reader: A Critique of Creative Industries*. Amsterdam: Institute of Network Cultures.

Lund, N. W. (2009). Document theory. *Annual Review of Information Science and Technology, 43*(1), 1–55.

Lundby, K. (2008). *Digital Storytelling, Mediatized Stories: Self-Representations in New Media* (vol. 52). New York: Peter Lang.

Lyon, D. (2013). *The Electronic Eye: The Rise of Surveillance Society-Computers and Social Control in Context*. Hoboken, N.J.: John Wiley & Sons.

Madrigal, A. C. (2013, April 19). #BostonBombing: The anatomy of a misinformation disaster. *Atlantic*. Retrieved from www.theatlantic.com

Manovich, L. (2001). *The Language of New Media*. Cambridge, Mass.: MIT Press.

———. (2013). *Software Takes Command* (vol. 5). London: Bloomsbury Academic; international edition.

Martinez-Torres, M. E. (2001). Civil society, the Internet, and the Zapatistas. *Peace Review, 13*(3), 347–355.

Marx, G. T., and G. W. Muschert (2007). Personal information, borders, and the new surveillance studies. *Annu. Rev. Law Soc. Sci., 3*, 375–395.

McAdam, D. (2006). Collective action. In G. Ritzer (ed.), *Encyclopedia of Sociology*. Malden, Mass.: Blackwell Press.

McChesney, R. W. (2013). *Digital Disconnect: How Capitalism Is Turning the Internet against Democracy*. New York: New Press.

McCracken, H. (2014a, January 29). How Twitter turned out to be the only second screen we really need. *TIME.com*. Retrieved from http://techland.time.com

———. (2014b, February 4). Facebook turns 10: What if it had never been invented? *TIME.com*. Retrieved from http://time.com

McLuhan, M. (1962). *The Gutenberg Galaxy: Making of Typographic Man*. Toronto: University of Toronto Press.

———. (1994), ed. *Understanding Media: The Extensions of Man*. Cambridge, Mass.: MIT Press.

Medina, E. (2011). *Cybernetic Revolutionaries: Technology and Politics in Allende's Chile.* Cambridge, Mass.: MIT Press.

Meinong, A. (1904). *The Theory of Objects.* Trans. I. Levi, D. B. Terrell, and R. M. Chisholm, in R. M. Chisholm (1960), *Realism and the Background of Phenomonology* (76–117). Glencoe: Free Press.

Michaels, E., D. Hebdige, and M. Langton (1994). *Bad Aboriginal Art: Tradition, Media, and Technological Horizons* (vol. 3). Minneapolis: University of Minnesota Press.

Miller, D., and D. Slater (2000). *The Internet: An Ethnographic Approach.* Oxford: Berg.

Miller, J. H., and S. E. Page (2009). *Complex Adaptive Systems: An Introduction to Computational Models of Social Life.* Princeton: Princeton University Press.

Minority Rights Group International. (2009). *State of the World's Minorities and Indigenous Peoples 2009—United States.* Retrieved from www.refworld.org

Minsky, M. (1988). *Society of Mind.* New York: Simon & Schuster.

Mitchell, M. (2009). *Complexity: A Guided Tour.* New York: Oxford University Press.

Mitchell, T. (1992). Orientalism and the exhibitionary order. In N. Dirks (ed.), *Colonialism and Culture* (289–317). Ann Arbor: University of Michigan Press.

Mitra, S. (2003). Minimally invasive education: A progress report on the "hole☒in☒the☒ wall" experiments. *British Journal of Educational Technology, 34*(3), 367–371.

———. (2005). Self organising systems for mass computer literacy: Findings from the "hole in the wall" experiments. *International Journal of Development Issues, 4*(1), 71–81.

Mol, A. (1999). Ontological politics. A word and some questions. *Sociological Review, 47*(S1), 74–89.

———. (2002). *The Body Multiple: Ontology in Medical Practice.* Durham, N.C.: Duke University Press.

Montfort, N. (2012). Programming for fun, together. Presented at the ELMCIP Conference on Remediating the Social. Retrieved from http://elmcip.net

Morozov, E. (2011). *The Net Delusion: How Not to Liberate the World.* London: Penguin U.K.

———. (2013a). *To Save Everything, Click Here: Technology, Solutionism, and the Urge to Fix Problems That Don't Exist.* London: Penguin U.K.

———. (2013b, May 27). Future shock meet the two-world hypothesis and its havoc. *New Republic.* Retrieved from www.newrepublic.com

Ndiwalana, A., O. Morawczynski, and O. Popov (2010). Mobile money use in Uganda: A preliminary study. *M4D 2010,* 121.

Negroponte, N. (2006). One laptop per child. Retrieved from www.ted.com

Negroponte, N., W. Bender, A. Battro, and D. Cavallo (2006). One laptop per child. *Podtech Podcast.*

Nelson, M. E., and G. A. Hull (2008). Self-presentation through multimedia: A Bakhtinian perspective on digital storytelling. In K. Lundby (ed.), *Digital Storytelling, Mediatized Stories: Self-Representations in New Media.* New York: Peter Lang.

Néret-Minet Tessier & Sarrou (2013, April 12). L.S. collection: 70 Katsinam masks of the Hopi Indians of Arizona. Press release, Drouot Richelieu. Retrieved from www. drouot.com

Nissen, J. (1998). Hackers: Masters of modernity and modern technology. In J. Stefton-Green (ed.), *Digital Diversions: Youth Culture in the Age of Multimedia* (149–171). London: University College.

Noble, S. U. (2011). *Searching for Black Girls: Ranking Race and Gender in Commercial Search Engines*. Urbana-Champaign: University of Illinois at Urbana-Champaign.

O'Brien, R. (2001). Um exame da abordagem metodológica da pesquisa ação [An Overview of the Methodological Approach of Action Research]. In R. Richardson (ed.), *Teoria e Prática da Pesquisa Ação [Theory and Practice of Action Research]*. João Pessoa, Brazil: Universidade Federal da Paraíba. Retrieved from www.web.ca

O'Doherty, B. (1999). *Inside the White Cube: The Ideology of the Gallery Space*. Berkeley: University of California Press.

O'Donnell, P. (2011, April 7). Natural Law "Externalism" v. Law as "Moral Aspiration." *Social Science Research Network*.

Olson, H. A. (2000). Difference, culture and change: The untapped potential of LCSH. *Cataloging and Classification Quarterly, 29*(1–2), 53–71.

——. (2007). How we construct subjects: A feminist analysis. *Library Trends, 56*(2), 509–541.

Orlikowski, W. J. (2008). Using technology and constituting structures: A practice lens for studying technology in organizations. In M. Ackerman, C. A. Halverson, T. Erickson, and W. A. Kellogg (eds.), *Resources, Co-Evolution and Artifacts* (255–305). New York: Springer.

Page, L. (2014). *Where's Google Going Next?* Retrieved from www.ted.com

Palfrey, J. G., and U. Gasser (2012). *Interop: The Promise and Perils of Highly Interconnected Systems*. New York: Basic Books.

Parikh, T. S., and E. D. Lazowska (2006). Designing an architecture for delivering mobile information services to the rural developing world. In *Proceedings of the 15th international conference on World Wide Web* (791–800). ACM.

Paris auction house sells Hopi masks despite tribe's objection. (2013, April 12). *Guardian*. Retrieved from www.theguardian.com

Pariser, E. (2011). *The Filter Bubble: How the New Personalized Web Is Changing What We Read and How We Think*. London: Penguin.

Parks, L. (2013). Zeroing in: Overheard Imagery, infrastructure ruins, and datalands in Afghanistan and Iraq. In N. Mirzoeff (ed.), *The Visual Culture Reader* (196–206). London: Routledge.

——. (2014a). Walking phone workers. In P. Adey, D. Bissell, K. Hannam, P. Merriman, and M. Sheller (eds.), *The Routledge Handbook of Mobilities* (243–255). Abingdon, U.K.: Routledge.

——. (2014b, April 10). Water, energy, access: Approaches for studying mobile phone and Internet use in rural Zambia. Presented at the Information Studies Colloquium Series, UCLA Department of Information Studies.

Pearce, S. M. (1994). *Museums, Objects and Collections: A Cultural Study*. Washington, D.C.: Smithsonian Press.

Philip, K., L. Irani, and P. Dourish (2010). Postcolonial computing: A tactical survey. *Science, Technology and Human Values*, 0162243910389594.

Pickering, A. (2010). *The Mangle of Practice: Time, Agency, and Science*. Chicago: University of Chicago Press.

Plumwood, V. (1993). The politics of reason: Towards a feminist logic. *Australasian Journal of Philosophy*, 71(4), 436–462.

Porteous, D. (2006). *The Enabling Environment for Mobile Banking in Africa*. Boston: Bankable Frontier Associates.

Poster, M. (2008). Global media and culture. *New Literary History*, 39(3), 685–703.

Prahalad, C. K. (2004). *The Fortune at the Bottom of the Pyramid: Eradicating Poverty through Profits*. Philadelphia: Wharton School Publishing.

Pratt, M. L. (1991). Arts of the contact zone. *Profession*, 91, 33–40.

Praxis (process). (n.d.). Retrieved from http://en.wikipedia.org

Puri, S. K., and S. Sahay (2003). Participation through communicative action: A case study of GIS for addressing land/water development in India. *Information Technology for Development*, 10(3), 179–199.

Putnam, R. D. (2000). *Bowling Alone: The Collapse and Revival of American Community*. New York: Simon & Schuster.

Rajagopal, A. (2013). Putting America in its place. *Public Culture*, 25(3 71), 387–399.

Reibel, D. B. (2008). *Registration Methods for the Small Museum*. Lanham, Md.: AltaMira Press.

Riles, A. (2006). *Documents: Artifacts of Modern Knowledge*. Ann Arbor: University of Michigan Press.

Ritzer, G., and N. Jurgenson (2010). Production, consumption, prosumption: The nature of capitalism in the age of the digital "prosumer." *Journal of Consumer Culture*, 10(1), 13–36.

Robbins, B. (1999). *Feeling Global: Internationalism in Distress*. New York: NYU Press.

Rogers, E. M. (2010). *Diffusion of Innovations*. New York: Simon & Schuster.

Rosaldo, R. (1993). *Culture and Truth: The Remaking of Social Analysis: With a New Introduction*. Boston: Beacon Press.

Rosaldo, R., H. Calderón, and J. D. Salvadívar (eds.). (1991). *Criticism in the Borderlands: Studies in Chicano Literature, Culture and Ideology*. Durham, N.C.: Duke University Press.

Rose, N. (1999). *Governing the Soul: The Shaping of the Private Self* (2nd ed.). London: Free Association Books.

Ross, F. (in preparation). *The Tribal Digital Village: Sovereignty, Technology and Collaboration in Indian Southern California*.

Rossiter, N. (2003). Report: Creative labour and the role of intellectual property. *Fibreculture Journal*, 1(1), 1–15.

Rousseau, J.-J. (2002). *The Social Contract: And, the First and Second Discourses*. New Haven: Yale University Press.

Rule, J. B. (2013, March 18). The search engine, for better or for worse. *New York Times*. Retrieved from www.nytimes.com

Russell, A. (2001). The Zapatistas online shifting the discourse of globalization. *International Communication Gazette, 63*(5), 399–413.

Said, E. (1978). *Orientalism: Western Concepts of the Orient*. New York: Vintage.

Samarajiva, R., and P. Shields (1990). Integration, telecommunication, and development: Power in the paradigms. *Journal of Communication, 40*(3), 84–105.

Sandvig, C. (2013). Connection at Ewiiaapaayp Mountain. In L. Nakamura and P. Chow-White (eds.), *Race after the Internet* (168–200). New York: Routledge.

Santos, B. de S., J. A. Nunes, and M. P. Meneses (2007). Opening up the canon of knowledge and recognition of difference. In B. de S. Santos (ed.), *Another Knowledge Is Possible: Beyond Northern Epistemologies*. London: Verso.

Sassen, S. (1998). *Globalization and Its Discontents: Essays on the New Mobility of People and Money*. New York: New Press.

———. (1999). Digital networks and power. In S. Lash and M. Featherstone (eds.), *Spaces of Culture: City, Nation, World* (49–63). London: Sage.

———. (2000). Spatialities and temporalities of the global: Elements for a theorization. *Public Culture, 12*(1), 215–232.

———. (2003). The state and globalization. *Interventions, 5*(2), 241–248.

Sawhney, H., and V. R. Suri (2008). Lateral connectivity at the margins: Ritual communication and liminality on aboriginal networks. *Science Technology and Society, 13*(2), 345–368.

Schiller, D. (2000). *Digital Capitalism: Networking the Global Market System*. Cambridge, Mass.: MIT Press.

Schmidt, E., and J. Cohen (2013). *The New Digital Age: Transforming Nations, Businesses, and Our Lives*. New York: Alfred A. Knopf.

Schultz, T. (2015). Cognitive redirective mapping. *Nordes, 6*.

Schumacker, E. F. (1973). *Small Is Beautiful: Economics as if People Mattered*. New York: Abacus.

Schwartz, H. (1996). *The Culture of the Copy*. New York: Zone.

Scott, J. C. (1998). *Seeing Like a State: How Certain Schemes to Improve the Human Condition Have Failed*. New Haven: Yale University Press.

Searle, J. (1990). Collective intentions and actions. In P. R. Cohen and J. L. Morgan (eds.), *Intentions in Communication* (401). Cambridge, Mass.: MIT Press.

Searls, D. (2008, December 16). The splinternet. Retrieved from http://blogs.law.harvard.edu

Seddon, J. (2011). Urban interstices: Statistical advocacy and urban infrastructure. *Cityscapes, 1*, 20–24.

Seddon, J., and R. Srinivasan (2014). Information and ontologies: Challenges in scaling knowledge for development. *Journal of the Association for Information Science and Technology, 65*(6), 1124–1133.

Sen, A. (1993). Markets and freedoms: Achievements and limitations of the market mechanism in promoting individual freedoms. *Oxford Economic Papers*, 519–541.

———. (1995). Rationality and social choice. *American Economic Review, 85*(1), 1–24.

———. (2007). *Identity and Violence: The Illusion of Destiny*. New Delhi: Penguin Books India.

Shalom, S. R. (2008). Parpolity: A political system for a good society. In C. Spannos (ed.), *Real Utopia: Participatory Society for the 21st Century*. Oakland, Calif.: AK Press.

Shannon, C. E., and W. Weaver (1949). *The Mathematical Theory of Communication*. Urbana: University of Illinois Press.

Shapiro, I. (1996). *Democracy's Place*. Ithaca, N.Y.: Cornell University Press.

Shipek, F. C. (1988). *Pushed into the Rocks: Southern California Indian Land Tenure, 1769–1986*. Lincoln, Nebr.: University of Nebraska Press.

Shirky, C. (2008). *Here Comes Everybody: The Power of Organizing without Organizations*. New York: Penguin.

———. (2010). *Cognitive Surplus: How Technology Makes Consumers into Collaborators*. New York: Penguin.

———. (2011). The political power of social media—Technology, the public sphere, and political change. *Foreign Affairs, 90*, 28.

Shome, R. (2006). Thinking through the diaspora: Call centers, India, and a new politics of hybridity. *International Journal of Cultural Studies, 9*(1), 105–124.

Silverstone, R., and L. Haddon (1996). Design and the domestication of ICTs: Technical change and everyday life. In R. Silverstone and R. Mansell (eds.), *Communicating by Design: The Politics of Information and Communication Technologies* (44–74). Oxford: Oxford University Press.

Silverstone, R., and E. Hirsch (1992). *Consuming Technologies: Media and Information in Domestic Spaces*. Hove, U.K.: Psychology Press.

Simpson, M. G. (2012). *Making Representations: Museums in the Post-Colonial Era*. New York: Routledge.

Slater, T. (2012). What is interoperability? *Network Centric Operations Industry Consortium* (NCOIC).

Slavin, Kevin. (2011, November 30). How algorithms shape our world. *Huffington Post*. Retrieved from www.huffingtonpost.com

Smith, L. T. (1999). *Decolonizing Methodologies: Research and Indigenous Peoples*. London: Zed Books.

Snijders, C., U. Matzat, and U.-D. Reips (2012). Big data: Big gaps of knowledge in the field of internet science. *International Journal of Internet Science, 7*(1), 1–5.

Spivak, G. C. (1988). Can the subaltern speak? In C. Nelson and L. Grossberg (eds.), *Marxism and the Interpretation of Culture* (271–313). Basingstoke, U.K.: Macmillian Education.

Spradley, J. P. (1980). *Participant Observation*. New York: Holt.

Srinivasan, M. (2016). Do attitudes toward societal structure predict beliefs about free will and achievement? Evidence from the Indian caste system. *Developmental Science, 19*(1), 109–125.

Srinivasan, R. (2006a). Indigenous, ethnic and cultural articulations of new media. *International Journal of Cultural Studies*, 9(4), 497–518.

———. (2006b). Where information society and community voice intersect. *Information Society*, 22(5), 355–365.

———. (2012a). Rethinking digital cultures and divides: The case for reflective media. *Information Society*, 28(1), 24–36.

———. (2012b, October 26). Taking power through technology in the Arab Spring. *Al Jazeera*. Retrieved from www.aljazeera.com

———. (2013a). Bridges between cultural and digital worlds in revolutionary Egypt. *Information Society*, 29(1), 49–60.

———. (2013b). Re-thinking the cultural codes of new media: The question concerning ontology. *New Media and Society*, 15(2), 203–223.

———. (2013c, July 15). How networks overpower states. *Al Jazeera*. Retrieved from www.aljazeera.com

Srinivasan, R., K. Becvar, R. Boast, and J. Enote (2010). Diverse knowledges and contact zones within the digital museum. *Science, Technology and Human Values*, 35, 735–768.

Srinivasan, R., and A. Fish (2011). Revolutionary tactics, media ecologies, and repressive states. *Public Culture*, 23(3 65), 505–510.

Srinivasan, R., and J. Huang (2005). Fluid ontologies for digital museums. *International Journal on Digital Libraries*, 5(3), 193–204.

Srinivasan, R., and L. Juliano (2012). Tagging it: Considering how ontologies limit the reading of identity. *International Journal of Cultural Studies*, 15(6), 615–627.

Standage, T. (1998). *The Victorian Internet: The Remarkable Story of the Telegraph and the Nineteenth Century's Online Pioneers*. London: Weidenfeld and Nicolson.

Star, S. L. (1983). Simplification in scientific work: An example from neuroscience research. *Social Studies of Science*, 13(2), 205–228.

———. (1999). The ethnography of infrastructure. *American Behavioral Scientist*, 43(3), 377–391.

———. (2002). Infrastructure and ethnographic practice: Working on the fringes. *Scandinavian Journal of Information Systems*, 14(2), 6.

Star, S. L., and J. R. Griesemer (1989). Institutional ecology, translations, and boundary objects: Amateurs and professionals in Berkeley's Museum of Vertebrate Zoology, 1907–39. *Social Studies of Science*, 19(3), 387–420.

Star, S. L., and A. Strauss (1999). Layers of silence, arenas of voice: The ecology of visible and invisible work. *Computer Supported Cooperative Work (CSCW)*, 8(1–2), 9–30.

Statement of Subcomandante Marcos to the Freeing the Media Teach-In. (1997). Retrieved from www.prometheusradio.org

Stevens, M., A. Flinn, and E. Shepherd (2010). New frameworks for community engagement in the archive sector: From handing over to handing on. *International Journal of Heritage Studies*, 16(1–2), 59–76.

Subcomandante Marcos/TKO/The Getaway Drivers. (1994, August 21). *60 Minutes*. Retrieved from www.imdb.com

Suchman, L. (1986). *Plans and Situated Actions*. New York: Cambridge University Press.

———. (2002). Located accountabilities in technology production. *Scandinavian Journal of Information Systems*, *14*(2), 7.

———. (2003). Figuring service in discourses of ICT: The case of software agents. In E. Wynn, E. Whitley, M. Myers, and J. DeGross (eds.), *Global and Organizational Discourse about Information Technology* (15–32). Dordrecht: Kluwer.

———. (2007). *Human-Machine Reconfigurations: Plans and Situated Actions*. New York: Cambridge University Press.

Sundaram, R. (1999). Recycling modernity: Pirate electronic cultures in India. *Third Text*, *13*(47), 59–65.

Suro, R. (1990, August 13). Zunis' effort to regain idols may alter views of Indian art. *New York Times*. Retrieved from www.nytimes.com

Taylor, D. (2003). *The Archive and the Repertoire: Performing Cultural Memory in the Americas*. Durham, N.C.: Duke University Press.

Taylor, F. W. (1911). *Shop Management*. New York: Harper and Brothers.

Terranova, T. (2000). Free labor: Producing culture for the digital economy. *Social Text*, *18*(2), 33–58.

———. (2004). *Network Culture: Politics for the Information Age*. London: Pluto Press.

Terranova, T., G. Thomas, and S. Wyatt (2002). They came, they saw, they went back to the beach: Conceptualizing use and non-use of the Internet. In S. Woolgar (ed.), *Virtual Society? Technology, Cyberbole, Reality* (23–40). Oxford: Oxford University Press.

Thierer, A. (2009, August 12). Cyber-libertarianism: The case for real Internet freedom. *The Technology Liberation Front*. Retrieved from http://techliberation.com

———. (2012, June 11). What is "optimal interoperability"? A review of Palfrey and Gasser's "Interop." Retrieved from http://techliberation.com

Thompson, C. (2013, August 20). Creating an alternative Internet to keep the NSA out. Retrieved from www.popularresistance.org

Tongia, R., and E. J. Wilson III (2011). Network theory, the flip side of Metcalfe's law: Multiple and growing costs of network exclusion. *International Journal of Communication*, *5*, 17.

Tufekci, Z. (2011). New media and the people-powered uprisings. *Technology Review*. Retrieved from www.technologyreview.com

Tulloch, J., and H. Jenkins (1995). *Science Fiction Audiences: Watching Doctor Who and Star Trek*. London: Psychology Press.

Turnbull, D. (2000). *Masons, Tricksters and Cartographers: Comparative Studies in the Sociology of Scientific and Indigenous Knowledge*. London: Taylor and Francis.

———. (2003). Assemblage and diversity: Working with incommensurability: Emergent knowledge, narrativity, performativity, mobility and synergy. Presented at the AAHPSSS, Melbourne.

———. (2009). Working with incommensurable knowledge: Traditions assemblage, diversity, emergent knowledge, narrativity, performativity, mobility and synergy. *Thoughtmesh.net*. Retrieved from http://thoughtmesh.net

———. (2011, November 14). Other knowledges: Reflections on recent archaeology in South America by David Turnbull. *Southern Perspectives*. Retrieved from www.southernperspectives.net

Turner, F. (2010). *From Counterculture to Cyberculture: Stewart Brand, the Whole Earth Network, and the Rise of Digital Utopianism*. Chicago: University of Chicago Press.

Turner, T. (1992). Defiant images: The Kayapo appropriation of video. *Anthropology Today*, 8(6), 5–16.

Tyler, G. (1995). *Look for the Union Label: A History of the International Ladies' Garment Workers' Union*. Armonk, N.Y.: M. E. Sharpe.

Ulluwishewa, R. (1993). Indigenous knowledge, national IK resource centres and sustainable development. *Indigenous Knowledge and Development Monitor*, 1(3), 11–13.

Ulrich, W. (2000). Reflective practice in the civil society: The contribution of critically systemic thinking. *Reflective Practice*, 1(2), 247–268.

Urban, T. M. (2007). Caracol de la Resistencia: Zapatista Symbol References Maya Past. Retrieved from http://traumwerk.stanford.edu

U.S. Census Bureau. (2008). *2005–2007 American Community Survey*. Retrieved from www.census.gov

U.S. Government Accountability Office. (2006). *Illegal Immigration: Border-Crossing Deaths Have Doubled since 1995; Border Patrol's Efforts to Prevent Deaths Have Not Been Fully Evaluated* (No. GAO-06-770).

Van Dijk, J., and K. Hacker (2003). The digital divide as a complex and dynamic phenomenon. *Information Society*, 19(4), 315–326.

Verran, H. (2002). A postcolonial moment in science studies alternative firing regimes of environmental scientists and aboriginal landowners. *Social Studies of Science*, 32(5–6), 729–762.

Virilio, P. (1986). *Speed and Politics: An Essay on Dromology*. (M. Polizzotti, trans.) New York: Semiotext(e).

———. (1995). Speed and information: Cyberspace alarm! *Ctheory*, 18. Retrieved from www.ctheory.net

Visvanathan, S. (2012). For a new epistemology of the South. Retrieved from www.india-seminar.com

Vítězslav, O. (1996). *Gregor Mendel: The First Geneticist*. Oxford: Oxford University Press.

Von Foerster, H. (1979). Cybernetics of cybernetics. In *Communication and Control in Society*. New York: Gordon and Breach.

Von Hippel, E. (2005). *Democratizing Innovation*. Cambridge, Mass.: MIT Press.

Wallack, J. S., and R. Srinivasan (2009). Local-global: Reconciling mismatched ontologies in development information systems. In *System Sciences*, 2009. HICSS'09. 42nd Hawaii International Conference on (1–10). IEEE.

Wardrip-Fruin, N., and N. Montfort (eds.) (2003). *The New Media Reader* (vol. 1). Cambridge, Mass.: MIT Press.

Warschauer, M. (2001). Millennialism and media: Language, literacy, and technology in the 21st century. *AILA Review, 14*, 49–59.

———. (2003). Demystifying the digital divide. *Scientific American, 289*(2), 42–47.

———. (2004). *Technology and Social Inclusion: Rethinking the Digital Divide.* Cambridge, Mass.: MIT Press.

———. (2006). *Laptops and Literacy: Learning in the Wireless Classroom.* New York: Teachers College Press.

Watkins, S. C. (2005). *Hip Hop Matters: Politics, Pop Culture, and the Struggle for the Soul of a Movement.* Boston: Beacon Press.

Weinberger, D. (2005). Tagging and why it matters. Berkman Center for Internet and Society. Retrieved from cyber.law.harvard.edu

Wells, H. G., and A. J. Mayne (1938). *World Brain.* London: Methuen and Company.

Whitehead, J., and J. McNiff (2006). *Action Research: Living Theory.* London: Sage.

Williams, R. (1985). *Keywords: A Vocabulary of Culture and Society.* New York: Oxford University Press.

Winsberg, E. (2010). *Science in the Age of Computer Simulation.* Chicago: University of Chicago Press.

Winter, R. (1996). Some principles and procedures for the conduct of action research. In O. Zuber-Skerritt (ed.), *New Directions in Action Research* (16–17). London: Falmer Press.

Woolgar, S., and J. Lezaun (2013). The wrong bin bag: A turn to ontology in science and technology studies? *Social Studies of Science, 43*(3), 321–340.

Zielinski, S. (2006). *Deep Time of the Media: Toward an Archaeology of Hearing and Seeing by Technical Means.* (G. Custance, trans.) Cambridge, Mass.: MIT Press.

Zillien, N., and E. Hargittai (2009). Digital distinction: Status-specific types of Internet usage*. *Social Science Quarterly, 90*(2), 274–291.

Zimmerman, U. (1998, December). Review of James C. Scott, Seeing Like a State: How Certain Schemes to Improve the Human Condition Have Failed. *H-Net: Humanities and Social Sciences Online,* (H-PCAACA). Retrieved from www.h-net.org

Zittrain, J. (2008). *The Future of the Internet—and How to Stop It.* New Haven: Yale University Press.

Zuckerman, E. (2008). Meet the bridgebloggers. *Public Choice, 134*(1–2), 47–65.

———. (2013). *Rewire: Digital Cosmopolitans in the Age of Connection.* New York: W. W. Norton.

INDEX

abstraction versus embodiment, in Zuni ways of knowing, 177. *See also* ontology

access: to Internet and technology, 1, 5, 26–27, 29–30, 78, 79, 206–207; to mobile phones, 1, 50, 56, 65–67, 68–69, 90

activism, 18, 72, 198, 219. *See also* Arab Spring

Advanced Research Projects Agency (ARPA), 19, 30

affirmative action, controversies of, 7

agency, community, 18, 105, 108, 178, 217, 223

Agrawal, Arun, 127

Agre, Phil, 9, 215–216

AirBnB, providing data to, 20, 21

Akrich, Madeleine, 145

algorithms, 132, 178–179, 184; personalization, 132; ethnographic algorithm, 215

Alibaba, 21

Amazon (company), 22, 209

Amidollane, 184–195

Anahoho, 187–195

Anderson, Chris, 22

Andhra Pradesh, India, 84, 88–90; Ardhavaram, 93–110, 181; Kesavaram, 91–110

Aneesh, A., 54

anomie, 142

Anselm, Saint, 34

anthropological work, in indigenous communities, 170. *See also* ethnography

Appadurai, Arjun, 55, 82–84, 119–120, 178

Apple, 22, 25

appropriate technology, 201

appropriation, 47–48, 69, 74–77, 113, 145, 153, 197–199, 217–219

apps, 22, 212, 227

Aquinas, Thomas, 34

Arab Spring, 17–18, 24, 218–222

A:shiwi A:wan Museum and Heritage Center, 118, 167, 168, 194

asset, as opposed to "need," 108

authenticity, cultural, 118

autoethnography, 11

autonomous networks, 181, 231; autonomous ontologies, 184. *See also* lateral connectivity; lateralize

Balsamo, Anne, 36–37

"banking education," 95. *See also* Freire, Paulo

Banksy, 200–201

Baran, Paul, 182

Baym, Nancy, 75–76

Beauchesne, Oliver, 27

Belkin, Nick, 191

Berger, Jonah, 5

Berners-Lee, Tim, 30

Bhabha, Homi, 214–215

Bhaskar, TLS, 88–90, 92–93, 95–99, 101–103, 105

big data, 113, 184, 203, 227

biodiversity, 8

biopolitical narratives, 127. *See also* Foucault, Michel; Haraway, Donna

black-boxing, 128–129. *See also* classification systems

Boast, Robin, 37–39, 162–164, 166–172, 175, 182, 184, 193

Boazizi, Mohammed, self-immolation, 24. *See also* Arab Spring

Boellstorff, Tom, 184

ABOUT THE AUTHOR

Ramesh Srinivasan is Director of the UC Digital Cultures Lab and a professor at UCLA who works across the world to study new technology's interactions with diverse cultures and communities. An active contributor to the mainstream media and press, Srinivasan has worked in the middle of Egypt's Arab Spring, with Native American and indigenous peoples across the Americas, within South Asia, and more to identify how new technologies can empower grassroots voices, equality, and the potential of democratic communication around the world.